The
Last Boat
On The
River

The
Last Boat
On The
River

Cycling Alongside the Mississippi River

Quentin van Marle
(assisted by Mark Twain)

PNEUMA SPRINGS PUBLISHING UK

First Published in 2008 by Pneuma Springs Publishing

Cover design, editing and typesetting by:
Pneuma Springs Publishing

A Subsidiary of Pneuma Springs Ltd.
7 Groveherst Road, Dartford Kent, DA1 5JD.
E: admin@pneumasprings.co.uk
W: www.pneumasprings.co.uk

Sketches by Daphne van Marle, a professional artist and the author's sister.

Cover design input by Bru Amey.

A catalogue record for this book is available from the British Library.

ACKNOWLEDGEMENTS

My sincere thanks for the assistance and support given by the tourist authorities in the states of Minnesota, Iowa, Missouri, Arkansas, and Louisiana: and in particular to Paul Sherburne and Beth Satrang (Minnesota); Chuck Martin, Cape Girardeau, Missouri; Jana Greenbaum (the gorgeous 'calling card' of Arkansas); Bill Serrat and Colleen Stafford May, respectively of Greenville and Vicksburg, Mississippi; and to Jeff Richards, the sharpshooting mouthpiece of Louisiana.

And by no means least, to all the wonderful, hospitable, and eccentric folks who inhabit the banks of the Mississippi River. They are proud, and they are unique.

Other books by the same author

Marooned
A 31 day ordeal on Dead Man's Chest

Boomerang Road
A Pedalling Pom's Australian Odyssey

Ride the Blazing Rainbow
Cycling across South Africa … Where Anything can Happen

DEDICATION
For my son Gavin, for his wife Alex, and for their adorable, mischievous little daughter, Evelyn (or 'V' as she is known).
I love you all.

Prologue

IMAGINE THIS IF YOU WILL: you go to bed one night inside the home you know so well - and wake up the next morning to find that your house has, quite literally, been moved to a different street, or even to another town entirely. This cannot be so, you say; it's impossible; a few too many last night, that must be it. But then you get dressed and walk out the front door - into totally unfamiliar surrounds.

These panic-stricken moments would have anyone seriously questioning their state of mind, or even believing they and their property had been abducted by aliens while sound asleep. Yet such an event has occurred many times, and in the only place it could do.

Beside the Mississippi River.

This, as you will see, is no tall story. Unlike most rivers of the world, the Mississippi does as it damn well pleases, including the overnight shifting of residences from one place to another. It has a mind of its own; an aquatic Action Man, a doer-of-deeds over which humans have no control; a flowing, enigmatic spirit that is the custodian of some amazing tales and dark secrets.

This alone makes it worth exploring more than any other river I can think of. From its tiny source near the Canadian border in northern Minnesota, my aim is to travel all the way to its estuary down in the swamplands of deepest-south

Louisiana: some 2,000 miles by road or 2,552 miles by water, along its twisting, snake-like river bends.

It is a deceptively friendly waterway, and in its own way, pretty schizophrenic: a river that is absolutely vital to mankind everywhere, and steeped in history and romance like no other; a river of folklore and culture; danger, violence, and tragedy. It delivers good times and terrible times. When in the mood, the Mississippi won't simply shift your house, it will transport you to that great place in the sky without warning. A serial killer with the warmest of smiles.

Three recent adventurers, all certifiable, have navigated its length by bizarre means. One guy rolled down it in a barrel; another juggled his legs on a log; and a hardened Slav actually swam the distance. Unlike them - and wimp-like by comparison - I shall do this by bicycle, alongside its banks.

I am a freelance writer, a hack, and this will be the fourth cycling marathon that I've undertaken for the BBC Radio 5 Live programme *Up All Night*, and for which I'll be making weekly broadcasts as I pedal along - hopefully an eclectic mix of stories covering a whole range of topics; the unusual, the striking, the tear jerking, the outrageous, and anything worthwhile that I happen to come across en-route, on the road and off it: stories which I'd be most unlikely to find had I been travelling by any other method than a simple bicycle. Just for the record, those previous BBC adventures were coast-to-coast America from Los Angeles to Key West; through Australia from far north Queensland down to Melbourne; and a much shorter hop from Durban to Cape Town in South Africa: only 1,000 miles, that one.

Such an obvious Mississippi character as Mark Twain clearly has to figure within these pages, and he will periodically do so. So to explain that bewildering opening paragraph, let's have this wise old scribe take up the slack. These are his words from 1882, and they remain as true today as they were back then.

'The Mississippi has a disposition to make prodigious jumps by cutting through narrow necks of land, and thus straightening and shortening itself. More than once it has shortened itself by 30 miles at a single jump. These cut-offs have thrown several river towns out into the rural districts, and built up sandbars and forests in front of them. The town of Delta used to be three miles below Vicksburg. A recent cut-off has radically changed the position, and Delta is now two miles *above* Vicksburg.

A cut-off plays havoc with boundary lines and jurisdictions: for instance, a man living in the State of Mississippi today for whom a cut-off occurs overnight, will tomorrow find himself and his land on the other side of the river, within the boundaries, and subject to, the laws of the State of Louisiana. Such a thing happening on the upper river in the old times, could have taken a slave from Missouri across to Illinois and made a free man of him'.

So I shall be taking nothing for granted, not even on dry land, as I make my way along the length of what is arguably the world's most mystical river. Far from it. For one thing, my bike is an untried entity in this instance. It is not the standard touring cycle, in so much as it has 'electric assist'. That is to say, there is a tiny one-horsepower electric motor tucked into the hub of the front wheel. Now perhaps I'm bowing to advancing years, but I like the idea of this device; something to give the rider a boost when the headwinds get high and the hills get higher still. But this journey is to be the longest ever made on such a machine and the battery capacity has yet to be tested on runs of up to 80 miles at a time.

I have not the slightest idea what lies in store as I make my way up to Lake Itasca, Minnesota - the actual source of the Mississippi. Assuming that I'm not killed in the process, all I hope for at this stage is that over the next eight or nine weeks my two wheels will spin alongside the big river, from the very top to the very bottom. As for what happens in between … well, you know as much as I do. So come on and explore. Pedal the pages with me from south of the Canadian border down to the sub-tropical warmth of the Gulf of Mexico.

Towards, and beyond, the last boat on the river.

One

NORTH BY NORTHWEST

PARK RAPIDS, population 3,500, lies about 180 miles northwest of the twin cities of Minneapolis/St Paul. It is in the very heart of Garrison Keillor's Lake Woebegone country and situated 22 miles due south of Lake Itasca, the actual source of the Mississippi; it is also the nearest place to the lake offering hotel accommodation. Park Rapids is typically small-town America, and first impressions suggest that finding the community's 'wow' factor might require a few months research.

Me and the bike have been driven up here from the Twin Cities by a senior Minnesota tourism official, who drops me off at the Red Bridge Inn, a pinkish-red timber mansion nestling on the shore of a miniature lake. This is to be home for the next couple of nights while I prepare to set off downriver. In the driveway is a shiny black gangster-style Cadillac from a bygone era, complete with the Thompson machine-gunner's running boards. It is a rare sight.

Rarer still is the ritual practiced by my host, Kevin Thyr. As this short, bald, plumpish man emerges from the house, he lunges forward and envelops me in an astonishingly powerful bear hug. "We like to embrace all our new guests" he explains. "Kinda breaks the ice."

"A few ribs too" I wheeze, coming out of his iron-like grip. If I've ever been greeted by a complete stranger in this manner before, I cannot remember where or when. But I take it as a gesture of the immediate friendliness almost unanimously offered by Americans who live far away from the big, impersonal cities.

I ask about the Cadillac, obviously a collector's item. "Back in the late 1940s, it was a popular car with mafia bosses and other criminal big shots" Kevin explains, while opening the trunk. "And here's why." I stare into a cavernous abyss in uncomprehending silence until he says, "They used all this space to carry bullet-riddled stiffs, up to five at a time. The hoodlums would then disperse the corpses on their rivals' doorsteps." He looks for my reaction which is not much more than a raised eyebrow. I've seen gangster movies too.

But the eyebrow rises another notch when he says, "You and me will take a little ride in it around sundown. Over to Lake Portage, a few miles out of town."

"So long as I'm not riding in the trunk."

For such a big car, it is surprisingly claustrophobic inside. A charming blonde woman called Jennie, Kevin's long term live-in, slides into the back beside me while Kevin does the driving. We come to a stop in the driveway of a spacious lakeshore home where Jennie's parents live, and who've kindly invited us over for dinner. The sun, a vast orange orb is gradually slipping down to the trees, and her father suggests a quick tour of the lake before it gets dark.

We climb aboard the pontoon boat moored at his private jetty and are soon out in the deep stuff. Houses lining the shore are set well apart from each other, ensuring cordial relations between fellow lakeside dwellers. As the blazing orb levels with the treetops, barbecue smoke wafts across the water and a huge walleye fish jumps high into the air. I cannot but admire the lifestyle of these people who live at water's edge. More than any race I know, Americans make the most of their surrounds.

By Minnesota standards, Lake Portage is a tiny stretch of water for a state in which every number plate bears the inscription 'The Land of 10,000 Lakes' (it's actually got 15,000 of them, but they reckoned that 10,000 just sounded better). Our slow and relaxed circumnavigation takes just half an hour, but it has already set the mood for my coming travels through this heavily wooded and lake-studded state. As we cruise back to the jetty, the first slight chills of a high latitude reminds me that the Canadian border is only a short distance to the north and that autumn is already on the way. After that, this lake will become one big sheet of ice for several months.

Next morning, with the bike resting in the Cadillac's chasm-like mortuary, Kevin drives me up to Lake Itasca, where the Mississippi River begins its long journey down to the Gulf of Mexico. The lake's parklands are immaculate, with well-surfaced roads cutting through forests of endless pine. But the source itself comes as something of a surprise. It is a tiny boulder-strewn corner that is just 18 feet wide - and in this almost rainless year, only four inches deep. It is hard to imagine that such a mighty river develops from this trickling little pond.

"They come from all over the world" explains a park ranger, "just so they can wade ankle-deep and cross the source. Forever afterwards, they'll tell everyone that they have actually *walked* across the Mississippi."

I make a similar walk myself. But not particularly wishing to get my feet wet on this grey morning, I use a makeshift wooden bridge instead. Wimp is my second name.

Hard to believe, but this trickling pond, just 18 feet across by four inches deep, is where the Mississippi River begins.

Later, in a sort of test-pilot exercise, I cycle the 22 miles back to Park Rapids in what is my first real outing astride the *eZee Torq* electric-assist bicycle. It is brand new, built in Shanghai, and was shipped directly to the USA for me. But by God, it is a heavy piece of kit. A modern touring bike weighs about 25lbs and has up to 28 gears. This one weighs in at 58lbs and has a mere eight gears. I can foresee that the electric motor inside the wheel hub is going to get as much exercise as my legs before this trip is done.

The sun eventually comes out and I'm soon pedalling along the undulating highway densely populated with pines on both sides of the road. On the flat, it is a surprisingly easy bike to pedal, but when the hills come, however slight, a little boost from the one-horsepower motor is needed. This is activated by a twist-grip throttle on the handlebars. And oh, what a difference it makes. I simply slip into second gear, keep on pedalling effortlessly, and let the motor do the rest. Piece of cake.

Which suddenly has me worried. This is too good to last. Since this is to be the longest-ever trek yet made on an electric bike, in one sense me and my new machine are little more than guinea pigs. Once I add my luggage to the rear pannier and the two pannier bags, the weight is going to rise significantly; so careful use of the 18lb battery (fitting snugly under the rear of the saddle) will be crucial. At this stage, I really do not know how far I'll get to travel on one charge. That will depend on the hills encountered, on the velocity of headwinds and crosswinds, on the constant use of the pedals, and on thrifty use of the motor.

While cruising leisurely back to Park Rapids, I sense that trouble lies ahead. Previous experience confirms that life on a bicycle just cannot be this easy. Ah well, I'll just do as I've always done - sail headlong into the mire, then try and get the hell out of it. This has been the abnormally-normal pattern of my entire life - in personal relationships, socially, and throughout a long, rewarding, and occasionally precarious career in journalism.

Precarious because of my own brutal impatience. I have always looked for ways to dodge the everyday tedium - which is doubtless why I'm here now, astride this unfamiliar machine that will either become my very best friend, or my direst enemy in the uncertain weeks to come.

Tonight it is Kevin and Jennie's turn to act host to her parents. We sit outside on the deck overlooking their own miniscule lake, which must be the smallest in all Minnesota. After dinner, guitars come out and I perform a calypso-style song that I wrote some while ago called *Dancing Highwayman*. It concerns the futility of traffic jams, and a couple of verses go thus:

Wanna go where the sun do shine
Coconut trees and plenty of wine
Down on the shore in a conga line
Dancing barefoot on the beach
Not a single car in reach.

Do the Limbo, under the bamboo
While magic man performs his voodoo
Putting the curse on every BMW
As I cha-cha in the sand
On my fantasy island.

If these words aptly reflect my antagonistic attitude to the car culture, then as of tomorrow - September 7, 2006 - America's motoring zealots have their chance for some bloody revenge. It's not merely the bike I've got to worry about. In rural, car-crazy USA, cyclists receive roughly the same amount of affection as a teetotal taxi driver has for the drunk who throws up in his cab.

On that steely thought, I go up to bed.

16

Two

THE TRICKLE

IT IS AN ODD GEOGRAPHICAL FACT that to follow the Mississippi southwards, you first have to follow it 35 miles north, to the city of Bemidji. From Lake Itasca, the river runs in little more than a non-navigable, northerly trickle. At Bemidji it does a u-turn, and from there on it's downhill all the way.

Metaphorically speaking, alas.

On a lovely sunny morning, I'm dropped off at the entrance to Itasca State Park. From here on in, I'm on my own - which is the way I like it anyway. So I do what I came here to do and start pedalling. The ride along the Mississippi River has begun.

Except there is no river in sight, no sign of the trickling stream. Highway 71 runs north, then east, then north again before reaching Bemidji in a series of low undulations slicing through the plethora of pine trees. Traffic is light and so far unthreatening. This first day is a pleasant, quiet ride in which I use the electric motor sparingly, occasionally glancing at the 'fuel gauge' - a tiny electronic instrument that indicates green for full, amber for low, and red for *'that's it, buddy; legs only'*. On arriving in Bemidji, it is still on green, a promising sign.

What is baffling me now, trivial as it may be, is that although I know the big river to be anything but at this stage, I nevertheless cross a bridge into town that announces I am crossing the Mississippi. On my right is the expanse of Lake Bemidji with a sailboat cruising in the distance; but on my left are broad, silent, reed-strewn waters resembling a derelict harbour for ghost ships.

Very odd. Where is my winding trickle? This, it clearly cannot be. Well, no matter. The Bemidji stopover is only a case of going through the motions because I don't think I'm going to find many alluring riverside stories, and certainly no riverboat tales until I hit the Twin Cities in a week's time. Minneapolis/St Paul is the terminus and turnaround for the Upper Mississippi's commercial fleet. Its headwaters north of there are pretty much a no-go zone.

I check into the Birchmont Lodge, a lakeside hotel on the northern edge of town, happy that the adventure is now finally underway. This is what it'll be like from now on: a different hotel or motel almost every night for the next eight or nine weeks; new faces and places, fleeting acquaintances, changing scenery, hidden stories. I am once again adopting the life of the professional stranger, and the one element that will link all this together is the river - wherever that may be.

The lodge is made up of cabin-style rooms facing the lake. From the next door patio comes the sound of laughter, clinking glasses and beer bottles. A young woman pokes her head around a sort of privacy wall and calls out, "We're gonna be making a lot of noise, man. For a good two hours. That alright with you?"

"That's fine" I reply, "enjoy yourselves." And so for the next couple of hours loud whooping and hollering, roaring music, and coarse laughter blast through the flimsy cabin walls and windows. I had made the right decision. To have said no, it's not alright, would have been an open invitation to double the volume.

Sleep comes easily to a weary body. I never train for these rides; I just let them grow organically. If I'm out of shape now, I'll be a lot fitter this time next week, and fitter still the week after. Tomorrow however, I know I'm going to ache like a bleeding heart because growing pains are all part of the process. The time I most dread is Day Three - always the most demanding on long, tough endeavours. Statistically and in reality, it is the day when all your previous dreams about the project on which you've embarked, come to a screeching halt. Early optimism can turn to downright pessimism: doubts set in, and confidence can drop to an unknown low. I don't know why this should be, but the third day is always a son of a bitch. After that, things will pick up again. I hope.

Before confronting this strange foe, there is Day Two to get through. The next morning is grey, windy, and cold. Rain threatens. The lake is dark, rough and unwelcoming. As I get my stiff body ready to leave Bemidji, I opt to ride in a rainproof jacket and jeans, rather than the tee-shirt and shorts of yesterday. I don't like doing this: it doesn't look right and it doesn't feel right, but it's better than having a chill wind slice through the body all day long.

Today's ride takes me 20 miles southwest down Highway 197 to Cass Lake, then a further 20 miles due south on 371 to Benedict, a one-horse town that I and almost everyone else it seems, have never heard of.

At this stage I should point out that I've already gone over the proposed route with *Explore Minnesota*, the state's official tourist department. In its appreciable efforts to assist, the department has lined up assorted accommodation for me as I go along. So I stop over according to the prepared schedule. Tonight it is to be in somewhere so small, it isn't even on my map. All I know is that Benedict is supposed to be seven miles north of a town called Walker.

Finding it is another matter. It lies somewhere off the main highway, but there are no signposts. I know it must be around here someplace because the computer on my handlebars says I've done the distance. The highway still runs through thick, engulfing pine forests where roadside houses are sparse, but I eventually come across one with a couple of pick-up trucks outside, an open front door, the sound of hammers driving nails, and two gruff male voices coming from within.

I rap on the open door. Inside, the building seems gutted.

"Yeah?" calls out a voice, "Whaddaya want?"

"Directions to Benedict" I call back.

"Where?"

"Benedict."

"Benedict? Never heard of it. Come on in, buddy."

I step into the gloom, clambering over loose planks, insulation foam, and a variety of building materials. Two men in logging shirts are kneeling on the crossbeams, nailing a floor into place.

"Where d'you say again? Benedict?" He looks at his pal, who shrugs. "Beats me" the man mutters.

I return to the bike and dig out my instructions. "Well maybe you know the Embracing Pines B&B? The address is 32287 Mississippi Road."

That switches a light on. "I know that road from somewhere" says the man. He thinks for a while and another light goes on. "Yeah, you gotta go down the highway for about a mile, then turn right for another three miles. Mississippi Road will come up on the left." He shakes his head. "Never knew it was called Benedict. I've never heard of anywhere with that name."

I follow his guidelines, and sure enough Mississippi Road appears to my left. This grandly named-and-numbered road is nothing more than a dirt track that goes around in a circle, dropping me back to where I started. There are a few houses here and there, and on the second attempt I find number 32287, a ranch-style homestead set well back from the track. There are no signs to say this is the Embracing Pines, and certainly no explanation as to why an unmade track accommodating no more than two dozen houses should adopt *thirty two thousand, two hundred and eighty seven* as a house number. I find this baffling.

I wheel up to the driveway and rap on the door. A middle aged woman with dark hair seems startled to see me. She is staring at the bike with a look of horror.

"Nobody said anything about you arriving here on a bicycle" she complains. "They just told me you're from the BBC. What's the matter? Can't the BBC afford you a damn car?"

I check the instructions again. "You are Charlyne, right? Well Charlyne, once I get inside and cleaned up, I'll explain." I hope I'm not going to get this dumbstruck reaction every night. There is an awful lot of Minnesota to hack my way through yet.

For some reason I find Charlyne hard going. She is married to a chap called Dennis, but by mid evening there is still no sign of him. I am the only guest here, and I think the B&B thing must be a sideline. I'm curious as to why they set up this sort of business in a place so far from anywhere and so difficult to find.

Charlyne shrugs. "Because this is where we live."

Conversation is clipped and in short supply. Or perhaps it is just the wrong sort of chemistry between us. Once or twice I catch her looking at me intensely, as though building up hostility. My explanation of cycling the length of the Mississippi had not gone down well, maybe because Charlyne hails from the wastelands of North Dakota where I gather that cyclists are shot on sight.

There is clearly no restaurant in Benedict, and she at least offers to drive me to a steakhouse five miles away. This will give both of us a period of personal space. She drops me off and tells me to call the house when I need picking up.

I find a nice little corner to tuck myself away in, notebook in hand. It is what I call my 'cheap date' because on trips like this I tend to use this time of night to write up the day's notes. But scribbling away, alone at a restaurant table, always seems to attract the curiosity of others. A big lady with a slight German accent comes over to enquire about such odd behaviour. It turns out she is the proprietor, who has lived around here for the past

30 years. If I want a story, she says, I should come here in midwinter, "when the ice has settled over the lakes, and those lakes become cities until melting time."

"Cities?"

"Sure they do" she says in her adopted American English. "Haven't you heard of ice fishing?"

The image of a lone Eskimo comes immediately to mind, sitting on a bleak and frozen expanse as he dangles a fishing line over a small hole in the ice. There is an igloo in the background. He doesn't look as if he's having much fun.

"Oh, they have fun alright, from January through to the end of March. It is 24/7 party time, you believe it. Or maybe you haven't seen *Grumpy Old Men*?"

I have, but not the one she is talking about. A movie apparently, set on an ice fishing camp and starring that perfectly matched yet ill-matched pair, Walter Matthau and Jack Lemon. I invite her to sit down and tell me about this winter-long party-on-ice. It appears that once the ice is two or three feet thick, in moves the human race in a fiery effort to beat off the winter blues. They bring with them mobile homes specially designed for ice-top living, which are then towed across the frozen lake on skis. Entire streets are formed, with their own street names and postcodes, which will then expand into small temporary cities that can include stores and post offices. A few rules are laid down and mayors are elected for the duration of the season.

And the reason for all this? To drill holes in the ice underneath the floorboards, set the fishing lines deep under the ice, and sit back with a bottle of bourbon in the well heated, cosy comfort of the dwelling and let the coldwater fish start biting.

God knows what the traditional Eskimos would make of this, but the American Indians of the region were not slow to cash in. One nearby lake borders a large Indian reservation that is permitted to operate casinos. A while ago, tribal elders approved the construction of a gaming house-on-ice to lure in the rich and retired couch-potato fishermen. Their savvy did not go unrewarded.

Until, that is, the ice melted unexpectedly. Everyone got out in time, but the tent-like casino, caught at an angle, gradually slipped and slithered into the water - taking the slot machines and literally millions of coins with it.

"Every summer, amateur divers go down to the lake looking for this sunken treasure, and they always find some" the restaurant owner says. She had told me her name, but I've already forgotten it and I don't quite have the bottle to ask her again, particularly since she remembers mine. There is something formidable about this woman, but she's given me a great radio piece.

Dennis, Charlyne's other half, is prowling around the house when we get back, waiting to meet me apparently. He seems a decent guy who I find easy to communicate with. Talking to his wife also becomes easier - because although I'm politely addressing the pair of them, he's the one who replies.

The next day, as I'm stacking up the bike and getting ready to wheel away, he comes outside for a brief chat. "I was going to do what you're doing" he says, letting the words float away in the breeze.

"So what stopped you?"

Dennis jerks a thumb towards the door. The same door that Charlyne had stood at yesterday, glaring at the bike with loathing. "I got married" he answers, eyeing me a little sadly.

I wait for about five seconds, then slowly say, "You *idiot*."

He laughs, nodding his head vigorously. We shake hands and I ride away, feeling a pair of envious eyes bore into my back. We all make our own beds, and we've all got to get laid in them.

*T*HE BED I HAVE made for myself today - day three - is a long 60 mile hike to the city of Baxter, which will surely test the battery issue. The road takes me through the town of Walker, and then on to Hackensack where I witness an unusual sight. It is a wood carving of a lumberjack, a painted statuette standing in a small patch of parkland. He's got a bushy beard and wears a redcheck shirt and blue jeans. An axe rests over his shoulder, his right hand gripping the handle. Unlike the normal statues of cold grey stone, this one is animated, striking, and a lifelike work of art.

Incredibly, this colourful figure was carved in less than an hour - by chainsaw. I learn this from a passer-by who tells me that every year Hackensack hosts a chainsaw-carving competition. Participants come from all over the place, he says, and so do the crowds. The rules are simple. Each contestant is given a raw log of identical size, and exactly 60 minutes to carve out something from the teeth of a chainsaw that is readily identifiable. The end result can be anything from this particular lumberjack to a leaping walleye fish; or the Golden Gate Bridge, or a grizzly bear, or even the crippled Twin Towers when 9/11 struck.

Some of the sculptors are full time professionals who tour from show to show across the country, selling their works to collectors for envious sums. Oddball ways to make a living, as this one surely is, have always intrigued me - largely because my own activities in life have emanated from the very same school of thought. It's called the University of Life, in which getting to grips with the Theory of Chaos is the most coveted subject.

With the battery on amber, I wheel into Baxter with some relief. It is one of those towns that is not so much a disappointment as merely a convenient overnight stop: to use the local spelling, a drive-thru kind of place, with drive-thru banks, drive-thru burger joints, and other fast-food outlets; soulless hotels and motels, Walmarts and Seven-Elevens, and countless billboards. The river is five miles distant, though apparently not yet worth the effort to go and look at since it is only now just beginning to widen out a little. By the time I reach my next stop, the city of Little Falls, it will, I'm told, actually begin to look the way a river should.

Wooden statuette of a lumberjack - carved by a chainsaw.

I seldom bother to seek inspiring stories in places like this. The ambience, or what there is of one, intuitively tells me when it's not worth the bother. Besides, this is the dreaded third day - which has actually been not too bad on this occasion. So tonight I'll buy a takeaway instead, watch a little CNN, and in the morning, just ride on thru.

Three

THE FIRST SUPERHERO

SOLUTIONS: this one has been staring me in the face for the past three days, but it is only now that it dawns on me. Today's ride to Little Falls is a mere 32 miles, but there are enough serious ups and downs on the road to keep me edgy about the battery. On an eight-gear machine of this weight, sudden electrical failure would be catastrophic.

Plug it in for an hour's recharge whenever you stop for a lunchtime snack, you dumb banana. Every gas station and every café will have a spare socket somewhere. I must be having senior moments not to have thought of this before. It takes four hours from zero to full charge, so an hour's worth pumped in during the day will be of some small help. It is a shame that the designers of these bikes haven't yet developed a way of automatically recharging while you ride, by using the energy generated from pedalling.

This lunchtime stop is the tiny settlement of Fort Ripley, a one-horse town if ever there was. I find a café, park the bike against the wall next to an outdoor socket, and plug it in. This simple act of common sense leaves me feeling extremely pleased with myself.

Fort Ripley is the halfway point to Little Falls, where I believe my next decent radio piece awaits; so I buy a sandwich and some coffee, take it outside to sit in the warm sunshine, and think while I munch. It may or may not be that easy to make a story out of someone who's been dead for 32 years. Also, the achievement for which he will always be remembered, incredible as it was, took place as far back as 1927.

But riding into Little Falls, the first thing I spot seems a hopeful omen. Outside an unremarkable house in an unremarkable street stands that odd American icon, the personal mailbox. And this one is odder than most. Cut from aluminum, it is made in the shape of an aircraft, complete with propeller. It represents the *Spirit of St Louis*, the plane in which the legendary aviator Charles Lindbergh became the first man to fly across the Atlantic - alone, and with just a single engine at that. Little Falls had been Lindbergh's hometown.

It is Sunday. Downtown, there's an annual arts and crafts festival going on. Stalls are everywhere and the streets are packed. An impatient cop on traffic duty is as busy keeping the swarm of pedestrians in order as he is the traffic. I give him a street name, asking for directions to my hotel. He shrugs, pure boredom etched on his face. "Dunno. I've been drafted in from elsewhere" he grunts. "Ask someone else."

I ask a pedestrian who also shrugs. "Haven't got a clue. I only came here for the day." It seems the residents of Little Falls follow the same sentiments as the citizens of New Orleans. When *Mardi Gras* comes to town, everyone leaves. It takes another half hour to find my hotel.

The hotel clerk draws me a map to Lindbergh's house, about a ten minute ride away. I go back downtown and cross the Mississippi Bridge, astonished to see that the river has now widened from its narrow slit to about 100 metres from bank to bank. Now it is beginning to resemble a proper waterway.

I locate 1620 Lindbergh Drive South, where a modern visitors' centre is set down in a dell off the road. The *Charles A. Lindbergh*

Historic Site is a state-of-the-art miniature museum dedicated to the man's transatlantic flight, and to the subsequent events of a controversial political and public career.

Gary Block, a former radio hack himself, is in charge of the site today and invites me to look around the showcase before we wander over to the Lindbergh house next door. A stack of information and photographs are mounted on placards; and there's a tiny seven-seat movie theatre, just press a button to start the show rolling; what's more, there is a lifelike replica of the aircraft's cockpit in which you can sit and imagine what the man went through during his wearisome, pioneering flight through uncertain skies. For one thing, the seat is non-cushioned wickerwork - pretty uncomfortable for a non-stop 33 hours. For another, the only exterior vision he had was via a pair of small side windows. The actual windscreen, if you can call it that, had been a blank sheet of aluminum.

As we tread over to the house, Gary asserts that the aviator was America's very first superhero. "By that I mean, *international* hero. All the others with hero-status in this country had been national icons only: George Washington, Abe Lincoln, a few Generals, and pioneers like Davy Crockett, all the way through to the Wright Brothers. Until Lindbergh came along - and with the dubious exception of Mark Twain - we had nobody at all up there on the world stage."

My, how the airplane and transatlantic flying has changed all that.

The house itself is modest; three bedrooms, lounge and library, kitchen, and a screened veranda at the rear, from where the Mississippi is visible through the trees, about 100 metres away down a wooded slope.

The veranda is bare, except for a single bed in one corner. "This" says Gary, "is what became Lindbergh's bedroom. He loved the view of the river, and he liked the sparseness of furniture. For him, a bed was all that was required. It says something about the man. He didn't need material possessions because he lived in his head." Which is where, of course, he dreamed up his wonderfully outrageous plan to fly across the Atlantic.

In the kitchen are more telling signs of the aviator's personality. The bare wooden floor contains a good number of axe marks. "If it was cold or snowy outside, he'd chop up the firewood here in the kitchen, with scant regard for the consequences, or for his mother's despair. I mean, take a look at this."

The house where Charles lived. The riverside home of legendary aviator, Charles Lindbergh.

Gary's finger stretches towards several holes in the upper part of the kitchen door. "He'd won a Colt .45 in a shooting competition. Once, when he was bored and it was too wet outside, Charles came in here to practice fast-draws from the holster. If you look closely, you'll see one of the bullets embedded into the wood. The others went clear through it and into other parts of the house."

If the axe marks are an example of exuberant youth, the bullet holes go further. "Both he and his mother were very upset about this incident" Gary goes on, "but for different reasons. She was madder than hell with him for shooting up the place with live ammo. Charles, on the other hand, was angry because the bullets had missed their mark. He had wanted to do a fast-draw that would kill his imagined opponent. But the bullets went too high and wide - and this *enraged* him."

Outside, a strange box-like dark green car is coming through the front gate, one that belongs to a bygone era. "Lindbergh's first automobile" Gary says. "Built during the first world war by Saxon Cars of Detroit. He was only 16 when he took delivery of it, a time when driving permits hadn't even been thought of."

It is clearly still in good working order, and an important item in this shrine to Charles Lindbergh. It has apparently been on display down at the Little Falls exposition going on today, and here it is rattling home again, still alive and handle-starting some 80 years on. It makes Kevin Thyr's corpse-carrying Cadillac seem like a teenage delinquent, and it must be worth an absolute fortune.

Gary thinks for a moment. "There is a story in that car that will leave you in no doubt of Lindbergh's determination and his strength of character."

It transpires that in the same year he acquired the vehicle, Lindbergh decided to take it for a 2000 mile spin across to coastal California. "Everyone thought he was just a young teenage idiot; that he'd get no more than 50 miles down the road before turning back. But to turn back would be to admit defeat, and that was not in his make up. He kept on going, going, and going ... "

Gary's voice trails off. He is eyeing me with a twinkling smirk.

"Until?"

"Until he reached the Rocky Mountains in Colorado. As the long climb became steeper, the engine began to splutter. Then it died out altogether, but he soon cottoned on to the problem. Back in those days, the fuel was gravity-fed into the carburettor, and therefore wouldn't flow if the car was at too steep an angle. So d'you know how he overcame that? Well, I'll tell you - he simply turned the car around and climbed the Rockies in *reverse* gear. The drive to California took him 40 days, but he made it there."

This is a terrific item, leading me to think that there may be something different about the people who live alongside the Mississippi. Where there's a will, there *is* a way. And they'll do it *their* way at that. Lindbergh proved that much on May 21, 1927 when the wheels of the *Spirit of St Louis* touched down at Le Bourget airfield in northern France, still with 85 gallons of fuel to spare.

I carry on towards St Cloud the next day, the last stopover before hitting the twin cities of Minneapolis/St Paul. A few miles into this lovely sunny day comes the reminder that life is not so sunny for everyone as I cycle along the length of a grim, grey prison wall to my right. I had passed this same prison on the way up from Minneapolis to Park Rapids and had been told that whatever misadventures might await en-route, to avoid this place at all costs. "It doesn't matter what you've done or how much time you've got to serve, anyone who receives a prison sentence in this part of the state will start his time in this penitentiary, be they serial traffic violators or mass murderers" my informant had said.

The rectangular walls are about 20 feet high, topped off with razor wire. At each corner is a tall turret housing the armed guards. I can only guess at the spike-like reality of life on the other side of those walls and it makes me shudder - bringing to mind a brief conversation I once had with a cab driver taking me to New York's JFK airport. As we passed Rykers Island - one of the grimmest looking jails in America - the driver said "I did three years in that place. Worse thing of all was being told to bend over for a good butt-ramming by this six-foot-six guy - or else I'd be a dead man. He meant it too."

I foolishly asked what followed. Before replying, he glared at me through his rear mirror and then said quietly, "I'm still here, ain't I?"

It is an easy 30 mile ride today along a more or less straight-and-level highway, where the pine forests have given way to relatively open farmland. The river is nowhere to be seen. I cruise into St Cloud in the early afternoon and find my way to a B&B called the Heritage House, a rambling mansion dating back to the 1880s, and so named because it was the first house in the state of Minnesota to have electricity. I guess it must have been owned by a politician.

Shortly, a middle aged woman called Jean Robbins comes calling. She is from St Cloud's Convention & Visitors Bureau and has come to take me for a drive around her pleasant city. She wants to show me museums, historic houses, and public gardens, but these are simply not radio pieces. I point out that what I'm really after is the unusual, the bizarre, and anything remotely interesting to do with the Mississippi River.

She thinks for a moment, shakes her head, then says, "Around here there's only one thing I can think of. I hate to say it, but Minnesota has always been a state of serious drinkers. It's been that way since long before Prohibition, and it's still that way now. So let me show you something."

She turns the car around and we head for the fringes of town. At a tall sign boasting the name *Anton's*, she swings into the parking lot of a bar and restaurant set in some seclusion from the road. Jean tells me to ignore the sign, because everyone in these parts knows the place under a somewhat different name. "*Fish and Whiskey*" she says, as if the two go together like fish & chips. "That is the bar's real name" Jean states. "It goes back to the place's links with Prohibition."

She's not kidding. In a corner sits a copper moonshine still, which looks to be in pretty good condition considering it's more than 80 years old. She introduces me to Anton Gaetz, the owner, who cannot be that much younger than his distilling contraption. He has grizzled looks, suspicious eyes, and a gruff way with words. There is something about Anton that suggests he's known people in his time who you might be inclined to give a wide berth to.

"It is the last surviving still that produced a moonshine known as Minnesota 13" he tells me over a glass of something a lot less blistering than raw corn spirit. "That was the very best firewater of the times, and always in demand." He gives me a shifty glance, as if sizing me up for a bootlegging deal. "Back in them days, the biggest customer by far was John Dillinger. Minnesota was his turf. Bootlegging this stuff to the rest of the state kept him in the money. He used to come in here real regular, back in the 1920s when it was a speakeasy called Ricky's. There was never a chance of the place being busted, on account of it was owned by the Chief of Police's son. Yeah, this is where he came to pick up his supplies from the local distillers."

"My grandfather was one of them" Jean volunteers.

Anton raises a bushy eyebrow. "That so? Then you oughta try a shot of the family produce." He calls for the bartender to bring a bottle over.

This takes me by surprise. "You've got leftover bottles from Prohibition?"

"No. But the same Minnesota 13 formula is applied in making today's liquor."

"What! You produce moonshine today?"

"Sure. As souvenirs and novelty gifts mostly. It sells well. And it's no longer illegal; not in this state anyhow."

A bottle arrives on our table. Jean declines the offer (she's driving, she says), but out of sheer curiosity I nervously accept. The first sip feels like it's been poured straight from a boiling kettle, and the aftertaste is extremely harsh. It's as if the water used in distilling Minnesota 13 came not from the Mississippi, but from Satan's own River Styx. I manage to finish the shot somehow. If this was the cream of the crop, God knows how anyone survived the rougher blends.

John Dillinger and his connection with Minnesota 13 should make a good enough radio item on this fifth anniversary of the 9/11 atrocities - about which I've heard not a single word all day.

An original moonshine still from the days of Prohibition.
A brand known as 'Minnesota 13' carries on distilling to this day.

On an unrelated topic, it is worth noting a reader's letter in today's edition of the *Pioneer Press*, the region's principal daily newspaper published in St Paul. In the build-up to the coming mid-term elections, the writer underlines a deep and growing cynicism here in the Midwest with the George W. Bush administration. Someone called Dutton Foster sarcastically writes:

" ... *Let me testify that it brings tears to my eyes to think just how lucky we are to have a government featuring incompetent military adventurers, security and disaster bunglers, diplomatic boors, science obstructionists, advocates of mass deportation, homophobes, and people who consider poverty to be a character defect. If this is mainstream America, we must conclude that the stream needs serious anti-pollution measures in the November elections ... "*

Well now, Amen to that.

Four

THE JUG OF EMPIRE

BEFORE SETTING OFF on the 60 mile ride to the twin cities, I take a call from Paul Sherburne, the international marketing manager for the state of Minnesota. He's going to somewhere called Monticello today, and since it is situated halfway from here to Minneapolis and only slightly off my route, how about we meet up for lunch. Afterwards he'll take me on to St Paul because "getting through Minneapolis and into St Paul is going to be a nightmare for you."

I am not pig headed about this. At my time of life I want as few self-induced nightmares as possible. This ride is proving tough enough as it is, and I've been battling a consistently powerful headwind since Bemidji. So for the final 30 miles into the Twin Cities, I'll happily put my feet up in Paul's 4x4.

Another sunny day. I wheel out onto Highway 10, pedalling along a relatively flat surface, through the settlement of Clear Lake, and then on to Big Lake where I turn onto an empty road for three or four miles to the small-town America that is

Monticello. The only evidence of the river this morning has been the occasional green-and-white road sign depicting a ship's wheel. This means I'm travelling along the 'Great River Road', the series of highways which (as best they can) follow the entire length of the meandering Mississippi.

But I look forward to getting ever-further south of here, where the river will surely start to open up its secrets. It's been mighty tight-lipped for these first few days.

ST PAUL OFFERS A PROMISING START. I'm dropped off at 100 Harriet Island Road, my lodgings for the next couple of nights. Except that this is no run-of-the-mill hotel; the Covington Inn is a 110-foot converted tugboat tied alongside a marina wharf, with the skyscrapers of St Paul towering across the river. At this point, the Mississippi is about 200 metres wide. Pleasure boats pass by in both directions, cruising gently towards a watery twilight. It is a serene sight.

And made all the better by my accommodation. I have an adequate sleeping cabin, plus the pilot house and top deck to myself. The pilot house, which is now a snug living room, still maintains its navigation instruments and controls. With the views it offers of the river and the city, I am much at home on this comfortable old banger.

The owner intrigues me. Her name is Liz Miller, an attractive 37 year old brunette, single, and 'between boyfriends'. She is also of independent and enterprising spirit. She hates getting up in the morning, refuses to answer the phone if she's not in the mood, and took out a $530,000 loan over 15 years to buy this little floating hotel.

"The previous owners found it in a junk yard" she tells me. "It was a derelict rust bucket which they picked up for $7,000 and on which they spent a fortune putting it into some kind of shape again. They then opened it up as a restaurant in 1995. I started work here as the waitress. But it didn't really work out as a restaurant, so when they talked of selling up, I thought …

yeah, why not go for it and make them an offer; I'll turn most of the ship into a B&B, and the rest into a home for myself."

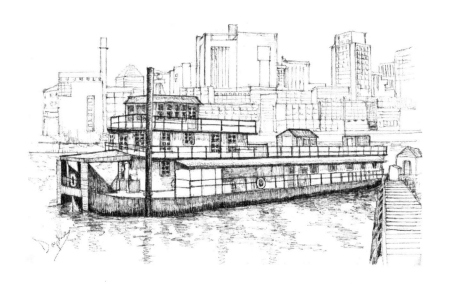

The Covington Inn, an old converted towboat, now a hotel near downtown St Paul.

The American Dream applies to every walk of life, it seems. That was 18 months ago. How is it working out?

She shrugs, seemingly unworried. "I'm a good swimmer. I don't think I'm gonna go under." Well, I for one hope that she stays afloat. This B&B is unique.

The next morning a chap called Brad Toll arrives at the boat. He's a big guy, tall and broad, in his late 30s, and who knows every square inch of the city, for which he is the vice-president of marketing. He has come to take me on a guided tour of gangland.

It is an illuminating morning. St Paul, the capital of Minnesota, is an elegant city and very different from its brasher neighbour, Minneapolis. I am pleasantly surprised to find at least as much greenery, woodland, and parks as there is glass and concrete. Some of the avenues and old houses are absolutely splendid. The city hums quietly, as if the river is its calming influence: a metropolis that appears to be wholly at peace with itself.

"It's got a raw side too" Brad says. "You'll see what I mean at lunchtime."

From a tourism perspective, much of the city's attraction lies in some violent history, during a time when St Paul was by no means at peace with itself. "The Gangster Tour is the most popular with our visitors" Brad states. "It traces the events from John Dillinger's time in the city."

I learn that Dillinger had the chief of police and the mayor in his pocket, so whenever the FBI came looking for him after a tip off, the police would smuggle Dillinger into a safe house in the area. The deal was that Dillinger and his gang undertook never to commit robberies or murders in St Paul - though he was at perfect liberty to engage in looting and killing sprees over in Minneapolis. In fact the police chief and the mayor encouraged it, because they both got instant payouts from the proceeds.

Brad takes me to a strange, cavernous building called Castle Royal on South Wabasha Street where the various rooms are like vast underground tombs. Amid the gloom is a long bar and dance floor. "This was Dillinger's favourite speakeasy where he did most of his deals" Brad explains. "The Tommy Dorsey band were resident musicians, playing to up to 300 guests while illicit gambling and drinking was going on in these other rooms. Today, we use it for conventions and private parties."

Later, we stop outside a dated red-brick apartment block on South Lexington Parkway, and Brad points to a third-floor window. "That's where Dillinger was holed up with his mistress for a few months. He used a disguise, but a neighbour grew suspicious and called the FBI. On March 13, 1934, a ferocious gun battle took place between the Feds and Dillinger right there in the hallways of the block. On that occasion, he managed to give them the slip."

After a few more gangster sites involving the no-less notorious Fred and Ma Barker, we cruise into a slightly run-down part of town where Brad leads me into a rough kind of bar-cum-eating house called the *Gopher Bar*, apparently a place known for its specialty hot dogs. "If you happen to order anything but a beer or bourbon to go with it, don't be offended if the waitress gives you a mouthful. It's all part of the charm" Brad advises.

I see his point. Pasted onto a mirror behind the bar are the following notices:

No fucking credit cards!
No fucking personal checks!
Fucking cash only!
   ... and ...
Be nice to your bartender. Even the toilet can only take one asshole at a time.

Almost everyone in here is drinking beer or bourbon or both. The waitress comes over to ask what we want with the hot dogs. I order a glass of white wine. She stares down at me, then her eyes start searching the floor as if she's lost something. She finally says, "I'm looking for the manhole you came out of, dude."

"No, no. It was the wine cellar" comes my rapid riposte.

"The last wine seller to come in here was run outta town. Never did come back."

It's just a bit of enjoyable banter. If this is St Paul's 'raw side', then this is one very civilised town. Sitting here in this hot dog-and-bourbon den (with a glass of wine now in front of me), seems an appropriate moment to reel off a few of Mark Twain's words when he last visited St Paul in 1882. After giving out some statistics of the city's impressive rate of growth, he added the following observation.

'How solemn and beautiful is the thought that the earliest pioneer of civilization, the van leader of civilization, is never the steamboat, never the railroad, never the Sabbath school, never the newspaper, never the missionary - but always whiskey! Look history over: you will see. The missionary comes after the whiskey has arrived; next comes the poor immigrant, with axe and hoe and rifle; next, the trader; next, the miscellaneous rush; next, the gambler, the desperado, the highwayman, and all their kindred in sin of both sexes; and next, the smart chap who has bought up an old grant that covers the land; this brings the lawyer tribe; the vigilance committee brings the undertaker. All these interests bring the newspaper; the newspaper starts up politics and a railroad; all hands turn to and build a church and a jail - and behold, civilization is established forever in the land. But whiskey, you see, was the van leader in this beneficent work. It always is. It was like a foreigner - and excusable in a foreigner - to be ignorant of this great truth. But if he had been conversant with the facts, he would have said *"Westward, the jug of empire takes its way."*

This great van leader arrived upon the ground which St Paul now occupies in June, 1837. Yes, at that date, Pierre Parrant, a French-Canadian, built the first cabin, uncorked his jug, and began selling whiskey to the Indians. The result is before us.'

This passage is extracted from Mark Twain's wonderful book, *Life on the Mississippi*. He had arrived in St Paul as a passenger aboard a steamboat, having made the long voyage from New Orleans. During Twain's much earlier incarnation as a steamboat pilot, his patch was strictly the Lower Mississippi, St Louis to New Orleans and back. I'll reflect further on this colourful scribe further down the line.

An amusing tale that Brad relates as we munch on our food concerns the former governor of Minnesota, a one-time heavyweight wrestler called Jesse Ventura and someone who would be very much at home in this little dive. Gaffe-prone, and not a man to think twice before speaking out, he had on several occasions been the cause of some embarrassment to this state which, until recently, he represented. During his tenure of office, the son of the Emperor of Japan paid a courtesy visit to St Paul. On being introduced to the Japanese heir to the throne, Ventura looked him up and down, then said, "*So tell me, boy - is your face on the money yet?*"

Once a month during the summer, Liz Miller holds a kind of outdoor hen party up on the wharf beside her boat, her way of keeping in regular touch with friends. Tonight is the night, and I'm invited to participate in a glass or two of wine. Surrounded by ten or more St Paul beauties, I'm somewhat reluctant to break off for my weekly BBC broadcast spot, but it's got to be done. Later, once that is out of the way, I go back outside. But alas, they have all dispersed into the night.

I stay outside for a while, watching the lights of St Paul flicker on the river like restless diamonds skimming over the ripples. In a sense, this city is the first milestone of the ride. The next will be St Louis, then Memphis, and finally New Orleans. But it is all the little river ports in between that I really want to discover, and tomorrow that will start in earnest as I head for the riverside city of Red Wing, some 50 miles south of the Covington Inn and its engaging, enigmatic mistress.

Five

REDEMPTION

I PEDAL FOR A FEW MILES alongside the river, into the industrial outskirts of St Paul, and then join Highway 61 South with its little green-and-white ship wheel signposts. For a while it is fairly flat, but then the hills and the headwinds begin, and the river fades from sight.

And the sun heats up to the boil. This is tough. The electric-assist gets more than normal use, and I'm relieved to pull in at the halfway stop of Hastings to plug in the battery charger. Later in the afternoon I come face to face with a really serious hill that seems to head right on up to the cloudless sky, and decide to walk it when the electric motor displays some obvious signs of fatigue. To my concern, here in the middle of nowhere, the fuel gauge has gone from green to amber already, and it suddenly seems a very long way to Red Wing, let alone to the end of the river. I am indeed starting to feel like a guinea pig in the cause of electric bikes.

At the top of this long steep hill the road levels off, and by using pedals only I manage to defeat what is now a strong crosswind. But that is only until I meet with a junction, where the sign pointing me towards the final 14 miles into Red Wing has me going into another head-on blast. I cannot adequately relate just how frustrating this is to the long-distance cyclist. It is a battlefield, where the advancing enemy hugely outnumber your own troops - which in my case totals a rapidly-fading battery and a pair of tiring legs. It is going to be a rout.

A couple of miles on, and not even daring to look at the gauge, something is very obviously wrong, and it doesn't take much analysis to see what. Not one, but two industrial size staples are wedged into my rear tyre and, what a surprise, it is as flat as a week-old beer.

What's more, my repair kit is nowhere to be found. I must have left it at the Covington Inn during one of my occasional clear-outs, damn it. I muse on the problem for a few moments. This is a case of somehow turning a negative into a positive.

There are still 12 miles left to Red Wing, so other than walking the distance with a wheel that jumps and hiccups twice per revolution, there is only one option. Three ranch houses are within eyesight. Someone might be going into town, or at least allow me to use a phone. So I walk the bike along the highway's shoulder towards the first homestead, a low-slung affair in the midst of outbuildings.

Nobody home.

It is the same with the next place, about 500 metres further along. There's a big 4x4 in the drive, but nobody answers the bell except for a barking dog. At the third ranch, there is activity. A group of workers are discussing something in the yard, and pulling on their gloves in preparation for some task or other. The boss man offers me his mobile phone. I fish out the number of the Golden Lantern Inn and speak to the lady in charge. She says don't worry, I'll send my husband out to get you - such is the friendly and instant helpfulness of small town America, which I know I can rely on. He'll be there before the hour is up, she adds.

The problem solved, I return to the ranch entrance and sprawl out on the grass in the warm sunshine of late afternoon, sip some fruit juice from my flask, and contentedly watch the traffic go by. The negative of 30 minutes ago has become a positive. Welcome to such events on the road - and to the line of least resistance.

Red Wing is an attractive, sloping kind of town where I've got just the one night. Gary McKenna, my rescuing Samaritan and host at the Golden Lantern Inn, gets us into town in time to drop the bike off at a cycle shop, where I'm told to come back sometime after 9am tomorrow. It is now in someone else's charge, freeing me up for a limited period to be a journalist, not a cyclist. This is a schizophrenic way of life, believe me.

After nightfall, I wander the town's quiet streets in search of a reasonable restaurant and/or bar, where the chances of striking up an illuminating conversation can make all the difference to the week's radio stories. Precious few of my pieces are pre-arranged on a ride such as this. To me, it is a question of spotting something and going for it, rather than relying on some PR opportunist to spin me a convenient line.

In the mood for a half-rack of spare ribs, I eventually find a place to satisfy both of tonight's requirements. I settle at a table in the bar area where I shall both eat and predatorily observe. I'll snatch someone with a story tonight. I can feel it.

It turns out to be the bartender himself. He is doubling as both bartender and waiter on this quiet night, and when he brings my plate of ribs over, he asks where I'm from. I tell him about my odd mission and he suggests that we go to the bar next door when he gets off work at 11pm. He's got a story, he says. A modern American story.

Come 11pm, we go next door to a small, seedy looking watering hole, painted all over in dark blue; the sort of place where you might expect to find sombre roughnecks lining the bar, staring miserably into their beers as if they might just contain the meaning of life.

Geordie Wilson is 28, a tall, fit young man with a lean face and dark hair, and distant family roots in Scotland and Northern Ireland, though he's not been to either. But such an explosive mixture of Celtic blood somehow sets the scene for a troubled life. His story is simultaneously uplifting and depressing.

"I was brought up in Bucks County, Pennsylvania" he says. "I went to a Catholic school, but had so many learning difficulties that they kicked me out. My inabilities must have been real bad, on account of the next school I went to was for kids *with* learning difficulties - and they kicked me out as well. I began to get into trouble after that, lots of vandalism and shit. By the time I was 14 I was not only on cocaine, I was dealing the stuff."

That led to 18 months of rehab in a detention centre. On returning home, his father threw him out of the house after just a few months, and he went back to selling LSD, marijuana, cocaine. "I only ever sold to actual dealers, never to kids. That's what made me so lousy at the job. I had a conscience."

He was caught once more and sentenced to a year in the county jail, where he finally managed to learn how to read and write. Strangely for a man of such non-academic background, the book that did it for him was George Orwell's *Nineteen Eighty Four*. But what happened next was typically tragic. "When I came out, I went to work at my uncle's roofing business in Philadelphia, and stayed far away from the drugs. But a few months later I broke my neck *and* my back in one big automobile smash and was laid out for months. It was during that period that my dad died as well. I was in a lot of emotional turmoil, as well as physical agony; and yeah, sure enough I went back on the stuff. To tell you the truth, I just didn't *care* any more, not about anything. Until I met Allison."

Allison, a professional artist plying her trade in Philadelphia, hailed from Red Wing. They took up together and three years ago she persuaded her man to move back here with her. So far, so good. He's held down the same job for all this time and believes that he's finally seen the last of the bad old days.

"There is no way I'd have come through all this without Allison. Or Red Wing for that matter. It's the river, man. It's got something that gets into your blood." He pauses for a reflective moment. "You know, whenever there's shit between me and Allison, we walk down to the river to sort things out, even in the dead of winter. It is like a healing agent, a go-between. I know it sounds cute, but the Mississippi has some kind of magic flowing in its water. I can't rightly explain it, but it's there alright."

I can make a neat radio piece out of this. Not just the mighty Mississippi, but the magic Mississippi. A river, that with a little help from a friend, has done its bit in the redemption of a once-futile drug dealer and addict - giving fresh hope to a human life that had written itself off as a lost cause.

*T*HE TYRE FIXED, I pedal away from Red Wing on the 30 mile ride to Wabasha, cursing myself a few miles on for completely forgetting to buy a new puncture kit while at the cycle shop. Hell, I'm not turning around now, so I carry on and hope for the best. At least the omens are good. The magic river is in plentiful view today, widening out in parts as to be more like a lake. A good number of mid-river islands are dotted here and there, as I pedal through sunshine and greenery. Today, Minnesota is dazzling. As against that, are the hills and this relentless headwind, but the electric-assist is in defiant mood and still on green as I wheel into Lake City for a lunchtime snack and an hour's plug-in. Dozens of boats are out there on the expanse spreading far and wide, their fortunate owners lazing the day away with fishing lines and chilled beer.

Around mid-afternoon I make it into Wabasha, and for some reason head straight for the river at the bottom of a downtown street. There is a lock-and-dam in the distance, one of 29 that exist on the Upper Mississippi between the Twin Cites and St. Louis. Closer in, is the Mississippi Bridge linking this Minnesotan river town with the state of Wisconsin to the east.

Below me, an old boy is sitting on a jetty and patiently waiting for his fishing rod to tug and jerk with a hooked fish. A few boats idle by. All is quiet and peaceful.

I pull myself away and go in search of the Andersen Heritage House, my lodgings for the night. I find it at the far end of Main Street, a big red-brick building apparently 150 years old. The receptionist hands me a chunky key to Room 10 - and then asks if I'd like to have a cat.

I must have misheard. "I'm sorry, what was that?"

"I said, would you like a cat?"

I am perplexed and it shows. "Look" she goes on, "the hotel has six or seven cats living here. They all love human company, so if you want to sleep with a cat tonight, we've got plenty."

In my wanderings over the years, I've many times been approached by shifty looking concierges and seedy hotel pimps offering women, or drugs, or visits to illegal gambling dens, or stolen goods at knock down prices. But never before has a hotel employee offered me a cat for the night.

"Yes, why not?" I shrug. Maybe I can shape a radio item out of this. I know of nowhere else that offers this eccentric service.

"I'll book one in for you" she replies, jotting it down on a notepad.

At around sundown a short, bespectacled woman of about 50 comes looking for me. "I'm Barbara - Barb for short - and I've come to take you to dinner."

This is news to me, welcome as it is. She is from Wabasha's Convention & Visitors Bureau, or CVBs as they're known, which appear to be tracking my journey with zeal. First off, she suggests, an aperitif down in the hotel's cellar bar. It is humming with people this Friday evening. We settle down at a spare table and along comes this waitress who is eagerly gulping a glass of red wine as she works.

"I'm the guest waitress" she explains. "Every Friday we have a guest barman and a guest waitress. We're volunteers. Since I'm doing it for nothing, I'm gonna drink as I work. Try and stop me."

Funny, but since visiting the Charles Lindbergh house, and then getting to know Liz Miller of the towboat B&B, and following last night's chat with Geordie Wilson, I am definitely forming the impression that there is something different about the people who live along the Mississippi; the offer of a cat for the night and this wine-toting waitress does nothing to dispel this notion. I cannot put my finger on what it is exactly, at least not yet; but these little ports nestling on the big river seem curiously detached from the rest of the USA, as though belonging to a vast body of water first, and to a huge nation as an afterthought.

Much later, when I go up to bed there's a sharp rap on my door. The receptionist stands in the hallway holding a big black five-kilo tomcat. I had forgotten all about it. I take the furry creature and bid her goodnight. She says, not so fast, buster. I'll be back. A few minutes later she returns with a cat litter tray. Great. Just what I wanted next to me in this cramped bedroom.

After lights out, the purring tom settles down on my chest. Each time I pull him off, he leaps right back on again. His weight makes breathing difficult and the volume of his purr must be waking the entire floor. Somehow I drift off to sleep with my new friend perched on top of me. At some point during the night, I awake to sharp pains. The cat has got its teeth into my fingers, and its claws are tearing into the duvet cover. I'm not sure this was such a good idea.

But I survive the night, plus the sight of a much-used litter tray in the morning. Before riding away, Barbara returns to take me to the Eagle Center - a kind of RSPCA for wounded bald eagles. Minnesota is very much bald eagle territory. It is a new venture, which at present has just three birds in captivity, to which they seem to have adapted well. One fell out of its nest and broke a wing; the other two are traffic victims. The talons on these creatures are simply awesome, as indeed are their eyries. I am told that a bald eagle nest can weigh up to a staggering four tons.

In theory, it should be a simple ride today, just 35 miles to the riverside city of Winona, my last stop in the state of Minnesota. On the road however, it is not that easy. A lovely sunny day, lush greenery, and the sparkling river are marred by a headwind so powerful I actually have to hard-pedal it when going downhill, otherwise the wind will bring me to a standstill.

I share the road with an abnormal number of motorbikes, some in loose packs of three or four, others in battalions of 30, 40, or even more. Their powerful thrust causes me not a little envy as they slice effortlessly through the wind, taking the steep hills with the charging strides of cavalry horses at the orders of their black-leathered hussars.

Coming on lunchtime, I notice a little settlement high up on a bluff overlooking the river, a place called Minneiska with a population of 116. I pedal up the steep incline towards it and notice several motorbikes parked outside a couple of neighbouring café/bars. I opt for the one called Buck's Bar and wheel into a patch of ground next to it - straight into some incredulous stares. If you want to travel on two wheels in America, then buddy, the machines come with engines, not pedals.

"That's one quiet bike you've got there, pal" opines one rider. He's got a hamburger in one hand and some hard liquor in the other. "Whaddaya get out of it - six miles an hour?"

I ignore the jibe. "What's with all the bikes?" I ask him. "There seems to be thousands on the road today."

"The Fall Flood Run" he answers, taking a belt of liquor and grimacing as it kicks him back. "We do it every year at this time, for charity."

Further probing reveals that Minnesota bikers make three or four charity runs a year. The way it works is that on a given day groups of bikers - be they large, small, or even solo - take to the roads of their choice and ride the day away in any manner they wish. "Some guys ride 500 miles, others only 50 or so. But whatever we spend, say 100 bucks per head in food, booze, and fuel, we'll match that amount for whichever charities we choose."

Bikers galore at Minneisk, Minnesota. Somehow the eZee Torq, foreground, is the loner in the pack.

Minneiska is suddenly filling up will fall flood runners. The machines are mainly Harleys, hugely powerful and daunting to behold. As each one arrives, they back into neatly parked lines on both sides of the road. One guy rolls up astride an ostentatious yellow three-wheeler which is the size of Bill Clinton's ego. He's a big chap, but dwarfed by his own machine. There were about 20 bikes when I rolled in here not ten minutes ago. Now there's more like 100, doubling the settlement's population and climbing by the second. Outside the bar, a hamburger stall is doing some serious business from this swarm of black leather. Inside, the pack is not worrying about any drink-driving laws today.

They are a mixed bunch. The men are anywhere between 25 and 70, though most have probably got more hair on their chests than their heads. Their women are all surprisingly feminine, though with an obvious penchant for the bar room way of life. I can only spot one amongst them who hasn't got a drink and a cigarette on the go.

The view of the river from up here is stunning. There's a smattering of woody, uninhabited mid-river islands and the water is an azure blue. A few boats are out and about, though I've still to spot any commercial traffic.

After giving the battery a decent boost, I take my leave of the bikers, feeling almost a target as I run the gauntlet of polished chrome that glints in the afternoon sun like theatre footlights. Once back on Highway 61, I follow the river into Winona, caring not about the unremitting headwind. With a recharged battery and only 15 miles more to ride, the bike and I cut through it with contempt.

Winona is actually situated on an island, and the last town of any size in Minnesota's river zone. The border with Iowa is just 12 miles south of here. I cross a short bridge onto the island and head downtown in search of tonight's accommodation, the Carriage House B&B at 420 Main Street. But first I ride down to the river and sit on the levee for a while, just watching the water roll by. Here, the Mississippi seems devoid of life, not a boat in sight nor anyone but me sitting on the levee. I find it odd that at certain stages, this once-so-busy river appears to be nothing more than a sleepy daydream. At this point it is about 600 metres wide - and what a lonely, empty 600 metres they are.

I locate the Carriage House - another rambling old property going back in time, and am designated the 'Toy Room', once a room for stable boys back when it was part of a horse stud. If this is 420 Main Street, Winona must have been little more than a few shacks back in 1870 when the house was built. Far from being a working lad's pit, the room is now adorned with teddy bears and other toys, which I find just a little silly.

It is going to be a quiet night. I'm unable to drum up the enthusiasm for the Heritage Fair going on at Winona State University; nor, I'm afraid, for the Jimmy Dorsey Orchestra playing inside the university's gymnasium. Instead, I'll simply find some place to eat, take my cheap-date notebook along for company, and later on cuddle up beside a teddy bear.

Six

WINGING IT THROUGH WISCONSIN

SUNDAY MORNING IS GREY AND DULL; rain is in the air. It starts as I'm crossing the Mississippi Bridge and by the time I arrive in Wisconsin a minute or two later, it is coming down like Niagara Falls. This is about as joyful as walking the plank, and just as drenching.

I pull in at a small service station and wait for brighter skies. Those travellers who call in are not necessarily after fuel. A good half of them seem to be leaving with six-packs of beer and other liquor you can buy at such places. Most have Minnesota number plates. In Wisconsin they can buy booze on a Sunday. In Minnesota, they cannot. A few bikers roll in, shaking the raindrops from their leathers. One of them says that if I think this sort of weather is bad on a pedal bike, then try being on a motorbike. "At 60 miles an hour, it's like speeding into an avalanche of flying nails" he grumbles.

The gloom eventually lifts. I get back in the saddle and make my way down Highway 35 South (which actually takes me due east for a few miles). For once, the wind is behind me and with a brightening sky I'm beginning to enjoy myself, not once having to use the electric-assist. I'm heading for the city of La Crosse about 50 miles away. Having pedalled 12 miles in seemingly no time, I should be there by ...

Phut.

Another rear-tyre puncture, again caused by a giant staple. What the hell are these items doing on the road anyway? And I'm extremely cross with myself because I've still to buy a repair kit. But where to find help on this quiet Sunday morning? I walk the bike along the shoulder until a building comes into view on the other side of the road. It looks to be a café or something. Closer scrutiny reveals it to be rather more than that. It is a lap-dance den situated on the side of a lonely road in the middle of nowhere. Even so, empty liquor bottles and beer cans litter the veranda, evidence of some wild trade into the wee hours. They'll all be sleeping it off right now. Nobody is around.

I walk another couple of miles and come across a small settlement of modest houses and trailer homes. One of them has the front door ajar, so I tap on it. An old boy of about 70 answers my knock.

"Yeah?" he says, looking at me suspiciously. I explain the problem and he allows me to use his phone. And I come up with the same solution as last time. Tonight's landlady is on her way. I really hate doing this, but right now I've no choice.

The old man's got the television trained on an NFL football game, the Green Bay Packers versus the Miami Dolphins. How anyone can call this sport football defeats me. But my lined and grizzled host invites me to sit and watch, and he slowly begins to open up.

His wife - or the 'old bitch' as he refers to her - has gone out. "It's why I turn the game on" he chuckles. "The old bitch can't stand football, so she goes off for the day. Dunno what she gets up to, and I don't care neither."

Stan, as he tells me to call him, has apparently lived around here for all his life other than for a spell in Vietnam. Even though the river is now some miles to the west and long out of sight, I ask him why it seems so quiet these days. It surely couldn't have always been like this.

"Nope, it wasn't. There was a time when you couldn't see across the other side for towboats and the like. But times changed, people moved away to the cities, money got tight, and the boats didn't stop around here no more. The river ain't dead yet, but it's down on its back, getting screwed, and I don't see it getting up again, not on the Upper Mississippi anyways. Could be different further down south, I wouldn't know. The railroads have stolen so much of the river trade, that I ain't holding my breath for some big revival. No sir, I ain't."

The railroads, which run along both sides of the river, are very much alive. The warning hoots and blasts of these massive diesel freighters, each hauling a good two miles of rolling stock, are routinely heard throughout the day and night.

Eventually a blonde woman in her late 30s swings into the old man's driveway. She is Dee Martin, owner of the Celtic Inn in the port of La Crosse, and another Samaritan for this hapless cyclist. Only half of my brute of a bike will fit into her little hatchback; the other half pokes out from the back with the hatch door held down by taut bungee cords. Old man Stan says to call in again when I pass through next, as if Highway 35 is a regular milk run for cyclists and other wayward types.

At a place called Centerville, Dee turns off towards the river and the delightful little town of Trempealeau, where some aesthetically-pleasing French colonial architecture lines the riverbank. The French were prolific in this region during the pioneering days. Many of Wisconsin's towns and cities bear witness to this, both in architecture and place names - Trempealeau and La Crosse being clear examples. As a brief aside, I know that there is a pair of French journalists from *Paris Match* in the area, tracing French history along the Mississippi. All the various CVBs have told me about them, and they apparently know about my own venture down the river. We are anxious to meet up and compare notes, but we keep missing one another by whisker margins.

La Crosse is a pleasant, medium sized town where river activity is more or less limited to private boats, and to short pleasure cruises in replica sternwheelers during the warm months. In a Wisconsin winter, the river freezes over. I would not want to live here. But it's the first place I've come across where a slight French influence hangs in the air, which in some strange way does make a difference from the run-of-the-mill. All the same, once that puncture is fixed, I'll be more than ready to leave because a honed instinct tells me I'm not going to find much here.

The La Crosse CVB dubs its own little stretch of the Mississippi as the 'River of Dreams'. Well that's as maybe; but if dreams equal imagination, then my own is not yet being tested enough. Where is the bizarre, the outrageous, the outstanding, for God's sake? Alas, I was never gifted with much patience.

The puncture repaired, I pedal on another 30 miles to an unscheduled stop in a one-horse river town called Genoa where there is one tiny hotel and an even smaller motel. The latter has the grand total of two rooms, and I can take my pick. After sundown I wander around town which takes all of five minutes - and that includes puffing my way up a short steep hill to the main street standing on a high bluff overlooking the river. It is Monday night. There are two bar/restaurants in town and one of them is shut. Having no choice, I saunter into the smaller of the two - and straight into the sight of a huge Union Jack pinned up on the wall, along with an assortment of London memorabilia: tube station signs, a silk-screened tee-shirt of Tower Bridge with the obligatory red-coated beefeater, a painting of Hampton Court.

There's a bargirl and one lone drinker sitting on a barstool. "I imagine the owner of this place is British" I opine.

"Yeah" says the bargirl. "Only he ain't in. Monday is his night off." Pity, I'd like to prise open the mind of a fellow Englishman who has chosen to settle in a tiny little spot like

Genoa. He would surely view the town, the river, the surrounds, and the people with the critical mind of an outsider. His opinions and local knowledge would probably make good listening.

"You a Brit too?" asks the guy on the barstool, seemingly pleased that a little company has arrived his way. I settle down next to him, view the limited menu with some despair, and order a cheeseburger and a glass of wine.

"Greg Roberts" he says, holding out his hand. "Genoa born and raised, and I wouldn't live anywhere else." He's about 40, of stocky build, and with a thick crop of wavy brown hair.

"Why not?" I enquire.

"Because I get to travel enough as it is. My job takes me all over the U.S. and sometimes overseas. I get to see a lot of shit out there. Returning to peaceful Genoa is like waking up from a goddam nightmare, every time."

I wonder if the river has anything to do with this, and ask as much.

He doesn't hesitate. "Oh Christ, yes. If Genoa was not on the Mississippi, I might just see the place differently. The river ... it kinda clears my head, if you know what I mean. The first thing I do when coming home from a business trip is to take a long, long walk down by the water. And it works."

He must have one hell of a stressful job, I suggest. And this much turns out to be true.

Greg's government-paid job is to get inside peoples' heads: not ordinary citizens, but returning U.S. servicemen from Iraq and Afghanistan. He flies from base to base around the country examining soldiers, sailors, and air force personnel for possible psychiatric troubles. "As a result of this god-awful war in Iraq, insanity is now as much a growth industry within the armed forces as it is in Washington DC" he says angrily. "Those guys go out there more or less normal, but half of them are coming back as real crazies, and with some lasting damage. One guy I saw last week howls at the moon. Another believes he's a reincarnated fish and wants to go live underwater. It's as bad as

Vietnam was, maybe worse."

The war is a frequent topic of conversation along this river, where people seem outraged by such a fruitless and bloody conflict, and I've yet to meet a single supporter. Unlike so much of rural USA, the residents of these Mississippi ports are independent free-thinkers, reinforcing my ever-growing belief that subconsciously at least, they belong far more to the big river than they ever will to the rest of the country.

The next morning I carry on to Prairie du Chien, 35 miles south of Genoa where I'll overnight and then re-cross the Mississippi into the state of Iowa. Well, that's the plan. But plans have a way of going awry sometimes, and I can feel this one trying to slip the net almost the moment I step into the Sportsman's Grill in the little port of Ferryville, the halfway point on today's ride.

The Sportsman's Bar & Grill, Ferryville, Wisconsin - where it takes about two minutes to become 'one of the boys'.

The sun is out and the river is a sparkling blue as I enter Ferryville, which looks to be every inch a frontier township. It has a 'buckskin and log cabin' feel about it, as if Davy Crockett might at any moment lurch out of the Wooden Nickel Saloon a few metres further up the street. For sure, he would have been right at home inside the Sportsman's Grill, where a handful of frontier types in lumberjack shirts and baseball caps are sitting around the three-sided bar swapping cheerful banter. At this point, the plan is to plug the battery in, order a light lunch, and then hit the road again.

But this is a small town on the banks of the Mississippi, where to make conversation with a total stranger is an automatic obligation. These days, I only very occasionally sip an alcoholic drink before nightfall, but in the few minutes it takes to become one of the gang the wine glasses just keep landing at my side. "This one's from Bill over there; that one's from Jake" says the plump bargirl, known to everyone simply as 'Bug'. ("It's become a nickname so well known around town, even my boss writes my weekly paycheck out to 'Bug'. The bank always cashes them, no problem.")

And then in walks her boss, the owner, a beefy individual who can spot a stranger a mile off. "Get that guy over there a drink" he says to Bug. "Who is he anyway?"

Where in England, or anywhere else, could you walk into a provincial pub as a complete unknown, and have everyone inside lining up to buy you a drink? Nowhere is the pretty safe answer to that. Nonetheless, this well-meaning hospitality has a few built-in problems. Quite apart from the danger of being nabbed by the cops as drunk in charge of a bicycle, ethics insist that I return the favour to each one of these generous barflies. I quickly learn that daytime drinking is pretty routine in Ferryville. Some are retired, some work part time, and others are either on welfare or of independent means. Jake, an 18-wheeler truck driver has just returned home from a long trip to Arkansas, and his next job up to Chicago isn't for three whole days.

"Damned if I'm gonna stare at the walls for all that time" he growls into his beer.

"What about the missus?"

"Hauled her ass elsewhere. Can't even remember what she looks like."

The owner comes round to my side of the bar, hand outstretched. "I'm Bruiser, the proprietor" he says genially. "Welcome to the big city, population all of 175 and falling." He is about 45, with arms like tree trunks, and an aura that suggests nothing ever fazes him.

With so small a population, there are no ferries in Ferryville any more, Bruiser tells me - despite the town being named as such because they were so plentiful in bygone times. To cross the Mississippi, Ferryville residents have to drive north to La Crosse or south to Prairie du Chien - another indication of the river's strange isolation in these northern parts.

"What do you do for entertainment around here?"

He sweeps an arm around the bar. "This is about it. We drink. Oh, and once a year, we'll go and watch the Outhouse Races."

"The what?"

"The Outhouses Races. You know what an outhouse is, don't you?"

The only outhouse that I've ever heard of is an outside loo. Bruiser nods and says "Yeah, that's right. The john, the can, the shithouse. We race 'em, every July."

I stare at him blankly, unable to fathom what he's on about. I mean, how do you enter an outside lavatory into a race? "Look, it's just a bit of fun" Bruiser explains. "We erect the outhouses out of wood, put a set of wheels on 'em, plus a toilet seat around the pan so that they look kinda like vertical coffins. The rider will sit on the john - trousers on or off, that's optional - and shout steering instructions to the guy pushing him from behind. On the downhill runs, they can get up speed."

I shake my head, trying to picture this idiotic sport - a sort of lavatorial version of the old soapboxes of yesteryear. I imagine sitting on a loo seat as the outhouse engulfing me rolls downhill, gathering speed. It's a scene that might have belonged to some bygone 'Carry On' disaster comedy. Bruiser says he doesn't know of anywhere else that goes in for outhouse racing. It's a home grown Ferryville activity that hasn't caught on elsewhere. Why ever not, I wonder.

Despite no less than three offers of a bed for the night, I finally pull myself away from all this wonderful company - though I confess to wavering for a while. But come the morning, there's a schedule to resume - something I've been free of the past couple of days. Starting the day 20 miles behind time, and unquestionably with a hangover, would be a strain.

Mindful of unplanned alcohol consumption, I climb onto the saddle and ride away. Less than two hours later I cruise into the spread-out port of Prairie du Chien, a city of low-rise buildings and broad streets which on first impressions doesn't quite match up to its alluring name. If it once had French influence, then they took it with them when they left.

I have no plans to socialise any more this evening. In any case, that Ferryville bunch would take some beating. I actually enjoy the nights I spend alone, grabbing a takeaway, flopping onto some motel bed, and gawping at the idiot box for a while. The mid-term elections are hotting up and there's a lot of political dirt and electioneering skulduggery on the small screen just now. George W. Bush is still prattling on about 'victory' in Iraq, unaware it seems, that he is becoming ever more despised over this burning issue. This gaffe-prone, oil mad warmonger could well take a real drubbing on the day - something the increasingly hostile people along this river say is nigh overdue - ever since his much publicised 'mission accomplished' statement became an undeniable case of 'mission impossible'.

Seven

STIRRING FROM THE DEAD

THERE ARE GOOD WAYS to start the day, and there are not-so-good ways. As I'm crossing the Mississippi Bridge into Marquette, Iowa, it happens again. I feel the front tyre go suddenly flat - and into it is firmly lodged *another* industrial staple. This sends me into an incandescent rage. If I find the bastard who's been depositing these metallic foes along these highways, I swear that I'll rip his ears off.

I've now got a repair kit, but there's a new problem. Taking the front wheel off this particular bike is going to be a headache because the hub houses the electric motor, from which assorted wiring is attached to several parts of the machine within its tubular frames. I grumpily decide to walk it into Iowa and find a quieter place than this windy bridge to do the necessary work. Relentless 18-wheelers are roaring in both directions.

At any other time I'd find Marquette to be a charming little place, named after one of the early French explorers. Unlike Prairie du Chien, it retains evidence of an obvious colonial past. Even the town's one and only bank is painted out in colourful pastels more likely to be seen around the harbour in St Tropez. The bank has a small courtyard outside, which is where I get down to it.

Removing the wheel proves easier than I thought and within half an hour I'm ready to get going again. But puncture repair is a grubby business; my hands, fingernails, and the front of my tee-shirt are filthy. The female teller inside the bank eyes me with some wariness as I approach, as if deciding between a professional smile or reaching for the emergency button. Stick-up merchants come in many guises, as do their getaway vehicles. But she kindly allows me to use the washroom facilities, and I'm soon on my way to today's destination, the port of Guttenberg, a 30 mile hop.

Just two miles on from Marquette along a shady riverside road, is the little port of McGregor, a great little place. It has a main street of old western-style buildings running parallel to the river, maybe 50 metres away. There are a couple of small marinas where a number of pleasure boats nestle alongside each other. McGregor is clearly somewhere that exists on tourism, and for the first time I get the feeling that the Mississippi River is at last opening up. I can feel this town breathe with robust health. My harsh annoyance of an hour or so ago has evaporated completely. I am a happy man again.

That is, until I leave the town and come face to face with a long winding hill that seems to get steeper as it goes along; so steep that I decide to walk it, using jolts of electric-assist to help me push the bike's weight uphill. The sun is out, and the day is hot. By the time I make the apex, I am boiling like a cauldron of chicken vindaloo.

The Great River Road, now Highway 52, cuts through fertile ranch land, allowing me occasional glimpses of the river from up high. At one point I get my first sight of a working towboat, pushing eight cargo-laden barges downriver. This lifts the spirits ever further. Things are finally beginning to happen down there on the water. The Mississippi is stirring from the dead.

Guttenberg is a smart little town with a main street that also follows the river. The rest of it is made up of quiet, tidy streets lined with single-storey homes and unfenced gardens, housing a population of just under 2,000. I seek out my riverside lodgings, a hotel known as The Landings - and so named because it is situated on Boat Landing Number 615. It is also the site of Lock & Dam 10, obviously the tenth such lock and dam since numbering began back up in the Twin Cities.

My spacious room overlooks the water. On the other side a towboat lies at rest. On my side, Landing 615 has several skiffs and fishing boats tied up alongside. One boat seems to be constantly coming and going between the dock and a pontoon moored out in mid-river. When I glance again, I see another towboat emerge from the lock, this one pushing 15 barges slowly southwards.

Jamie Gamerdinger, my 31 year old host at The Landings, is an amazing character. He first came to Guttenberg six years ago in his capacity as a carpenter, to assist with the conversion of a disused 19th Century factory into this classy 19 room hotel. As time went on, he persuaded the owner to let him buy into the place, and he is now at the stage where he's almost bought her out entirely. Jamie lives with his wife on a working ranch a short way out of town, where he helps out in what spare time he has. But hotel management and ranching are not his sole occupations.

"The thing about living in Guttenberg" he says, "is that you can be whoever and whatever the hell you want. If you take me as an example, I'm a hotelier, a rancher, a boat captain, a fishing guide, a hunting guide, and still in demand as a carpenter. I dunno how, but I always find the time to fit everything in. I thrive on the variety, and I thrive on this river, which I love. Once you've lived beside the Mississippi for a few months there is no other place you could ever live again. Why that should be exactly, I don't know. But it's true."

(Maybe I can help him there. This week's edition of the *Guttenberg Press* contains not a single crime account, except for a short police note reporting just four petty motoring offences.)

It is heading for early evening. Jamie has to collect a group of fishermen from the mid-river pontoon, and I join him for the ride. It seems that they've had a rewarding afternoon, each with catches of the prize walleye fish. This close to the dam, the roar of the water rushing through its multiple sluices is loud indeed, highlighting the natural power and energy of the river.

Going on dark, Jamie introduces me to another hotel guest - Captain Mike Mallone, a civilian towboat pilot employed by the U.S. Army Corps of Engineers, the body that has responsibility for overseeing all 29 locks and dams, and for every engineering necessity on the Upper and Lower Mississippi. Guttenberg is Mike's home base for the next few days.

We sit out on the terrace, him with a beer on the go, me with a glass of wine. Mike is 50, and his greying hair somehow enhances those middle-age movie star looks. He has been on and around the river all his life, and for 16 years operated Lock & Dam 11, the next one down. "Towboats came and went all day and all night, so I got to know most everyone on the river. For a change of scenery, I joined one of the boats as a deckhand for a couple of years, then took the pilot's exam 18 months ago.

"Man, on my very first watch as a pilot, I had a tow that was 435 feet long by 95 wide. It was like trying to control some giant goddam snake and I was very nervous because it takes a lot of getting used to. Anyhow, while negotiating Lock 14 on this first watch, my cell phone rang. It was the Corps of Engineers offering me this job, my first captain's post, and the guy wanted a decision there and then. I said yeah, I'll take it, because at that moment all I wanted was to get rid of him and steer my barges safely back into mid-river." He goes on to say that his new job is not towboating in the commercial sense, but "the creating of wing dams."

"Excuse me?"

"Special channels. We call 'em wing dams. Which is to say that I have to ensure that the towboat channels are at least nine feet deep at all times - the very least amount of water that a loaded barge requires. Because otherwise they're gonna buy real estate. You know, come aground with a crunch."

And what does such work entail, I wonder aloud.

"It means that four times a day, my boat will push barges laden with six tons of rocks and boulders to places in the river where the depth needs attention. The low rainfall this year hasn't helped matters, and we're kept real busy dumping the rocks at appropriate spots in order to raise the level of water through the channels. Without wing dams, there'd be no towboats operating on this part of the Mississippi, which would be a total and complete disaster. Not just for the industry, but for the environment, the economy, and ultimately for the entire United States."

This is a profound statement, requiring explanation for my tiny layman's brain. And Mike comes back with a staggering statistic.

"A boat pushing 15 fully laden barges is shifting the same amount of cargo as *eight hundred and seventy* 18-wheelers, don't you know? Those barges represent a quarter-mile in length - yet they are carrying the equivalent freight of *thirty five miles* of bumper-to-bumper trucks. If we can't keep the river deep enough to keep them afloat, then all that cargo is gonna go onto the highways - and that would be catastrophic. Trucks, trucks, and more trucks thundering along our highways 24 hours a day, as if we haven't got enough already."

I can vouch for that. Even on the quietest roads, never will a full minute pass without at least one 18-wheeler bellowing by, usually several more. And that's just on my side of the road.

This is a gem of a radio piece, and one that I'll investigate further as the ride goes on. Perhaps I might be allowed to join a towboat for a day or so, just to see how it all works at first hand.

"Do it south of St Louis" Mike advises. "There are another 19 locks and dams between here and there, where 15 barges is the maximum permitted. Beyond St Louis, where the river is open all the way down to the Gulf, they get to push up to 40 barges at a time. Every single day is an adventure on the Mississippi, and you'll get to have real fun on one of those suckers, take it from me."

This, I decide, is what I'll do. I'm sure one of the towboat companies will allow me to tag along, so long as I press my case hard enough. It won't be the first time.

I have a broadcast this evening. I'm bubbling with enthusiasm over these towboat figures and Mike Mallone's wing dams, somehow managing to present the stories with an appreciable dash of Mississippi legend and colour. In these green-conscious times, Mike's statistics are going to make a few people sit up and think.

I hope.

Another eco-aspect to this part of the river is the 29 locks and dams. They were built to last 60 years, but already they are into 70 and more. More worrying though, is the clearly-desirable targets they must be for terrorist attacks. Blow up just one of them, and you've not only ruined the river trading, you've also got guaranteed floods on a massive scale. Mike Mallone wears a tight, grim smile about this, asserting that "the Homeland Security guys have got this threat under the tightest possible surveillance." He eyes me up and down, then says, "If you think they don't know all about you and your bicycle ride, then think again, my friend."

The next day Jamie takes me through Lock & Dam 10 just for the experience. It is nothing like the tight, gloomy locks found on UK waterways. It is over a quarter-mile long to accommodate the barges and towboats, and the rapidity with which the water falls and rises is astonishing - millions and millions of gallons per minute. Annually, more than 22 million tons of cargo passes through this lock, plus around 7000 cruising boats. The obliging round-the-clock keepers will open and close it for a single voyaging canoe, or even for some weirdo rolling downriver in a barrel. The Mississippi's lock keepers have seen it all.

Inside Lock & Dam 10, Guttenberg, Iowa.

THE NEXT PORT OF CALL is the city of Dubuque, which means a tough 40 mile ride along a hilly, curving highway accompanied by the usual blasting headwinds. I pedal through open ranching country, devoid of civilisation except for the two tiny communities of North Buena Vista and Balltown. By comparison, Dubuque, population 57,000, swarms like a rat carnival.

If I want to learn about the river, then this is the place to be. Dubuque is the site of the National Mississippi River Museum & Aquarium which is, I'm told, a state-of-the-art class act (I just wish they'd drop the word 'museum', which to me brings in drab thoughts of dusty archaeological relics and specimens). But apparently it's a real humdinger of a show which I'll go and visit in the morning.

My accommodation here is apt. A cramped cabin on a 1934 steam-powered river dredger, the *William H. Black*, and all part of the museum's display. On the other side of this well sheltered port lies a replica sternwheeler that earns its keep as a floating casino, where no doubt I'll chance my arm on the slot machines while I'm here. I simply do not have the necessary skills or concentration required for success on the green baize tables.

Iowa's communications manager for tourism has driven from Des Moines, the state capital, to meet up for the evening, along with Sue Czeshinski from the Dubuque CVB. I can't remember the last time I've been so well entertained by two young ladies, if indeed there was a last time. The hospitality everyone is showing me along the river goes far, far beyond expectations.

As does the Nation Mississippi River Museum. Normally I'd give theme parks a pretty wide berth, but this one is truly something else. Inside this clean, modern building is just about everything you'll find in, on, and along the Mississippi - even a pair of live alligators. Its theme follows the history of the river in minute detail - but in a way where learning becomes high entertainment rather than a yawning drudge. This especially applies to its three movie theatres where the latest technology simulates with striking clarity the devastating storms, floods, and earthquakes to have hit the river at one time or another. In a film call *Mississippi Journey* you really do duck for cover when deadly lightning streaks down to earth; you urgently look around for cover when the floods come bearing down on you; and your seat shakes and shudders with the earthquake, until you're certain that you are going to drop through the floor at any moment.

Another film puts you into the pilot house of a towboat, as if the viewer is literally aboard, guiding all its barges in and out of a lock, and around the many twists and bends of the open water. A third, *River of Dreams*, is narrated by Garrison Keillor, he of *Lake Woebegone Days*. I'm told that this somewhat difficult man had at first declined the offer to narrate the picture - until he learned that he'd not been the director's first choice in any case, something that miffed him deeply. Nevertheless, he adopted a certain amount of humility when he was informed that the only reason he'd been asked was because 'Mark Twain happens not to be available'.

I could even have saved myself the trouble of cycling the length of the Mississippi by taking a virtual-reality tour from one end to the other - as slowly or as rapidly as I wish. On the museum's utterly lifelike computer simulation, I can travel from Lake Itasca to the Gulf of Mexico in precisely two minutes.

It is greatly encouraging to note the volume of visitors coming and going today. Interest in this great waterway is alive and vibrant, and I'm grateful to have experienced this place for myself. In some way, it has consolidated my own journey downriver and given me a far greater understanding of not only the Mississippi and its many dangers, but of why I found the idea of making this ride so exciting in the first place.

Terri Hawks Goodman, an elegant middle aged brunette, is appreciative of my praise for the place. As development director, it was she who was set the daunting task of raising the millions needed to build it, let alone pack it with such a vast array of hi-tech attractions. With justified pride, she tells me it has won several awards and accolades all over the USA.

"But the money issue never goes away" she utters. "We are forever out there raising funds from corporate sponsors and private individuals. But I really believe in what we are doing here … if I didn't, then I'd have found it impossible to ask for a single dollar."

Her passion for her job, this river, this excellent showcase, is catching. I understand there are a few other river museums along the Mississippi, but none are on a scale as grand, as imaginative, or as technically superior as this one. Without her, probably none of this would have happened. My admiration for this sparkling dark-eyed woman is growing by the moment, and I ever-so-slightly begin to rue the wedding ring fixed on the appropriate finger.

"You know what?" I say during a rare moment of inspiration. "I think that I'll bill you on the radio as the living Queen of the Mississippi. The new monarch of the river."

Oh, she likes that alright. Never has a woman smiled at me with such tantalising delight. But the thing is, I actually mean it. I have covered about 600 miles since starting out, and until these past few days the river has pretty much been yawning in my face. Now it has suddenly woken up, and Teri Hawks Goodman is part of the reason for that. Her formidable fundraising efforts for this most absorbing of exhibitions have, in my view, earned her such majestic status. Besides, she has the poise and elegance of a queen, and I like the look of her.

In the evening, Sue Czeshenski of the local CVB invites me for a dinner-cruise on the river, aboard the *Spirit of Dubuque*, another diesel powered replica steamboat. It is heading into late September and the tourist season is slowly drawing to a close. The boat is about half-full and there's a slight chill in the air as we sit out on an upper deck, sipping wine. Every now and then, the captain comes over the speakers to offer information about this and that. When dusk falls over the ship, Sue goes down into the warmth while I puff on a cigarette and gaze at the revolving stern paddle as it goes around, around, and around, chucking constant spray while it propels us along. I cannot think why such a simple, repetitive sight should be so captivating, but it is.

At dinner, we sit opposite a couple from Chicago. Conversation is relaxed, the way it should be when total strangers meet in mid-river - because every passenger and couple has this one thing in common: they do not know one another, they will never meet again, and they are all out here on the water slap bang in the middle of no-man's land - the perfect recipe for people to open up and let rip.

A one-man-band musician sets up his rig and launches into a promising rendition of *Moon River* - until, that is, the captain automatically cuts off his amplification with some banal river statistic coming through the intercom. The poor guy stops, waits, and starts again when the announcement ceases. He gets as far as the second verse when the captain breaks in again. I can see the pain in his eyes. The skipper's droning statement - all of which our performer has heard a thousand times before - appears to be driving him towards the edge. When it happens a third time, a thunderous look on his face suggests that he's getting ready to take a big running leap overboard. The guy has been plugged in for a full 15 minutes and he hasn't yet got through his first song.

Inside a Dubuque gambling boat, where the machines and atmosphere are really quite addictive.

Once Sue has gone home to the husband and kids, I amble around to the floating casino, which is lit up like a miniature city of its own. Liberally populated with punters, the boat hums with burping slot machines, flashing lights, and clanging bells. But no longer do you get the inviting sound of small change clattering into the trays. It is all electronic now. If you win something, you either use the credit digits to continue playing, or take the pay slip to the cashier's desk.

When I finally tear myself away from this addictive atmosphere, I'm $300 the richer. But as I wander off, a strange thought crosses my mind. Why, I wonder, would the casino's fully-qualified ship's captain want to take command of a boat that never shifts from its moorings? He surely did not study for his ocean-going master's ticket - which is required by law for the captain of a floating casino - for the sole purpose of going absolutely nowhere?

I surmise that it probably has something to do with his wife. Or maybe the money. These Mississippi gambling boats rake in upwards of $11 million a month - *each*.

Eight

THE SAMARITAN OF THE RIVER

I STAY ON HIGHWAY 52 which leads me directly to the next stopover, the tiny town of Bellevue via the even tinier town of St Donatus. Leaving Dubuque, the river disappears from sight and doesn't come back into focus until Bellevue some 30 miles on. The day is warm, the scenery utterly rural, and strong headwinds have come out to play again. But on a short hop like this, I use the electric-assist liberally. The bike rips through the blow with the ease of a switchblade slicing into soft cheese.

There isn't much in Bellevue. A main street with one supermarket, a couple of bars, a law firm or two, a real estate outfit, a medical practice conveniently situated close to a funeral parlour. And the obligatory local newspaper, the *Bellevue Herald-Leader*. I stop outside it with the intent of seeking directions to the Old Pepper Mill B&B. But a man in his early 60s comes dashing out before I've even dismounted.

"Hey, you must be Quentin!" he calls, pacing towards me. Well, I am stunned. In this quiet little town that few people have ever heard of, somebody knows the name of this total stranger. I've not been here for more than five minutes, and I've spoken to nobody.

"Lowell Carlson" he enthuses, holding out his hand, "editor of the town's newspaper. Heard all about your Mississippi tour and figured you'd be passing through about now. Been keeping an eye out, and I just now seen you from my office window. Your bike's a dead giveaway, see. So you wanna come inside and do me an interview?"

I must have done at least half a dozen such interviews with these small town papers since leaving Lake Itasca, so I suppose that a small awareness of this oddball ride is making its way downriver with me. I've received plenty of knowing toots on the road - although they come nowhere close to matching the amount of angry blasts from truckers and other anti-cycling drivers, to which I have become all but immune. Along this river, the furious roadster by day, will be the first to buy me a beer by night - which is all to do with the immediate transformation of the driver's perception once he (or she) gets behind the wheel. And the curious re-transformation when he (or she) emerges from the vehicle. You do not get such extreme psychological shifts on a bicycle; you merely observe them in others.

Inside the *Herald-Leader* are just three women working the computer screens and the phones. Lowell Carlson has his own office to one side. This crew of four write the paper's copy, take the photographs, answer the phones, sell the advertisements, design all the layouts, check to-and-fro with the printer on the weekly press day, and distribute the end product around the town and outlying areas. By UK standards, America's small town newspapers are pretty amateur and something of an eyesore to read. Yet they have that proverbial license to print buckets and buckets of money, even in a community of this size.

He is a nice chap, this Lowell Carlson - and ecstatic to have something as unusual as a freelance BBC journalist pedal into his patch on an electric bike - a machine that nobody along the river has ever seen before. "Can't remember the last time something real different happened in Bellevue" he says. "Unless you regard the railroad trains being issued with speeding tickets as unusual."

I've not heard of this before. Now I'm going to interview him.

"Well" he says, leaning back in his swivel chair. "You must have noticed that the tracks run alongside the river mostly. But here in Bellevue they go through town. Back when the railroad was laid through here, the agreement with the townsfolk was that the trains do only five miles an hour through the town itself - and that they wouldn't blast their darn whistles neither. I dunno if the diesel drivers these days are just plain impatient or if some of them are unaware that the speed and noise restrictions still exist to this day. Well anyway, a few times a year, some offended citizen or other will report a speeding freighter to the cops, maybe doing 15 or 20 miles an hour. And the cops will never miss the opportunity. They'll hurry along to the next railroad stop to slap a speeding ticket in the driver's hand. And the thing is, the railroad companies always pay up."

Another quirky riverbank story for me, for which I thank him. "No, no" he comes back, "it's my thanks to *you*, pal. We don't get enough murders around here, see. There's nothing that excites folk more than a real good killing, which always lifts the paper's circulation. Your story's gonna make a decent substitute."

I am not exactly sure how to take that statement; but as a hack myself, I get his drift.

After dark I wander from my lodgings, a converted waterside mill, back into town in search of a bite. Bellevue is so small and quiet that the only place I can find open tonight is a rough and ready bar that's prepared to bung a pizza in the microwave, but that's all. Better than nothing I guess.

On another fine and sunny day, I begin the 40 mile ride to the industrial port of Clinton. A mile or two out of Bellevue, the highway's shoulder switches from tarmac to dirt and gravel, which is nigh impossible to ride along. Very reluctantly I join the mainstream traffic - an act that invites not only hoots of protest from other road users, but also a truly boneshaking experience. This section of Highway 52 seems to have been totally ignored by maintenance crews - for the past 30 years at a rough guess. The surface is cracked, potholed, and so uneven it could have been carved out by a drunk with a chisel.

With the headwinds roaring in my ears, I have to rely on a kind of sixth-sense to know when an 18-wheeler is bearing down on me. Some blast their horns, but others attempt to bring on a heart attack as they fly past, missing me by inches. More than once I lurch wildly onto the dirt and gravel, my heart thumping like a jackhammer. Today's ride is downright dangerous, and no fun at all. I'm glad indeed to stop for a break at the midway point of Sabula - a tight and slightly unpleasant place that is wholly in keeping with the unpromising trend of the day. For some reason, it does not surprise me to see piles of garbage and a streaky oil slick moving downriver - a sight that I've not witnessed anywhere else.

The road surface goes from bad to worse as it becomes Highway 67 outside Sebula. So hostile is the traffic, particularly the endless stream of trucks that I honestly wonder if I'm going to make it to Clinton in one piece, or even make it there at all. There's been so many near-misses today, that surely my name has to be on one of these 18-wheel monsters so intent on hounding the hell out of me.

Somehow I survive the ordeal - and ordeal is the precise word. But more is to come as I pedal into Clinton. Riding the sidewalks is akin to bouncing up and down on a concrete trampoline. Pavement slabs have been dumped next to one another in no real semblance of order and with absolutely no regard for a pedestrian's well being. Thick tufts of weed protrude from deep cracks, and I feel as much for my machine as for myself. The jarring and shuddering is migraine-inducing.

This is a mean city, industrial and run-down. There is an atmosphere, and it's not a good one either. I make my way down the long main street lined with tired old brick buildings, some of them boarded up as if resigned to the notion that better times are a long way off. I locate the CVB at the far end of town just as the receptionist is trying to lock up for the day, and she is not pleased by this unexpected intrusion. I've no lodgings lined up for tonight, and all I want to do is get to some motel or other. Any old fleabag place will do, so long as it's south of here and far enough out of this awful city. She gives me unenthusiastic directions to an out-of-town strip apparently lined with motel chains and hamburger joints. Compared to downtown Clinton, it sounds like Utopia.

On the way, I pass a riverside power station belching thick fumes into the air. If that doesn't say it all, then a signpost with a giant arrow pointing to the power plant certainly does. In addition to the power station eyesore, it points the way to the Union Pacific Railroad Depot, to ADM Corn Sweeteners, to the Clinton Sewage Treatment Plant, to the Alliant Energy Company, and to the factory of National By-Products Inc.

I hate to think how much industrial pollution is flowing into the Mississippi from all this. Clinton has to be the worst city along the entire river, and makes no apparent attempt to hide the fact. I feel like blowing it up. I'll not trouble myself looking for a story in this place. Anyone from Clinton who is remotely interesting would have quit town long ago.

MERCY ARRIVES with the morning - insofar as that when Clinton is well behind me, so too is the wind for once. I barely use the electric-assist, even though the road remains as rough as they come. But the traffic is a little calmer today, and I've only got 30 miles to get through as I head for the little port of Le Claire, where the cleanliness and friendliness of the Mississippi resumes normal service.

Le Claire, population 2,875, has a sloping main street with colourful colonial-style buildings showing their backs to the river. Unlike last night's choice between burgers or pizzas, at least in this cheery little place I can opt between freshly caught walleye and catfish at the Riverside Roadhouse, or maybe something lighter at the Faithful Pilot, or a thick sizzler at Sneaky Pete's Cowboy Steaks.

Cowboy themes run through town, for Le Claire was the boyhood home of William 'Buffalo Bill' Cody, born here on February 26, 1846. Buffalo Bill went on to become a legendary Pony Express rider, a wagon trail scout, a dead-eyed-dick of a marksman, and a flamboyant public performer in his own Wild West show that toured throughout the USA, and which I believe he once brought to the UK. In photographs and sketches of the man, he looks uncannily like another 'William' showman - namely funny guy, Billy Connolly: the same beard, the same angular face, the same tall, slim build. From what I can glean about the chap, he shared Connolly's same sense of absurdity too. But then he was born a native of the Mississippi - and that makes him different.

A huge and famous Dutch elm nicknamed the 'Green Tree Hotel' once stood on Le Claire's riverbank, back in the steamboat days when local river pilots congregated under its leafy boughs, waiting for the boats to come calling. Downriver from here is a series of rapids which the steamboat men found too perilous to tackle without the aid of some local knowledge. The tree was the place to recruit such assistance, and it became a navigational landmark on the upper river. To be a Le Claire pilot must have been a great way to earn a living - one minute smoking and joking with colleagues sitting beside the tree, and the next guiding some lumbering steamboat through the swirling currents to safety. Alas, the tree is no longer. Dutch elm disease killed it off in the 1960s.

Le Claire has one other claim to fame - an unusual tug-of-war competition held every August. On the other side of the river lies the corresponding town of Port Byron, Illinois. Teams from both towns compete - across the water. This requires a rope that is 2,400 feet long and 680 lbs in weight. The side that gets dragged into the Mississippi are the clear losers, and the target of much derision from both riverbanks.

After a peaceful night in this relaxed town, I move on towards Davenport. Just outside Le Claire, the river turns sharply in a west by southwest direction and will stay that way for the next 50 miles. After only a few miles pedalling, the urban sprawl of a conurbation known as the Quad Cities quickly swallows me up. The four ports which make up this well populated area are Bettendorf and Davenport on the Iowa side, with Moline and Rock Island over in Illinois.

Davenport is a clean, friendly city and with a 100,000 population a fairly busy place - especially out there on the river. Any number of towboats are coming and going. The same can be said of the tourists, a constant stream of humanity going in and out of the floating casino called *Rhythm City*, moored next to my riverside hotel. Across the bridge is a second gambling boat over in Rock Island. At night they light up like glittering fun parks, tickling me once more to pay my respects to the slot machines.

But that can wait. What cannot wait is my hunt for a decent story. The Quad City CVB has all the usual stale ideas for visiting journalists - historic houses, museums, aquatic parks, botanical gardens and so on - but I've not much time for that kind of tourist stuff. So I'll cruise the city and try to find something meaty. Translated, that means a suitable bar where I'll keep the eyes peeled and the ears cocked.

Later that evening, I find the bones of what I'm looking for in a downtown pub when a local shoe salesman called Pete plonks himself next to me at a counter that is long enough for the bartender to show off his skills by expertly sliding full glasses of beer along its polished surface. Pete talks about this and that for a while; his lousy job and lousy boss; his grumpy wife and their ailing marriage; and the used car dealer who has sold him a lemon. He refers to his purchase as "a dirt sandwich on four worn tyres".

When Pete is through with griping, he becomes curious enough to ask what brings me to his city. I give him an edited rundown and he nods solemnly. "The guy you should talk to is called … ah, what's his goddam name? Some real strange European word." He turns and shouts down the room to the bartender. "Hey, Jerry! What's the name of that guy who's been cleaning up the river? Write it down for me, will you."

The barman scribbles on a scrap of paper and hands it over. "Yeah, that's the name" Pete growls. "Chad Pgradik. He's become a sort of folk hero along the upper river by drawing attention to the volume of garbage washing up along the banks. He's got himself a team of volunteers cleaning it all up, and there's some rock 'n' roll bigshot involved with his project as well, I forget which one. But I wouldn't know how to get a hold of Pgradik. You'll have to do that for yourself."

This has the promise of a cracking piece, and I'm surprised I've not heard of him before now. If the CVB don't know where to find this man with the strange name, the Davenport newspaper certainly will. I'm here for two nights, so I'll get right on to this in the morning.

Wandering back to the hotel, I decide on a brief flutter on the good ship *Rhythm City* before hitting the sack. Mistake. I leave two hours later, tail between legs, over $200 the lighter. Knowing exactly when to quit is a difficult art, but maybe I'll try and win it back tomorrow. I'm not keen on losing to these places.

I make contact with Chad Pgradik's office the next day. He is out of town on speaking engagements in Washington and New York I'm informed, but they'll ask him to give me a ring between airplane flights later this afternoon.

Which he does. And it is a story worth the wait. Pgradik, 32, once made his living as a pearl shell diver, for which the Mississippi is a surprisingly rich source. Some ten years ago, while setting up an overnight camp on a mid-river island, he became alarmed - and then angry - at the amount of human-generated flotsam and jetsam washing up on the island's shores: truck tyres, plastic bottles, tin cans, crates, shoes, old clothing, soggy books and magazines, discarded briefcases and suitcases, agricultural chemicals, and more.

"That same night I made up my mind to do something about this. Chucking things away in America's disposable society is one thing. But dumping them in the river - *my river* - was too much for me to stomach. So I quit the pearl shell business and set about raising a few bucks to buy a small towboat and some barges. The intent was to spend the rest of my days patrolling up and down the Mississippi to clean the damn thing up, and to recycle all those millions of tons of waste material."

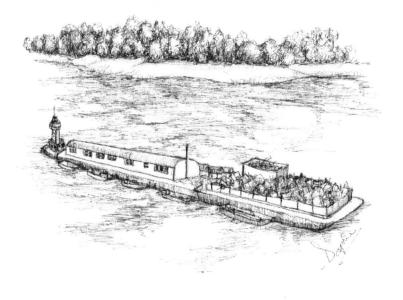

Cleaning up the river: towboat, volunteers' living quarters, and a barge crammed with human-generated trash.

His efforts came to the attention of a rock star, if that's the right term for the river-loving Billy Joel. He supported Pgradik at news conferences and photo-shoots. Word spread. Volunteers signed up on an expenses-only basis. Billy Joel's influence brought in the Budweiser beer label (which happens to be based on the river, down in St Louis), and which now supports Pgradik's mission with an annual grant. Chemical manufacturers and assorted barge companies also chip in. From zero funding a decade ago, Pgradik's *Living Lands and Waters* organisation currently pulls in $750,000 per year.

Inevitably he has a few stories from his wanderings on the Mississippi. "Well so far I've only fished one dead body from the water, which was a none-too-pleasant experience. Dunno if the police ever found out who he was. But we get to find some interesting pickings from time to time. Like a surveillance tape from a bank heist, and all the money bags that were stolen. Unfortunately they'd been emptied. And we pick up messages in bottles quite regularly. Mostly crass love letters, but some disturbing suicide notes too."

Chad's profile is growing. *National Geographic* has commissioned a book from him to be called *From the Bottom Up*. He is in demand as a speaker on environmental issues, especially with those Washington politicians suddenly jumping on the green bandwagon. The latter are particularly aware of his publicity-potential following the Katrina disaster in New Orleans when Pgradik immediately loaded up his barges with vital relief supplies - paid for by his organisation - and steamed all the way downriver from his Iowa base at Fort Madison to donate his essential cargo among the hordes of abandoned victims.

Such instantaneous action caused a decent chunk of embarrassment to George W. Bush over his inept handling of the crisis. The finger-pointing turbulence that followed in the hurricane's aftermath was both savage and damning.

If this remarkable man manages to complete his next project, then his place in this river's rich history is assured with five permanent stars. It is a two-parter; firstly, the planting of 55,000 trees on the hundreds of mid-river islands which dot the Mississippi - to be followed by the planting of a further *one million* trees along the waterway's entire 2,552 mile winding length.

"We want to put the river firmly back on America's environmental map" he goes on, with an anger seemingly undiminished from ten years previously. "It is probably the most important stretch of water in the whole world, and it deserves respect. The Mississippi is not a damn trashcan, it's a living entity. What it does *not* deserve is the scornful disdain of materialistic consumers."

I don't think I can add to that. This saint of the Mississippi has not merely said it all - he is actually doing it all. It is a privilege to talk with him, even if it is over the phone. America needs this guy.

And as a roving hack, I realise just how much I need the boozers and losers who occupy the barstools of dark saloons. A disgruntled shoe salesman with none too much going for him, has been my link to a rising environmental star whose self-made career is a world away from the likes of Pete - yet he was the man who had imparted that first vital scrap of information.

Nine

SNAKE ALLEY

*F*ROM DAVENPORT, Highway 22 becomes the Great River Road, running alongside the Mississippi for all of today's 40 mile ride to Muscatine. But whenever I've spent a day or two out of the saddle, my body lets me know, and it's doing just that today. It takes several miles for the aching to stop, only to return after my usual hour's break at lunchtime. It is a slow journey to the city that Mark Twain described as the 'home of summer sunsets'.

If he was right, then I'm denied the spectacle. The motel I'm in is set amid a row of depressingly similar buildings which block access to the lowering sun on this Saturday evening. Inside it's worse. The room faces an indoor swimming pool where half a million excited, pre-puberty kids are splashing, yelling, and running around - right next to my only window. If I want privacy, then even in daylight I have to draw the curtains and switch on the lights.

But it's the next day, Sunday, October 1st, that really provides the test. The river turns due south again and the headwind is just vicious on what is now Highway 61; in fact, it is so strong that even when going downhill, I have to pedal *and* use the electric assist. I know that today's 50-miler to the city of Burlington is going to be an evil experience - not helped by the fact that the highway has reverted to type, with no shoulder at all, and a surface that might have been laid by a vengeful chain gang with a real grudge against the outside world.

This is purgatory. There seem to be more angry trucks on the road than on storming weekdays, and they're not up for mercy either. Any church-like thoughts harboured by the drivers of these 18-wheelers and speeding pick-up trucks have been forgotten with the last Amen.

I think it wise to make at least two plug-in stops today. The first is at the inaptly named one horse town of Grandview, 18 miles out of Muscatine. The river is way to the left of me and far from sight, but what I do see from this gas station-cum-café is a strange triangular vista. On one side stands a helicopter gunship from the Vietnam War, supported several metres in the air by a steel girder. On the other side are a number of patriotic Stars & Stripes, their fabrics stretched rigid by the wind. Between the flags and the chopper is a memorial stone engraved with the names of this region's fallen men from that futile conflict. And ahead of me, a brief distance away but visually in the centre of all this, is a church sporting a huge neon sign that says, *Jesus Saves*.

Hmm. The irony of it.

Some miles later I decide to stop again for a second battery boost in the depressing little settlement of Wapello, and do the same again at a place called Mediapolis just 12 miles on. I'm using up so much juice today that in all, the battery gets three hours of recharge, which surely must be enough to get me to Burlington a further 15 miles away.

But later, while climbing a really steep hill in the rapidly fading light, the one thing that I dread most suddenly happens. The fuel gauge goes from amber to red, and the motor stops purring. The power supply has given out for the first time. Cursing, I strain on foot to push my load to the top of the hill - and once there, very nearly get down on my knees in a prayer of thanks. For below me, downhill all the way, the lights of Burlington glow and flicker in the dark. Phew.

This is a hilly town that knew its boom times via the timber industry. Leafy streets up on the bluffs are generously lined with the renovated mansions of bygone timber barons, giving the place a distinct air of grace and dignity. Whenever someone like me hits town, Lyle Magneson, widely regarded as the city's most authoritative historian, is assigned by the CVB to offer the guided tour. This one is worth the experience, particularly Mosquito Park and Snake Alley.

The former is probably America's smallest parkland, maybe 80x15 metres of rough lawn. Set high on a bluff, it has truly stupendous views of the river and its islands. But when the city officials first designated the land as a park, one of them was heard to grumble, "Nobody's gonna use it. It's got as much open space as a mosquito's ass." The analogy stuck, and the little park became a local landmark, second only to Snake Alley.

Burlington is locked in a war of words with San Francisco over which of the two cities has the most crooked street in the world. Burlington thinks it does, and I wouldn't argue. Snake Alley begins atop of the steepest hill in town; a pedestrian-only, forever twisting cobbled lane which, because of the sheer gradient, would be nigh impossible to ascend or descend were it to follow a straight line. So it snakes to the left, then sharply to the right, then to the left again and so on, until it eventually merges with the downtown area. Even if cars were allowed, they could not possible manoeuvre around those bends.

As for cyclists … well, every summer Snake Alley becomes part of the course for the city's annual bike race - uphill. No less a cycling ace than Lance Armstrong has said that he wouldn't want to tackle Snake Alley again. Staring down at this giddy lane, I know that I'd only attempt a downhill run, and with extreme caution at that.

Snake Alley, Burlington, Iowa. The crookedest street in the world.

Lyle has a wry grin on his craggy face. "Actually, neither Burlington nor San Francisco should claim to have the most crooked street in the world" he states. "That honour should undoubtedly go to ... Wall Street."

Ha! Good one, Lyle.

Some of the riverside buildings in Burlington are so old, you can easily envisage the steamboat era as if it had only slipped around the next bend in the river and will be back any minute now. In its heyday, the waterfront was stacked three-deep with boats picking up and dropping off passengers, and filling their holds with Burlington's timber produce. Amid such activity, other industries built up around the comings and goings of the steamboats. Lyle points towards three disused 19th Century red-brick buildings standing at water's edge.

"The nearest building was a real busy hotel, always booked up with river travellers. The centre one was the steam packet office, where all the business-end of things were done and where money changed hands. And the third, which did even better trade than either of them, was the bawdiest whorehouse on the whole of the Upper Mississippi: a round-the-clock honkytonk of gamblers, dancing girls, and rough sex."

This I can picture only too well. The cheroot-smoking men with their Derby hats and twirled moustaches; the women, adept at the professional come-on, moving among prospective clients in suggestive, though calculating manner - and almost certainly in cahoots with the port's gauntlet of pickpockets and card sharps. It's an image that bolsters the river's raw pioneering tradition, and well in keeping with the 'anything goes' zeitgeist of those frontier times.

However, things were not always so good around here. The Arrowhead Motel where I'm staying began life as the White Mill Tourist Cabins in 1925, and its present owner has written a brief but interesting history of the place. When the Great Depression came the steamboats, and thereby places like Burlington, sorely felt its dire effects. Trade all but grinded to a halt, and it wasn't going to improve anytime soon.

"Tough times got tougher still" says today's owner, Dennis Dietch. "If anyone had any money at all, they'd stash it away into a sock or something - and keep pretty damn quiet about it too. Money became pretty much non-existent. What few travellers there were at the cabins, paid their bills in other ways, like in pocket watches or other items. The owners of the day considered their options - and came to the conclusion that there weren't any, because most of their guests were unemployed, out on the road looking for work." Dennis adds that the price of a night's stay back then, including a hot meal, was just 75 cents - which hardly anyone possessed in cash. Rough times indeed.

I RIDE OFF THE FOLLOWING DAY, another 40 mile ordeal of juddering and jarring down Highway 61 to the city of Keokuk, via Fort Madison. Keokuk is only a couple of miles from the Missouri border, and my last stop in Iowa. I'll not be at all rueful to leave the appalling roads of this state behind.

Keokuk is a busy town with a long main street of mostly modern buildings. As I pedal down it in late afternoon, another cyclist draws alongside and starts up a conversation as we wheel along. He is fair haired, somewhere in his late 30s, and says that he always travels the city by bike. "Right now I'm on my way home to my mother's place" he says. "She thinks I've been hard at work, and I'm not about to tell her otherwise. The fact is that I've been in a bar all day because I'm addicted to drink; an alcoholic."

Amazing what people will tell you before you even know their names, but I soon see where this is heading - into another bar, if I'm not mistaken. Sure enough, he asks me to buy him a drink, and I'm agreeable to that. Who knows, he might have a good local story for me.

Jeff, it transpires, has only been in his new job as an apartment block janitor for two weeks - and he's already skipped three or four working days. Beforehand, he'd been a bartender, but there is no bar in town that will hire him any more because he was the guy doing all the drinking, which he candidly admits. In this darkened little dive where Jeff has brought me to, his old boss bears no grudges and seems pleased to see him - as a customer. But he can't put anything on the slate. It's cash only, and mine by the sound of it.

If Jeff has been consuming liquor since early light, then he's handled the day's intake fairly well. There had been no wobbling on his bike, and all these hours later, there's no slurring of the words. And boy, can he talk, jumping from one fanciful topic to another. When he at last grasps what it is that I'm doing in his city, Jeff spots an immediate opportunity.

"Buy me another bourbon, and I'll take you down to the river and show you something that I guarantee you haven't seen anywhere else along the Mississippi. In my own 37 years of living here, it's the first time that I've come across anything like it."

"Which is?" I ask, intrigued.

Jeff shakes his head. There is a cheeky twinkle in his eyes. "Uh, uh. You'll have to wait and see."

I ask the barman for bourbon number two. Jeff sinks it in less than a minute, and tells his old boss that he will be back shortly. Not with me, he won't. We mount our bikes and make the short trip down to the river. He rummages around the rocks and weeds for a few frantic moments, and then with a panic-stricken look on his face, suddenly erupts. "It's gone!" he yells. "Some bastard has stolen my wine! I keep a bottle of red wine hidden down here for emergencies, and some asshole has taken it!"

My reply is acidic. "Is that what you wanted to show me - a hidden bottle of red wine?"

"Hell no. I just wanted a few gulps is all, now that I'm here." He bends down again and continues the rummaging - fruitfully this time, and literally so. "I was gonna show you *these*" he adds triumphantly. In his hands are two enormous watermelons, still attached to their roots and growing wild at river's edge. "Not a bad find, eh? They're not quite ripe yet; give 'em another week."

In its way, the watermelons might pan out as a reasonable radio yarn, and certainly worth the price of a drink or two. Jeff had been right. This is the first time I've heard of such luscious fruit growing naturally on the riverbank - another unexpected aspect of this extraordinary body of water.

As for Jeff ... well, I guess he views his discovery from another angle altogether. He is already planning to ferment his fruity discovery into rough, barely drinkable alcohol.

Ten

MARK TWAIN

IT IS A RELIEF to cross into the 'Show Me' state, where Highway 61 marginally improves, yet remains dangerously short of shoulder space. A road sign welcoming me to Missouri is immediately followed by another notice: *$1000 Maximum Fine and/or a Year in Jail for Littering. NO MORE TRASH!*

Missouri, I think, is going to be interesting. Unlike say, Florida which calls itself the 'Sunshine State' or Texas, the 'Lone Star State', Missouri has adopted itself as the 'Show Me State'. It is born from a natural cynicism that Missourians are noted for. If someone says, 'Hey, I'm a hotshot billionaire, and don't you forget it', the Missourian response is likely to be, 'Oh yeah? Then show me. Prove it, buddy'.

To my delight, the wind is with me today and I'm going to take as much advantage of this asset as it will allow. It is blowing hard; so hard, that if I stop pedalling, it is strong enough to propel me along on its own, with my back acting as a kind of sail. There's a bit of rain in the air, but to hell with that.

I'll go for the full 65 miles today, to the city of Hannibal - the boyhood home of Mark Twain.

It is an effortless ride down to Canton, where I stop for a brief snack; then on to La Grange, Palmyra, and eventually into Hannibal itself. This two-faced wind has for once been a true ally today, as against a sworn enemy. I only have to use the electric-assist on the occasional long hill. Why can't it always be like this? If only.

From high up, Hannibal slopes sharply down to the river. Old mansions, hundreds of them, line its quiet, leafy residential streets. Even the main street appears to pay a certain homage to the wealth and style of bygone times; a broad, spacious commercial boulevard that whispers rather than shouts. In fact, the only person doing any yelling is Mark Twain himself. His presence is just about everywhere. The city trades, lives, and breathes on the man's image. It surprises me not at all to find 'twainburgers' listed on a café menu.

Writers of class are revered in America, be they dead or alive: Ernest Hemingway, William Faulkner, Tennessee Williams, F. Scott Fitzgerald, Arthur Miller, Kurt Vonnegut, Norman Mailer, Gore Vidal, John Updike, and all the rest. It seems to me that Mark Twain leads this illustrious elite, and not simply because of his Mississippi creations (*Tom Sawyer* and *Huckleberry Finn*). His instant wit and wisdom had later generations comparing Winston Churchill's frequent acerbic ripostes and witticisms with the sayings of this former runaway urchin and steamboat pilot hailing from an obscure Mississippi river town.

After checking in at Reagan's Queen Anne B&B - another mansion standing high in the residential hills - I ride back to the far end of downtown where I'm eager to visit an obvious attraction: the house where Twain lived. It is a modest green-and-white two storey clapboard building, and probably the biggest money spinner in town.

Unlike the Charles Lindbergh home back up in Little Falls, the Twain residence strictly regulates the visitor's movements.

The aviator's house has no roped-off areas, no barriers of any sort, not even any anti-theft devices to prevent the stealing of artefacts. It is now, as it was then; you may roam around freely, sit in the chairs, peruse the bookshelves, or inspect the family cutlery, if that's what you want to do. Incredibly, never has there been an abuse from its steady stream of tourists.

By comparison, the writer's home seems like a gentler version of Fort Knox. From the cobbled street outside, a plastic image of the man gazes back down on you from a high window. Inside, you follow a set trail, starting with your payment at the ticket counter. All the rooms are screened off by thick plexiglass, and all you can do is to peer inside them from narrow corridors. Typically, the tour ends at the souvenir store. I do not know what Mark Twain makes of this from wherever

Mark Twain's modest boyhood home, Hannibal, Missouri.

he is now, but I reckon he might be scornfully dismissive.

In 1839, the then four year old Samuel Langhorne Clemens,

aka Mark Twain, moved with his sickly family from the town of
Florida, Missouri to Hannibal. His sister Margaret had already
died before the move. But it wasn't until 1844 that his father, a
county judge, completed the construction of the new family
home. In between, they lived in rented accommodation. Two
years later, the judge died from pneumonia, forcing young
Samuel to leave school at the age of 12 and find employment as
a printer and odd-job boy on the local newspaper, which he did
until 1853. Thus this house, not 200 metres from the riverbank,
was home to Twain from the age of nine through to 18. At that
point, the ailing Mrs Clemens sold up, moved to Keokuk, while
her son decided to make a break for it by making his way
downriver to New Orleans where his time as a steamboat
apprentice began.

A poignant extract from his book, *Life on the Mississippi*,
concerns his boyhood yearnings in Hannibal - then little more
than a village, and which he describes as such:

'When I was a boy, there was but one permanent ambition
among my comrades in our village on the west bank of the
Mississippi River. That was to be a steamboat man. We had
transient ambitions of other sorts, but they were only transient.
When a circus came and went, it left us all burning to become
clowns; the first Negro minstrel show that came to our section
left us all suffering to try that kind of life; now and then we had
a hope that if we lived and were good, God would permit us to
become pirates. These ambitions faded out, each in turn; but the
ambition to be a steamboat man always remained.

Once a day, a cheap, gaudy steam packet arrived upward
from St Louis, and another downward from Keokuk. Before
these events, the day was glorious with expectancy; after them,
the day was a dead and empty thing. Not only the boys, but the
whole village felt this. After all these years I can picture that old
time to myself now, just as it was then: the white town
drowsing in the sunshine of a summer morning; the streets
empty, or pretty nearly so; one or two clerks sitting in front of
the Water Street stores, with their splint-bottomed chairs tilted

back against the wall, chins on breasts, hats slouched over their faces, asleep; a sow and her litter of piglets loafing along the sidewalk'.

Twain goes on, 'A pile of "skids" on the slope of the stone-paved wharf, and the fragrant town drunkard asleep in the shadow of them; two or three wood flats at the head of the wharf, but nobody to listen to the peaceful slapping of the wavelets against them; the great Mississippi, the majestic, the magnificent Mississippi, rolling its mile-wide tide along, shining in the sun; the dense forest away on the other side; the "point" above the town, and the "point" below, bounding the river-glimpse, and turning it into a sort of sea, and withal a very still and brilliant and lonely one. Presently, a film of dark smoke appears above one of these remote "points"; instantly a Negro drayman, famous for his quick eye and prodigious voice, lifts up the cry, "S-t-e-a-m-b-o-a-t a'comin!" and the scene changes! The town drunkard stirs, the clerks wake up, a furious clatter of drays follows, every house and store pours out a human contribution, and all in a twinkling the dead town is alive and moving. Drays, carts, men, boys, all go hurrying from many quarters to a common centre, the wharf. Assembled there, the people fasten their eyes upon the coming boat as upon a wonder they are seeing it for the first time. And the boat *is* a rather handsome sight, too. She is long and sharp and trim and pretty; she has two tall, fancy-topped chimneys, with a gilded device of some kind swung between them; a fanciful pilot house, all the glass and "gingerbread" perched on top of the "texas" deck behind them; the paddle boxes are gorgeous with a picture or with gilded rays above the boat's name; the boiler deck, the hurricane deck, and the texas deck are fenced and ornamented with clean white railings; there is a flag gallantly flying from the jack-staff; the furnace doors are open and the fires glaring bravely; the upper decks are black with passengers; the captain stands by the big bell, calm, imposing, the envy of all; great volumes of the blackest smoke are rolling and tumbling out of the chimneys - a husbanded grandeur created with a bit of pitch-pine just before arriving at a town; the crew is grouped on the forecastle; the broad stage is run far out over the port bow, and an envied deckhand stands picturesquely on the end of it with a coil of rope in his hand; the pent-up steam is screaming through the gauge-cocks; the captain lifts his hand, a bell rings, the paddlewheels stop; then they turn back, turning the water to foam, and the steamer is at rest. Then such a scramble as there is to get aboard, and to get ashore, and to take in freight and to discharge freight, all at one and the same time; and such a yelling and cursing as the mates facilitate it all with! Ten minutes later the steamer is under way again, with no flag on the jack-staff and no black smoke issuing from the chimneys. After another ten minutes the town is dead again, and the town drunkard is asleep by the "skids" once more'.

I continue on down to the waterfront, presumably getting much the same view that a young Samuel Clemens had of the river some 150 years before. It is visible for less than a mile in each direction, and I can only imagine his youthful itching as he watched the steamboats disappear around the next bend, rolling from adventure to adventure along this broad, twisting waterway. As a lad, he could only dream of such distant places, so frustratingly unknown to him.

I strongly believe that if you want something badly enough you'll find a way to get it, regardless of circumstances. Samuel Clemens wanted above all else to be a steamboat pilot, and at the age of 18, with just a few dollars in his pocket, he found his way down to New Orleans - initially with the intention of going further south still, to that other mighty river, the Amazon. But boats heading down that way were rare, and he didn't have the fare anyway. So he spent his days down on the wharfs of New Orleans trying to secure an apprentice-berth on a Mississippi steamer - only to be greeted with gruff refusals. But where there is a will, there really is a way. After several days of pestering the pilot of a boat called the *Paul Jones*, he finally got his way. The pilot, a certain Mr Bixby, agreed to teach him 'all he knew' in return for $500, payable over time from the meagre pay packet of an apprentice.

Twain's stories of his 18 months as a cub pilot make absorbing reading, yet he was only to follow this much sought-after occupation for a total of four years. The Civil War put a premature end to his career on a river blockaded by Yankee gunboats. For the period of that war, steamboating on the Mississippi more or less died out. In later reflections, Twain said of his brief time on the river that it was "the most worthwhile thing I have ever done, before or since."

To quote him once more: 'I had to seek another livelihood. So I became a silver miner in Nevada; next a newspaper reporter; then a gold miner in California; next a reporter in San Francisco; next a special correspondent in the Sandwich Islands (now Hawaii); next a roving correspondent in Europe and the East; next an instructional torch-bearer on the lecture platform; and finally, I became a scribbler of books, and an immovable feature among the other rocks of New England'. (He eventually settled in Connecticut.)

I'm sure to make further references to this unforgettable character as I continue heading downriver, but for now there remains just one other detail - which is how Samuel Clemens became Mark Twain. When taking soundings of the river's depth, especially at night, the guy poking his long pole down to the river bed would call out to the pilot "Mark Three Quarters!" When it got a little deeper, "Mark One!". And when it doubled that, "Mark Twain!"

I imagine that Samuel Clemens heard that yell so many times, it embedded itself inside his skull. The name has certainly served himself and his readers well over all these years.

Apart from Twain, the city of Hannibal had at least one other resident with a claim to fame. She was known as the 'Unsinkable Molly Brown', and her life story was made into both a Broadway musical and a Hollywood hit movie, the latter starring Debbie Reynolds. Molly Brown was a wealthy and notable Midwest socialite and philanthropist - but why unsinkable? The answer to that is she was one of the survivors of the *Titanic* disaster - and apparently a dominating force when it came to organising other survivors into the lifeboats. The crew, panic stricken themselves on that dark, freezing night, simply did what this unflappable woman told them to do.

By now, there is one observation immovably embedded into my own skull - which is that this river has bred, and continues to breed, some truly extraordinary people.

Eleven

THE SHOOTING GALLERY

*R*ON AND LOUISE RIGGS are a charming couple. Ron is a retired engineer who takes a real interest in the eZee Torq, eager to strip it down to all its bits and parts simply to understand for certain how it all works. The machine becomes a focal point of interest wherever I go, but for none so much as this man.

His wife Louise works at the Hannibal CVB. They are early 60s and both possess a noticeable 'parental' element. By that I mean, they take me under their wing as if I'm a kind of surrogate son or brother. Ron is concerned for my safety on the road, while Louise fusses over things like diet and clean clothes. And like only a mother can, she tut-tuts at my penchant for roll your owns. Somehow it is a refreshing change to have two people make a big deal of you; it certainly beats truck drivers having a go at you.

Ron informs me that the 35 miles to my next stop - a town called Louisiana - is strewn with difficult hills and that I'd be better off riding along the Illinois side of the river, where it is almost flat. It is early evening, and he suddenly suggests that we pile into his 4x4, drive to Louisiana on the Missouri side, and return via Illinois. That way, he says, I'll know my alternatives.

About three miles out of Hannibal, a strange white building comes up on a spare patch of land to our left. If this was England, I'd take it to be a public lavatory. It is about seven metres long by four wide, with a couple of small, mean windows embedded into walls a good two feet thick. Ron pulls to a halt.

No, not a public loo - but a nasty little jail outside Hannibal.

"During the 1920s, this area employed a whole lot of East European immigrants to work in the cement factories: Poles, Romanians, Bulgarians, those kind of people. Coming from where they did, I guess they had a strong liking for vodka - and for some vicious fighting among themselves. Every weekend, this place would fill up with bloodied Slavic drunks. It's a jail, you see. If you look inside, you'll see why it became an effective deterrent."

I wander over to its heavily-barred door. It is locked, but I can see enough of the inside to know I'd be absolutely determined to remain on the outside, were the jail still in use. Through the gloom, I note a tight and tiny corridor facing three small cells. The bars are thick, and painted in satanic black. The bunks are austere. There is an overwhelming grimness and misery about it. Banged up in here, time would have gone by agonisingly.

There is not much between Hannibal and Louisiana, just a lot of hills; some of them are seriously steep, but they offer resplendent views of the river from on high. If I take this route tomorrow, I'll be using a lot of juice with no place to plug in the battery. Illinois would be a safer bet.

Louisiana seems another pleasant, hilly Mississippi port with plenty of old red-brick buildings suggesting more frontier history of the big river. We pass through it leisurely and then drive onto the single-lane Mississippi Bridge where I spot an instant drawback. There is no sidewalk and no shoulder at all. On this Friday evening, trucks are belting across it. If I travel the Illinois option, this half-mile span of the river will guarantee more harrowing moments. Ah well, I tell myself, cross that bridge when you come to it.

Dusk falls over Illinois. The hunting season is quickly approaching and a road sign warns drivers to keep a lookout for deer darting across the road. In the gathering dark I see them everywhere, roaming and grazing the flat, open land on either side of us. Headlights switch on in those curious moments when it's too dark to drive without them, and still too light to make much difference. Suddenly a deer makes a run for it. The driver of a pick-up truck coming the other way has no time to hit the anchors. The animal leaps out in front of its bull-bars and an instant later it is flying way up in the air. The driver pulls over and so does Ron.

"Just want to see what he does" Ron mutters, staring into his wing mirror. I go one further by getting out of the 4x4 and crossing the highway, where the driver of the pick-up is dragging the fresh carcass to the back of his vehicle. He then calmly pulls out a fold-up hunting knife from his jeans, and with a few swift slices of the blade, he cuts the deer's throat. Blood gushes at the roadside. At least there is no pain, not any more.

"Dinner for the next few days" he says, looking up at me with a grin. "This one saved me a bullet. I'll skin-and-gut it when I get back to my ranch."

There and then it strikes me how different attitudes are on either side of the Atlantic. In Europe, a driver who collides with a deer will only get out of his or her car to inspect any damage to the precious tin-can-on-wheels. In America, or this part of it anyway, a scrape or scratch on the pick-up is of no importance, but the dead animal is. It will not go to waste. The deer is food for this man's family; and its skin, once cured, will make another rug for the ranch house floor.

I cross Hannibal's bridge the next morning and back into Illinois, heading east for ten miles, then south along Highway 96. There will be no sight of the river again until Louisiana. I pass through the settlement of Kinderhook, then New Canton, through to a dot on the map known as Rockport, and finally the strange little settlement of Atlas before turning west again for the remaining seven miles into Louisiana. Between these points, it is just acres and acres of flat, open farmland. In Atlas I stop for a light snack and some fruit juice, standing outside in the café's forecourt and taking in the place's odd setting. What few businesses there are in Atlas are all located at a T-junction: this café, an arts & crafts shop across the road, a small general store, a real estate office, and that's about it. A pair of leather-clad bikers emerge from the café, ambling towards their gleaming black-and-silver Harleys. One of them eyes up my own bike for a few moments, looks at me with just a hint of hostility, shakes his head, and mounts his powerful machine. There is no mistaking the meaning in his revving-up, soon to be doubled by his colleague. The engines roar, drowning out all other sound. When they hit the road and speed off towards Louisiana, it is in an ostentatious display of near-demonic superiority.

I remount and set off again. Shortly the Mississippi Bridge comes into sight and this, I know, is going to be a problem. The traffic is not too heavy, but what there is of it seems mostly to consist of 18-wheels, coming from both directions. I am justifiably nervous because there is not a spare inch to be had along that narrow bridge. Also, the several accidents requiring hospitalisation which I've had during my life have all, for some reason, occurred on a Saturday afternoon. This is Saturday afternoon. Working on the theory that history repeats itself, crossing that bridge on my bike seems to be really asking for it. It is as though the two bikers from the Atlas café are waiting on the other side, like scouts and outriders for the Grim Reaper.

I stop at the base of the rise leading up to the bridge and take a look around. To my right is a small marina, a yacht club of sorts. I freewheel down to it and enter a riverside restaurant which apart from a couple of staff members is empty. A blonde woman in her 30s sits by the cash till counting the money. When she eventually looks up at me, I can almost read her mind. 'Another boat bum' she's thinking. 'This one's been washed up with the tide.' Not too far wrong, I suppose.

This may seem like trifling minutiae, but I've convinced myself that a lift across the bridge is more or less vital. I've got the strongest gut-feeling about it and I think it shows. The woman nods in solemn understanding, tells me to wait five minutes, and she'll run me across in the marina's pick-up.

She is as good as her word. We swoop onto the highway, up onto the bridge - and do not meet with a single vehicle in either direction. I feel like an idiot. But the woman says I've done the right thing because last year a local cyclist was killed on it by an impatient overtaking truck. Not only that, a car coming the other way got mangled too. Ever since, the bridge has been regarded as a black spot.

My motel is right by the bridge and at water's edge. When darkness falls a huge orange moon lights up the river as if inviting me to put pen to paper and write some moonlight lullaby. It is a sight that lures the guests outside, and soon an impromptu party begins beneath its glow. I've no idea where all the alcohol is coming from, but someone thrusts a giant paper cup into my hand and fills it to the brim with wine, and another Saturday night begins. I do not recall how it ends.

I wake later than normal on Sunday, and with something of a thick head to boot. But I've got a 60 mile trek today to a place called St Charles, north east of St Louis, and part of that city's massive conurbation. I need to get cracking. I make my way out of town and onto Highway 79, following the river for 12 miles down to Clarksville where I wallow in the luxury of several glasses of fruit juice at an outdoor riverside café. Local families are already tucking in to the Sunday brunch, while watching the river flow and the boats cruise in and out of Lock & Dam 24 in the bright sunlight. I'd stay here all day if I could.

Outside Clarksville the road veers away from the water, and I carry on through quiet ranch land, stopping again at Elsberry for an hour's plug-in. Headwinds are on the attack once more and electric-assist is required. Midway between Elsberry and the small town of Winfield, thick smoke looms up ahead. Soon I'm caught up in it all. An entire paddock is ablaze. Firefighters tackle it with powerful hoses while orange lights flash and sirens wail. The smoke is stinging my eyes and bringing on a brief asthma attack which I'm occasionally prone to. This I can do without.

It is turning into a pretty tough day. I plug-in again at Winfield for the remaining 25 miles to St Charles. Distance is going by slowly and the sun is already on its way down. I figure to make my destination by the latter part of dusk - but that turns into wishful thinking when the sun slides from view with at least another 12 miles to go. Soon darkness enwraps me on a narrow, single-lane, no-shoulder highway. Cars and trucks speed past, some slamming their horns. For the sake of my nerves, I have to pull over for a break from this. On its own, cycling through the dark is bad enough. Cycling through the dark amid impatient, ever growing traffic closing in on the St Louis conurbation is as close to hell as it gets. I have a front light which is of some small help in spotting the stones and potholes, but that is not enough. There are times in all our lives when we need a bit of extra help from the Big Man Upstairs, and this is one of them - for tonight I am one very vulnerable human being indeed.

I pedal on, stopping whenever it all becomes too much, and wait for the next break in this charging stream of traffic. Eventually I arrive at a confusing junction, where I am relieved - mightily so - to see that this is my turn-off for St Charles. I wheel into a nearby gas station to ask directions to my hotel, the Country Inn.

The young chap at the counter scratches his stubble. "You've still got a long way to go, pal. About 18 miles is my guess."

"What!"

He turns to his colleague at another counter. "Hey, Joe. How far is it to St Charles from here? About 18 miles?"

Joe says, "Could be that. Not much less."

This cannot be right, and I'm warming myself up to throttle someone. A bad day is about to get worse it seems. Just then a woman comes in to pay for her fuel. Maybe it's the look of thunder on my face that prompts the counter clerk to ask, "Lady, d'yuh know how far it is to St Charles?"

She thinks for a moment, then nods to herself. "If you take the service roads and a couple of short cuts, it's about five miles." Now that is manageable, and my relief must be evident because the clerk is looking relieved himself. She gives me some complicated directions which I take with me back into the night. Actually, well into the night. After a few more stops to re-check her instructions - and taking a number of modified routes - I finally wheel into the cobbled main street of St Charles, astonished to see that my watch is reading 9.30pm.

I ask the desk clerk for room service. No such thing on a Sunday, she says. Try one of the restaurants further down the street. I clean up, change clothes, and take a short walk downtown. Three restaurants are still open, but last-orders have come and gone. One waitress tells me to go another five miles to an all-night joint, and I cannot be bothered to explain. I'll just go hungry.

In daylight, St Charles seems a prosperous, tourist-oriented sort of place. The river, to the north of here, runs in an east-west direction at this point where soon it will be joined by the equally mighty Missouri River upon which this town stands, and which pours into the Mississippi some 20 miles due east of here. It is about 35 miles to downtown St Louis - and today I'm ensuring the distance is made in daylight.

I cross the Missouri River and get onto Highway 364, a multi-lane road with a merciful amount of shoulder space. The area soon becomes rural again, and for a doubtful moment I think I must be on the wrong road. I'll ask whoever is in the pick-up truck parked further along. The driver's window is open, but the man himself is sound asleep, his head stretched back, his mouth wide open, and snoring like a heavyweight wrestler might after consuming an entire bottle of bourbon. I'm unsure if I should wake him, but his sixth-sense kicks in and he suddenly opens his eyes, alarmed.

"Uh … ah … who the hell … waddayawant?"

I ask my question, which seems to have a real wake-up effect on him. "Buddy, you're on the Page Avenue Extension, so just keep on going down the highway. Sooner or later it becomes Page Avenue for real, which will take you straight downtown. *But …*"

"But what?"

He shakes his head. "You be careful, my friend. Page Avenue is a stronghold for gangs and drugs, if you know what I'm saying. They don't call it the Shooting Gallery for nothing."

"The what?"

"Yeah, the Shooting Gallery: *bang, bang*. The whole goddam

avenue is awash with guns, knives, drug gangs, murderers, and street muggers. It is Missouri's Murder Row. Watch yourself on that bicycle. And that is real good advice."

Hmm. This doesn't sound good. Then again, I was given the same warning every day over the five weeks it took me to pedal from Durban to Cape Town in South Africa. I was not threatened once, but of course there's always a first time. I could get myself onto a nearby Interstate where cyclists are strictly forbidden, but that would almost certainly mean some unwelcome police attention. No, I'll run the Shooting Gallery's gauntlet and hopefully bluff my way through it by appearing steely and bold.

"Are you carrying?" the man asks.

I know what he means, but guns are not my thing. I shake my head. He says, "Too bad. Good luck, buddy."

The miles roll on, easier and faster than yesterday. The Page Avenue Extension ends, and piece by piece the urban sprawl begins. A big grey cloud blocks the sunshine as if overcast conditions automatically go with the territory. The sprawl thickens, and the avenue becomes a combination of poor residential and business districts. Some of the houses are in tumbledown condition, barely worth barring-up. All the stores and the bigger houses have taken the opposite view. Groups of black youths loiter on street corners; burned-out car wrecks line its side-streets, and rusty old bangers belching fumes are prolific. It is 3pm, and a group of old men clustered by the door of a liquor store are passing a bottle around. It is wrapped in a brown paper bag, from which they each take long swigs. At a set of red lights, an argument is going on in a dented, beat-up vehicle next to me. The passenger suddenly leaps out and starts running away fast. The driver abandons his car right there and chases after him, shouting murderous threats. I am extremely vigilant at red lights, but it's okay once I get moving again. So far, nobody has taken much interest in me.

The avenue seems to go on forever, a sorry vista of urban neglect with a feeling of helplessness and futility floating along its dirty, littered sidewalks. I can too easily imagine what Friday and Saturday nights would be like in this ghetto of a place. As the man said, *bang, bang*. And it probably isn't much better on weeknights either.

I think about getting my camera out, then think the better of it. No point in tempting fate. The sooner I put the Shooting Gallery behind me, the better. Things improve dramatically when the avenue joins up with King Boulevard, leading me straight into a downtown area of tall, modern buildings, parklands, and the giant Gateway Arch which is the city's international landmark. What a difference a mile makes.

After checking into my hotel, I go for a short wander of the city. St Louis is the halfway mark of this ride down the river, and the end of the Upper Mississippi. I've got almost 1,100 miles on the clock. Park Rapids and Lake Itasca seem like faraway places right now. As of tomorrow, I'll be heading ever more towards and into the Deep South. The second half of the ride is going to be different along the Lower Mississippi, I'm sure of that. In what way, I'm not so sure.

After dark I call in at a bar/restaurant for something to eat. Two cops, one white, the other black, are sipping coffee in silence. On a whim I walk over to their table and introduce myself as a UK journalist. Having survived the Shooting Gallery myself, these two guys must have stories of those who didn't.

"One or two" grunts the white cop, who does not want to be named. He is early 40s, with a tough, pockmarked face and prematurely greying hair. "We got a call out a few days ago to investigate a body found in a dumpster. He was a cab driver who'd been shot in the back of the head."

He falls silent. "And?" I prod.

He shrugs. "We think we know who shot him. A drug dealer who is currently out on parole. We're trying to establish proof. I guess the victim owed him money or double-crossed him in some way. Happens all the time."

The black cop, a big rotund man also in his 40s, says, "There was one time when we was called to a house off Page Avenue.

114

Someone was worried about the neighbours who hadn't been seen for 48 hours. We forced the door and went inside. There was five dead bodies, three men and two women, sprawled around the television set which was still switched on. The Cartoon Channel, as I remember. Someone had gained access to the house and blown the occupants away with a .38 handgun. I dunno if anyone was ever charged, and I dunno what the killings was over, but we found 30lbs of cannabis in the place."

I suppose that when ghetto dwellers turn to guns and drugs as a means to an end, it can so often become a sticky one. The outcome of that way of life will only ever be negative.

I leave these two cynical cops to their own devices, in the knowledge that this is one shooting gallery that is anything but a fairground attraction.

Twelve

THE CITY OF SOBRIQUETS

THE PHONE RINGS in my hotel room. The desk clerk downstairs says, "Your driver is here, sir."

He is? What driver? I know nothing of this. I go down to the lobby and am approached by a casually dressed young black woman named Donna Andrews who says she has come to take me for breakfast. She is from the St Louis CVB, and didn't I get her message? No, I did not. "The desk clerk said something about a driver. You don't much look like a chauffcur to me."

She laughs. "Yes, I heard him say that. It's because I'm wearing jeans and I'm black. He doesn't expect me to be in an executive position. So welcome to St Louis - where the south begins and attitudes change."

It is a grey morning outside. Donna drives us to a former warehouse district that is now undergoing some tasteful regeneration; expensive apartments, restaurants, curio shops. From the restaurant window, the Gateway Arch spans the city skyline. She asks if I want to go up it, which I don't. She seems relieved. God knows how many times she has had to escort journalists up and down the arch. All I want in fact is to get myself the hell out of here and back to the smaller river ports.

I tell Donna about my ride down Page Avenue and she gives me a reproving look. "You evidently enjoy living dangerously."

I think back to Sunday's nerve-wracking ride into St Charles. "No, not always. I've had so many close calls since I started, that I sometimes wonder when my luck is going to run out."

"You're not gonna have much fun getting out of St Louis either" she says. "There's about 30 miles of complicated suburb to get through unless you take the Interstate, which I don't think is allowed." That's the trouble with my map. It pinpoints St Louis, but seems to disregard the miles and miles of outer city areas. It also shows no other way of heading south, other than on Interstate 55.

Donna says, "Why don't I take you to the edge of town? I'm not in the mood for the office today."

If she wants to do that, I'm not going to argue. Riding the endless sprawling suburbs is hell on wheels, and in this case could take up most of the day. So she is my driver after all.

An hour later the bike is resting in the back of her 4x4. We quickly leave downtown St Louis behind and get onto the Interstate, where the four-lane traffic streams like a flow of deranged racing snakes. There is a kind of madness in the air, as if the collective traffic has entered a competition in self-destruction in which there are no prizes and everyone is a loser. Some more so than others: across the barrier, there's been a pile-up, and a nasty one by the look of it. I am grateful for the lift, but will be glad for a return to quieter byways.

That soon comes. Donna drops me off at a gas station outside Crystal City at the southern end of the St Louis conurbation. I give her a big hug and a peck on the cheek. She has done me a big favour today. When she's gone, I grab a coffee and stand outside, studying the map and basking in what is now glorious sunshine. I am going to head for Sainte Genevieve today, a little river port just 30 miles away down Highway 61.

And what a peaceful road it is too. This is when cycling is the fun that it should be: warm sunshine, light traffic, and some stunning Missouri scenery. The blazing red and gold of autumn are lighting up these rolling hills, almost as if they are on fire for real.

Twelve miles from Ste Genevieve is the town of Bloomsdale, actually more of a clustered village with a population of just 419. As I wheel into it, a cop car wrecks the silence with a howling siren and squealing tyres. It is speeding my way. Two grim faced officers are inside, and they whoosh by in an anxious blur. When I pull up at the town's only bar and café, the regulars are standing outside discussing this unexpected breach of the peace.

"Was them cops or an ambulance?" asks one grizzled oldster in a check shirt and red baseball cap. "They was come-and-gone so goddam fast, we didn't get to see."

"Cops" I answer. "Two of them. They didn't look happy."

"Wouldn't know what a happy cop looks like" he retorts. "That's got to be the first time in months that the sirens have gone off around here."

One by one they shuffle back inside. I stand the bike next to the entrance and join them. I've long stopped worrying about theft from my baggage in places like these, although I always remove my essential pouch, the one that carries the money, passport, and so on. Inside I plonk myself down at the bar, order a toasted sandwich and a coffee to go with it.

With the exception of me and the barmaid, everyone else in here has long passed retirement age. This place must be their daytime gathering point and a refuge from the wives. The speeding cop car is still on their minds. "Last time the cops came thisaway with them sirens blowing, was when the bank was robbed" says one. "It took 'em so long to get here, the robbers had already reached Ste Genevieve by the time the county sheriff was leaving there."

How, I wonder, would he know that?

"On account of it came out in the newspaper. Witnesses saw

the robbers' car racing through town. They got clean away and were never caught because we don't have any cops here in Bloomsdale to give chase. No need, not as a rule anyhow."

I enjoy these moments. A new town, new faces, all of them friendly. In an hour from now I'll be gone and will never see them again. They don't know it, but they're all a part of this Mississippi marathon, providing me with insight and local colour. I suddenly notice something else. The accent has subtly altered from that of St Louis and all points north of there. It is not yet the southern drawl, but there is a leaning towards it. It particularly comes out in the word 'Missouri', which has now become 'Missoura'. And this detail leads me to ask a curious question.

"Tell me something" I say to anyone who'll listen. "During the Civil War, which side was Bloomsdale on?"

That brings a sudden silence and some blank looks. It also starts a debate among the old timers. One says that it wouldn't have made any difference since the population back then was about three people, and it isn't much more now. Another opines that anywhere south of St Louis would likely have been sympathetic to the southern cause, while anywhere north of there would have been on the Yankee side. A third says that the south will live to fight another day - and he voices that improbability with a clear conviction. Donna had been right. The north-south dividing line along the Mississippi is St Louis. The upper river versus the lower river, with St Louis as the buffer-zone for an antipathy that exists to this day. Damn Yankees versus Southern Rednecks.

I press on to Ste Genevieve, climbing a long, steep hill, and then enjoy a five mile downhill glide into town. Some of these ports are really two towns in one, the old and the new. The new is built along the main highway, lined with motels, restaurants, burger bars, gas stations, and convenience stores. The old, always down by the water, is where history seeps out from the walls of early buildings and quaint downtown streets. Ste Genevieve is such a place, the last remaining French colonial settlement in the USA with all its original houses still intact from as far back as 1749.

Along this river, that is quite a miracle. When in dark mood, the Mississippi is dastardly to man, beast, property, and anything else that gets in its way. I'll return to this point after a quick tour through a town that seems more aware of its past than of the present. Just as most everything in Hannibal is 'Mark Twain', in Ste Genevieve, all is 'historic'. I pedal along its tight streets. The old, low buildings that were once emporiums, steam packet offices, small hotels, and whorehouses are now bistro-type restaurants, antique stores, art galleries, and other tourist-related concerns. No downtown street lasts for much more than 100 metres before continuing as a tidy line of pastel-painted clapboard houses with white picket fences.

A young lad of about 12 emerges from one of them astride a chopper bike. He instantly spots my electric machine and coos. "Seen 'em in the bike magazines" he wistfully says. "Gonna get one, and I am too." I ask him the way to my hotel and he just says to follow him. I have trouble keeping up, as he leaps and bounces his sturdy little bike along badly-paved sidewalks at a jarring pace. At a fork in the road, the boy stops and points out the hotel. "I'm going the other way" he says. I thank him and offer a five dollar bill, but he smiles pleasantly and says, no sir, no need, it's been a pleasure. And with that he's gone, pedalling towards whatever polite 12 year olds get up to in this little town in the late afternoon.

There is a package waiting for me at the front desk containing general information about Ste Genevieve. Up in my room, I idly flick through the pages and take note of a few interesting details, some of which bring me back to my earlier point that the big river takes no prisoners when in a raging temper.

Over time, its floodwaters have obliterated cities, settlements, and islands, and the citizens of Ste Genevieve thought that they might be in for such a fate back in March, 1993. An extraordinary amount of rain had been falling, five

121

times the seasonal average, which in turn melted the snow from a late and heavy snowfall. The river quickly reached flood stage, 27 feet. It can actually go a lot higher than that without causing too much damage, but at 27 feet, people begin to get edgy. By late April it had reached 37.7 feet, flooding the town and its surrounding ranch land. At that stage, everyone figured the worst was over, with the water receding slowly as it gushed towards the Gulf of Mexico in a dirty brown torrent. But then the rains blew in again, lasting all through the months of May and June, and the river went on the rise once more. Urgent requests to the Corps of Engineers to establish higher levees were turned down on the grounds of cost. By early June it was up to 32.5 feet and rising. Sandbagging began again in earnest - emergency, temporary levees in the form of thousands of 35lb bags of sand. This time the National Guard was drafted in to aid the town's band of volunteers, and the Salvation Army stepped in to give support to the 100 families that had been evacuated for a second time from their homes on the low-lying parts of the riverbank.

Preventive activity became ever more frantic as the river rose further still. The sandbag walls were just about coping, but an impending feeling of doom set over the town once it reached 47.9 feet. By this time, the national media had descended upon Ste Genevieve. Although all the other ports on both banks of the Mississippi had similar problems, the TV crews spotted a real story in this town by watching its inhabitants attempt to save not only their own properties, but all the historic French colonial buildings too - the one entity that makes Ste Genevieve unique in the United States. When, at 2pm on August 6, the river level reached an unprecedented 49.67 feet, they knew that anytime now they might well be reporting one of the great tragedies this river has ever caused. The sandbag levees would not be able to hold 50 feet, which would then leave the Mississippi free to surge into town and virtually destroy it for all time.

Flood devastation, Ste Genevieve, Missouri. In 1993, it came close to being a lot worse than this.

The townsfolk held their breath. Then, mercifully, the rain eased and then stopped altogether; inch by important inch, hour by fretful hour, and day by endless day, the water level ever-so-slowly lessened. It had been a very, very close thing. Just five miles south of here, the little town of St Mary was not so lucky. It was wiped out; only a handful of buildings remained. The sodden citizens of Ste Genevieve were ordered to use boiled water only - an edict that lasted through to the end of September. It took over a year to clean up and return to normality - a normality subtly adjusted by the experience. Come each spring, when the northern snows melt and pour their liquid content into the river, Ste Genevieve becomes nervous. In these days of acknowledged climate change, they know those rains can come again, and again, and again.

MICHAEL BOYD JNR, the sports editor of the *Ste Genevieve Herald* wants to interview me the next morning, somehow equating my sort of cycling with sport. We meet late morning in a café in the old town and sip coffee while he asks all the usual questions. It is not just the bike ride that's of interest to the riverside media; it is that for the duration of the trip, it is linked to that global giant of the broadcasting business, the BBC. It's not every day that the BBC passes through a place like this, especially not on a bicycle, and I've noticed that all the newspapers I talk to make quite a deal out of it. Michael Boyd Jnr, a young black man with ambition, is no different. He is building up a portfolio, he tells me. It consists of clippings from the sports names and other notables he's managed to collar at one time or another, and which will, he hopes, eventually help land him a job on the *Washington Post* or the *New York Times*. He thinks that adding the BBC to his credits will do his cause no harm at all.

There is an old man standing alone at the bar, nursing a beer and a bourbon chaser. His eyes are fixed on us intensely, and his ear is cocked our way as if whatever we're saying is of crucial importance to his day. I am unsure of why I feel a small discomfort at his presence, but I do. Once the interview is over, I get out of there and wander down to the river. It is quiet and empty today. I try to imagine what it must have been like during the flood, with days, weeks and months of tumbling rain. Not just worrying, but pretty damn miserable too.

According to my info-pack back at the hotel, the spot where I now stand was the scene for another Mississippi disaster, this one way back in August, 1852. It was an incident that did nothing to enhance the perceived glamour of the steamboat era.

The steam packet *Dr Franklin No.11*, with a full complement of passengers aboard, was on its way from Memphis to St Louis when about four miles from Ste Genevieve one of the chimney flukes suddenly collapsed, resulting in a violent explosion of steam. The scene was described by a prominent townsman of the day as thus:

'She was towed down to the Ste Genevieve wharf. Among the passengers was the famous novel writer Ned Buntline, who escaped unhurt. The sight on board the steamer was a depressing and mournful one. The cabin of the boat was strewn with men and women, uttering the most fearful cries, and undergoing the most cruel sufferings. Strong men were blistered with steam, yet cold in death. Both engineers were blown into the river, and at the time of the explosion, some jumped overboard and were lost. In one berth lay a wife and mother dead, with a child still clasped in her arms, while others lay frightfully mutilated. The citizens of Ste Genevieve rendered all the aid and assistance to those unfortunate persons, and had the dead decently buried in the graveyard'.

The death toll was 32. As stated, one lucky survivor was Ned Buntline - which goes some way to proving the theory that only the good die young. Buntline was the chap who commissioned the Colt handgun company to make what became known as the Buntline Special, which among others, became the favoured weapon of Wyatt Earp and Bat Masterton. Ned Buntline (1823-1886) was a writer of cheap 'dime' novels, an adventurer, a showman, and a notorious troublemaker who had more than once been tried for murder. Yet he toured all over the place, relentlessly preaching the necessity for temperance in thundering fire-and-brimstone deliveries. But after each one of these moral outbursts, he would then go on a massive bender himself, which always landed him in big trouble. A few of his 'dime' novels became big sellers, though mostly they flopped. His big success came when he met William Cody - the frontiersman from Le Claire, Iowa - and renamed him 'Buffalo Bill'. They travelled the country together, putting on those famous Wild West shows and raking in the money. Then they fell out over just that and went their separate ways.

I get lost in the history of it all, daydreaming by the side of the river. Eventually I amble back into town in search of a light lunch, settling down at the bar of the Anvil Saloon and Restaurant. I've not been there more than a minute when someone slips onto the next stool. It is the eavesdropping old man again.

"I been watching you" he grunts. Up close, his hair is grey and unkempt, his stubble untidy. His clothes are rumpled and shabby. What teeth he has left are yellowing and long. He resembles the human equivalent of a plane crash. "It's been a time since someone interesting came to town, and I'm gonna buy you a drink."

My first thoughts are that he's simply after someone to talk to, and such people are normally the town's bore. I can tell by the looks he's getting from the barmaid that he is not Mr Popularity around here. Yet I hesitate to be impolite or offensive, and unwillingly accept a glass of wine. And that's when he starts on me.

"I got more money than I know what to do with" he brags against all visible evidence. "Yes sir I do, and that's the truth. And I'll tell you something else. My wife has gotta be the best and biggest bang in town. Ask any man, and he'll tell you that is so."

I look at his lined face. It contains a small sadness beneath the bluff and bravado. In my travels around the world, I have met this man before in different towns and countries.

"Why would I want to do that?" I ask in reply.

"Because my wife would like you. I know so. Go ahead and screw her, be my guest."

This is ridiculous. He looks to be close to 70 and I don't suppose his wife would be much younger; nor much prettier for that matter. I shake my head and ask him if he's serious. "Sure I'm serious. It's what makes her happy. If she's happy, then I'm happy. If she's unhappy, well now, that's another thing, and it ain't good for my health."

"Is this what you do all day - go about hustling strange men for the wife?"

He nods. "Pretty much. Out-of-towners like you, if I can find 'em: truckers, salesmen, tourists. Satisfaction guaranteed, and not a cent to pay. Don't need money, I got plenty of that."

I am most certainly not going to take matters to his desired conclusion, but I am debating with myself if I should turn this into a radio piece. It isn't the first time that someone has suggested that I might care to give his wife a once-over. There are some men who get a strange kick out of that. But it's a real first when it comes to someone who makes this his life's work - and for no reward other than a sated partner. It must be a most disorientated marriage.

His cell phone rings. I'm surprised he owns such an item. He turns his back to me and mumbles something into it. Then he swivels round and says, "That was her. She needs something from the pharmacy, urgent. I gotta go. I'm gonna tell her you're in town so don't go away. I'll be back."

I don't even know his name, or he mine. When he's gone, a kind of relief settles over the bar area. The barmaid, who could not possibly have missed our brief conversation, says to me, "Don't you believe all that shit about money. The guy lives on welfare and spends near all of it on drink. How old do you think he is?"

Around 70 is my guess. The barmaid laughs harshly. "Try mid-50s or younger still. It's the booze. He never eats."

Somehow that does not surprise me. "Does he really round up total strangers to have sex with his wife?"

"Yeah, that much is for real. He's supposed to be impotent, but she ... well, she can't get enough. Finding other men for her, it's like fulfilling an alternative role. I hear that she never leaves the house."

I think this not to be a radio item. I see it instead as a sort of human tragedy, albeit with a funny side to the wreckage. Two afflicted people, trapped with one another, neither with a means of escape. But they get through each day somehow, he with drink, her with sex from strangers. I had to come across a black comedy sooner or later along the Mississippi. It just happens to be here in Ste Genevieve.

Talking of comedy, Michael Boyd Jnr had earlier given me the name and number of a woman named Lorraine Stange. She

127

apparently knows every amusing and bizarre story associated with the town and I want to say hello. I have a broadcast this evening, and I need to follow up the flood story with something more lighthearted. We are to meet in the lobby of my hotel when she knocks off work as director of the town's historic homes.

*I*T COULD ONLY HAPPEN beside the Mississippi. By the time Lorraine is through with her story of Ste Genevieve's penchant for nicknames, my laughter is almost painful. It is a tradition that's been around this town for over 200 years and is still going strong today.

No matter what name you were born with, in Ste Genevieve it is going to get changed by others - and the new name will stick. If you were born, say, John Smith, it will only stay John Smith until something happens to warrant a bizarre sobriquet. The new name will spread across town and in no time become an everyday reality. Fiction becomes fact, and that name will appear in the phone directory, in bank accounts, on license plates and mailboxes, on wedding and death certificates, and on epitaphs.

An example of how a seriously-quirky nickname can befall you comes from the Mark Twain era when a local youngster with the surname of La Rose applied for a job on a riverboat. He took with him his meagre wardrobe in the hope of being far gone up the river that same day. While signing the ship's register, a gust of wind blew his valise clean off the table, causing the comment, 'Mister, you must have very few damn clothes if the wind blew it away so easily'. Forever after, he was called 'Few Clothes La Rose'. Whatever his given name had been, it was no longer. 'Few Clothes' became his regular moniker and nothing was going to change it. I do not know how his brothers became 'Sparrow' and 'Cocky' but they did.

Three brothers from a Jewish family began life as Raymond, Marion, and Leo. Over time they became Dizzy, Izzy, and Nuts.

Izzy, I'm informed, somehow arose from yet another nickname. As an elementary student, Izzy could run faster than any other kid in school, and became 'Hebrew the Wind Away'. Other members of the same family are known as Noonie, Cap, and Goofie, whether they like it or not. The Basler kin are known respectively throughout the town as Chipper, Beck, Big Foot, Little Big Foot, Batch, Moosey, Porky, and Schnay.

Here is how Schnay acquired his nickname. As a boy, playing out in the snow, he would frequently relieve himself into the white stuff - and in the process, spell out his name, then Ray. One day a neighbour of German descent spotted his artful urination and instantly nicknamed him *Schnee* - German for snow. To rhyme with 'Ray' the name quickly became Schnay.

The Scherers, another local family, are known as Kee Kee, Poogie, Piggy, Butts, Bossy, and Hammer. Bossy had once been called Goo-Goo Eyes, of which he disapproved. He told Lorraine Stang that it was 'a name that could only have been started by Flower Pot' - which is his own name for Flower Pot Rhem, the town florist.

Animals feature significantly in Ste Genevieve sobriquets: brothers Mouse and Rat Schwent, Moose Jokerst, Horse Morice, Snakes Grass, Hippo Sadler, Wonder Warthog Kertz, Catfish Ruttler, Squirrel Irlbeck, Froggie K. My pet favourite in this category is Toad Grieshaber, which by popular demand was modified to Toad Greasehopper.

The list goes on. Knock-Out Vineyard because of his penchant for starting fights. In similar vein, Crusher Vaeth, Two Gun Goverrau, Killer Brown, and Tarzan Arnold. To balance out the tough guys, are Smiley Taylor, Sweet Pea Vaeth, Honey Wehner, Fluff Martin, Powder Buff, Funny Mayer and his daughter Wee Wee (whatever that implies).

Ste Genevieve can boast a near-complete A-to-Z of current nicknames with the exception of the letters 'V' and 'X'. Apple Knocker Schwent, Bots Grieshaber, Chevvy Gendron, Do-Do Wehner, Ernie Schmeltz, Flakes Bahr, Grump Roth, High Pockets Kreitler, Itchy Rudloff, Jazbo Scherer, Kilowatt Greg,

Lemon Klein, Moon Williams, Nooks Oberle, Ockie Geisler, Peck Wehner, Quick Start, Ratsy Bahr, Snew Fallert, Toothpick Bollinger, Ugh Wilson, Waddie Schmeltz, Yitty Wehmeyer, and someone who is simply known as Zombie.

Were I to stay in town for a week, I reckon the missing 'V' would get filled. Quite some time ago, following a sharp exchange of words over the phone with someone, the person in question sent me a letter. It was addressed to 'Mr Quentin von Snarl'. I do believe it may be time to continue on my travels.

Thirteen

WHERE THE RIVER IS MIGHTY

I GET MOVING early in the morning; next stop Cape Girardeau, a city that Mark Twain once referred to as the 'Athens of the Mississippi'. By Interstate it is 60 miles distant, but on Highway 61 - a road that does its fair share of twisting and weaving - I have to add another 15 miles. But I'm in luck today. The wind is at my back and I'll Go for the full 75 miles. If my map and my suspicions are anything to go by, the nine settlements en-route are unlikely to have overnight accommodation. They may not even have cafes or gas stations either.

This following wind is making all the difference. The river has disappeared from view, and I pedal along yet more open, undulating ranch land, passing through some oddly-named places set a few miles apart: Belgique, Menfro, Farrar, Brazeau, Frohna, Pocahontas. I'm using so little electric-assist today that I simply decide to keep on going; to stop only for a pee and to munch a banana or two. Lost in assorted thoughts, the miles sweep by. At somewhere called Fruitland I turn east onto Highway 177 which takes me back to the river, and then due south for the final few miles to Cape Girardeau. I arrive feeling rather pleased with myself. And with the bike. It has become such a true and trusty friend.

Pedalling along clean and pleasant downtown streets which rise sharply from the river, I see nothing that remotely resembles Athens (unless Twain was referring to Athens, Georgia), but there is a unique ambience here that strikes me immediately. The place has something special that I cannot yet put my finger on.

At the Rose Bed Inn on South Sprigg St - yet another renovated old building dating from way back - a young man comes bouncing down some steps to greet me, insisting on helping with my bags. By the time I've stashed the bike away and am ensconced in my upstairs room, I realise that in him I have already got a superb little radio item.

J.C. Harris ("just call me JC") is a musician. After dumping my bags onto the huge bed, the slim, fair haired 30 year old tells me that he's played piano duets with the one and only Jerry Lee Lewis and has done backing keyboards for Kris Kristoffersen among others. So what is he doing in Cape Girardeau, hauling luggage?

"It's a bit of a story. Let's just say I took a fall, but now I'm on the way back. Say, what are you doing later?"

I shrug. "Get something to eat; maybe go for a drink somewhere."

"I get off work around nine. We can go to a place just down the road. Have a drink and a talk. It's got a piano. I'll play a few tunes if you want."

I want. Anyone who duets with Jerry Lee Lewis must be good; very good.

After showering away the day's accumulated offerings of dirt, dust, oil, and sweat, I nip downstairs to meet with my hosts, Eldon and James. They are middle aged, openly gay, and as welcoming as it is possible to be. I warm to them instantly.

They are busy in the kitchen, preparing a set menu for tonight when a TV advertising crew will be present with a cast of extras to shoot a commercial. The extras will be getting a free meal and free wine while they pose as satisfied diners in the Rose Bed's restaurant.

Also showing up anytime soon, Eldon says, is a man called Chuck Martin, the boss of Cape Girardeau's CVB, who is apparently going to take me to dinner somewhere. I may have pedalled enough miles to have possibly earned that today.

Chuck is a tall, broad man in his 40s with thick glasses and a decent beard, and who bears the responsibility of promoting this city to the wider world. He kindly takes me to a restaurant in a converted warehouse down by the river, where we eat spare ribs and sip tea. He's got a batch of ideas for me and says that tomorrow we'll be going here, there, everywhere so keep the day free. Suits me. I've an inkling that Cape Girardeau is going to be a gold mine for good stories. It has that 'feel' about it.

The first item has to be J.C. Harris though. Chuck drops me off back at the inn, where the camera crew are hard at it and the extras, all dressed in semi-formal evening wear, are pretending to have a good time. Well, maybe they're not pretending. They are eating, drinking, laughing, and talking naturally among themselves as if the camera and the hot glaring lights do not exist.

Shortly, JC and me settle at the bar of a private club just 100 metres from the inn. Eldon has given him the inn's credit card with the instruction that tonight is on them and we're simply to enjoy ourselves. What have I done to merit all the wonderful hospitality I'm receiving along this river?

I press him on Jerry Lee Lewis, whose music I more or less grew up with and which still makes me want to get out there on the floor and rock my socks off. "I met him through a friend of mine, Kenny Lovelace, who plays fiddle in Jerry's band" he explains. "It was on the night of his 40th anniversary in showbiz and the guy put on one hell of a show to celebrate it. Then

Kenny suggested that the boss might like to hear me play - and that was that. Jerry Lee had a second piano put up there on the stage. Together we did *Great Balls of Fire*, and *It'll Be Me* ... "

" ... *and I'll be lookin' for you*" I croon, finishing off the line.

"Ha, you got it, man. Anyhow, Sam Phillips was in the audience. He was the guy from Sun Records, who launched the careers of Elvis, Roy Orbison, Johnny Cash, Carl Perkins, and the rest. He came up to me afterwards and said, 'I'm gonna keep my eye on you, boy. Because you're gonna make it, and I think you're gonna make it big'."

Also in the audience was Kris Kristoffersen. JC's performance with Jerry Lee was enough to earn him a tour in Kristoffersen's backing group, and playing piano on his next album. Offers of session work poured in from various studios, as did the offers to join other touring bands. Through all this, he stayed in touch with Jerry Lee via his friend Kenny Lovelace. J.C. Harris, then in his mid 20s, was on his way.

But on his way to where? The rock music business is full of such tales.

"It was the usual rock 'n'roll lifestyle. The usual volume of women, booze, drugs; the usual partying until dawn. I climbed too far, too fast. The big fall had to come, but I couldn't see it; not at the time." That happened when a certain band fired him after a drunken argument. Word spread. J.C. Harris suddenly had 'trouble' written across his forehead. When the money ran out, he found himself out on the streets, where he lived rough for two years.

By then, JC had drifted up to Cape Girardeau. Enter Eldon and James, proprietors of the Rose Bed Inn. They took him in, gave him a job, and actively encouraged JC to get back to writing songs and playing piano again. The upshot of their help is a forthcoming album called *Southern Roots*, a compilation of what JC calls 'alternative country music': a blend of blues, gospel, country, and bar room honkytonk.

All I need now is to hear him play. He leads me to an ante-room at the back of the club and settles down at the piano.

Suddenly his fingers become a sweeping blur as he lets rip with a real belter, Jerry Lee's *Whole Lotta Shakin' Goin' On*. The lad is a wizard. He not only plays and sings as well as Jerry Lee Lewis ever did, he seems to transform into a younger incarnation of the big bad bruiser of rock 'n'roll. I understand why Sam Phillips had been bowled over by his performance. I don't think I've seen anyone, Jerry Lee and Jools Holland included, hit the keys with such lightning speed, and not a single bum note throughout. He is an outstanding talent, young enough to climb back up there once more and hopefully wise enough to have absorbed the harsh lessons of the past.

We return to the bar and talk some more. He tells me his next live date is here in 'the Cape', as the city is locally termed, set for Friday week; a Democrat fundraising dinner where he's been booked to strut his stuff in front of those with the big cheque books. I am already trying to figure out a way to have him play on the BBC.

J.C. Harris, a youthful version of Jerry Lee Lewis.

135

During the course of the evening, I ask about Eldon and James. They are so very openly gay - James in particular - and I'm curious at what the attitude might be towards them down in what is ever more becoming the American south. Is there still prejudice, or has the Cape gone beyond that?

"Is there *prejudice*?" JC retorts with emphasis. "Oh, there's whole lot of that, plus tax."

I can see him chewing something over. Then he says, "They've got a story, those two. I really can't go into it because it is real personal. But if you're looking for human-interest material, you might be able to prise it out of them."

So what am I supposed to be looking for? If JC thinks he's going to escape with only those few teasing words, he is mistaken. I apply a subtle and well-oiled questioning technique developed over my many years in journalism. It usually produces the desired effect.

"I can't tell you the full story, honest. That will have to come from them. But they both did time in prison. It involves embezzlement - $500,000 or damn near that - attempted murder, and more. Just be careful how you tackle it."

NEXT MORNING, Chuck Martin picks me up and we drive to a tourist centre that has the 'Trail of Tears' as its theme. It is a little known episode in American history, which is now looked upon in shame. In 1830, Congress passed the Indian Removal Act that allowed the government to forcibly eject eastern tribes from their ancestral land and move them into the hinterlands west of the Mississippi (to what eventually became Oklahoma). Thus, in the winter of 1838 some 16,000 Cherokees were rounded up in the state of Georgia and unwillingly commenced the 1,000 mile hike west. Divided into 16 groups of 1,000 people, 15 of those groups crossed the river at Cape Girardeau. Except by then, the numbers were down to 12,000, the others having died along the way through cold, illness, exhaustion, and downright misery. It is a moving exhibition, intended not simply as an uncomfortable item of learning, but also as a 'lest we forget' tribute.

Next we go to the downtown riverfront where a professional artist is busy painting huge colourful murals on the 16-foot high floodwall. "It used to look more like the Berlin Wall" Chuck grunts, "and had roughly the same effect. It deterred people from coming down here. We hope these murals will help to reconnect our citizens with the river."

They are superb works of art, featuring old steamboats, past presidents, a scene from the Cape's great fire of 1916, and another from the 1927 flood, which had been the worst of them all. They do much to brighten up a necessary evil.

Next on this illuminating tour is a light lunch at the River Ridge Winery. Whenever I think of American wine, I also automatically think of California. In fact, New York was the first state to produce wine in the USA, and Missouri the second. It is big business for the state, worth some $35 million per year. What's more, it is first class stuff.

Later, following a few media interviews (the Cape, population 35,000, is big enough to house a regional TV station, two radio stations, and a daily newspaper called the *Southeast Missourian*), Chuck suggests that we cross the bridge into Illinois and take a 30 mile drive south to the city of Cairo, where the Ohio River pours into the Mississippi. This I have to see, though Chuck has an additional reason. "I'd like to show you why I regard Cape Girardeau as a kind of paradise. You'll see what I mean when you compare it with Cairo. It'll be interesting to note your reaction."

We drive through a flat and empty Illinois landscape. There is a railroad bridge that spans the entrance to town with the single word CAIRO written across its arch. Beyond the bridge, the city itself sprawls into an untidy tumbledown mess. Youths, loiter by fast food outlets and liquor stores. "I think I get your reasoning" I mutter to my host.

"Not yet, you don't. Wait until you see the main street."

We drive to a poorly-kept parkland and walk to the point

where the two rivers meet. It is an incredible sight, here at the southernmost tip of Illinois. To my right, the Mississippi flows around the point, with the shining state of Missouri on the other side. To my left, the rolling Ohio River tumbles into the big river, the two meeting up with each other like a powerful, slithering pair of titanic anacondas joining in copulation. Beyond lies the state of Kentucky, aglow in its autumnal colours. Having already added the Missouri River to its flowing volume, this is the point at which the Mississippi becomes mighty indeed. The rip tides of the confluence shimmer, bubble, and boil in the sunlight where the two waterways collide, jostling and elbowing one another like Manhattan's rush-hour commuters pouring down into the subway.

At water's edge assorted trash is strewn around the point: beer cans, plastic bottles, torn wrapping paper, and the inner tube of a truck tyre. I cannot understand it. This exact spot, a rough patch of unkempt wasteland with such stunning views, surely ought to be the most valuable piece of real estate on the entire river. It should be to the Mississippi what Las Vegas is to Nevada, what Disneyland is to Florida, or what the pyramids are to that other city of Cairo. This spot is just begging to become the playground of the river - fun nightclubs, cabarets and top acts, gambling boats, cruise boats, smart restaurants and international hotels; a 24-hour resort set slap-bang in the middle of where two mighty rivers meet.

Instead, it is nothing more than patchy scrub and forlorn rocks. How has the state of Illinois missed such a trick? I am honestly baffled and intensely curious. There has to be a reason for this neglect, and I potentially see this as a really interesting radio piece.

Back in the car, Chuck explains as best he can. "From what I gather, it all goes back to 1969 and the Civil Rights Movement. This used to be a city of around 15,000 people, but now it's down to 3,000 or less. The city experienced some of the worst race riots in the country, and it has never properly recovered from them. People were killed, black and white. Hatred and mistrust simmered through the city, and if my antenna is on track, I'd say it's only just under the surface today - on both sides of the divide. The riots have left a nasty and continuing aftertaste."

This is as astonishing as it is disturbing. Close to 40 years has passed since then. With the confluence of the two rivers, Cairo has so much tourism potential that I'd have thought a Walt Disney or a Howard Hughes or a Donald Trump would have invaded the city by now and sorted everyone out.

"It's not as simplistic as that" Chuck argues. "The riots led to a boycott of all white-owned businesses by the black population. In retaliation, the whites fired their black employees, boarded up their stores, and left town, waiting for matters to calm down. But the depth of feeling was such that neither side was prepared to give an inch. The traders never came back."

The empty, crumbling main street of Cairo, Illinois. This city should have been the 'Playground of the Mississippi'.

139

Times clearly went from bad to worse. Factories closed and even the towboats began to give the place a miss. There is just one main industry left in town, a plant that processes soybeans, but apparently its owners are wearying of Cairo and talking of locating elsewhere.

A city without purpose. That much is startlingly plain when Chuck swings into the main street. It is really quite shocking. The entire street, which runs along a shallow slope, is an empty sea of peeling paintwork, boarded-up buildings, crumbling sidewalks. There is nobody - *nobody* - about, apart from ourselves and one old man in a wheelchair. He is rolling down the middle of the street, and in no danger at all of meeting any oncoming traffic. Chuck tells me the story of a well known film director who thought about using Cairo for a particular sequence in a movie he was shooting, an adaptation of a hardboiled Elmore Leonard novel. "I drove him here, just like you and I have done today. He took one look at this street, with his mouth hanging agape. In the end, he said 'This place is like Beirut during its civil war. I don't think we'll be doing any shooting here - at least, not of the filming kind'."

Beirut. I was there myself towards the end of its 15 years of disturbance, and the analogy is a reasonable one. That too had been a playground before the civil war blew a see-through hole from one end of the city to the other. And now Cairo, Illinois. The Beirut of the Mississippi. What a terrible waste.

For the sake of balance, not to mention contrast, we drive to a district where the houses are big, magnificent even. Not surprisingly, it covers only a small area of town. "This is where most of the remaining whites live" Chuck says. "If they sell up and leave, they'll be lucky to get about one-tenth of the true value. That would not be enough for them to buy elsewhere. They are trapped."

To be trapped in Cairo, Illinois, would be akin to having a PhD in the Meaning of Futility. By comparison, Cape Girardeau really is paradise - an entire world away from a city that could, and should, have been just that itself.

Back in Missouri, and against a setting sun, we drive to that point by the river where the Cape got its title. In the old days, it had been a giant slab of rock jutting out from a riverside bluff, and a navigational landmark for the steam packets. Alas, it is no more, having been broken up when the railroad came to town. But at this peaceful, lonely part of the river, there is such serene beauty down there that the missing rock doesn't seem to matter very much. A towboat is slowly nudging its load upriver; in the near distance, a lush and green mid-river island is fringed by white sand; the sun is glinting on water that, at this moment, is a lovely shade of blue; and the sky, still blue but fading into dusk, is tinted with the red hues of early evening. The Cape is in a calm, alluring mood.

ELDON AND JAMES are also in agreeable mood this evening and perfectly willing to talk of their troubled past. James is the younger, taller, and broader of the two; he has a light voice, smooth features, and a distinctly camp manner. Eldon, his partner, you would not necessarily suspect is gay. In fact, he's been married twice and has a son living somewhere in Louisiana. He is older than James, in his mid-50s, carrying a slight stoop that somehow gives the impression of an occasional word-weariness.

They met some 12 years ago. Eldon, having extricated himself from the second and final marriage, and still coming to terms with the fact that he was gay, went on a 'grand drive to anywhere' to clear his head and work out what to do with his new life; to try and find himself, in other words. One day, while filling up at a gas station in a small town a long way west of here, he was approached by a hitchhiker who asked if he might be heading for his hometown of St Louis, or anywhere thereabouts.

"He wasn't my type" Eldon explains, "but I could see at once that he was also gay. Since I'd no real idea where I was heading for myself, I made a snap decision. I said to him, 'I don't know anybody in St Louis, but I'm prepared to take you all the way - on one condition: which is that *you* will introduce *me* to the gay scene in that city'. The guy stuck to the agreement, so in an indirect way it was through him that I met James, who was living there at the time."

As the relationship established itself they talked of moving to a smaller city, some place like Cape Girardeau where property was still affordable; maybe buy up an old building and turn it into an hotel. But at some stage during this period, what surely must be one of the most difficult of human triangles entered the equation. Eldon's son by his first marriage - who never had an inkling that his father might be gay - turned up in St Louis.

He reacted badly to his father's new status. In fact, he tried to stab him to death not once, but three times. Eldon says that his son has always been a loose cannon with a violent streak and an unbalanced mind. But he remained sane enough to devise a way to get rich quick, and to get perceived revenge on his father and James at the same time.

Good with numbers, he got himself a job in a St Louis bank - the same bank where Eldon and James kept a joint business account. Over a period of time, he embezzled almost $500,000 from his employers, which he quietly laundered through the unwitting pair's account. The fraud was eventually discovered, the police were called, and all three men were charged. When it came to court, Eldon and James entered a not guilty plea, still dazed by events and the predicament they suddenly found themselves in. Eldon's son on the other hand, plea-bargained with the prosecution which demanded that he give damning evidence against the two in return for a couple of years in prison and repayment of the stolen money.

He did just that, apparently lying through his teeth in the witness box. The jury, which possibly thought that no son would give false evidence against his own father, chose to believe his version of events. Or, equally possible, maybe its members just didn't like gays, who knows. Either way, it returned a guilty verdict and the two men were sent to separate prisons for five years each.

"The worst of it was the time spent in the county jail" Eldon says. "Oddly, the federal prisons were reasonably tolerable. Nobody gave us any hassle, not even the guards."

They stayed in touch through cryptic notes. Mainly they would contain morale-boosting ideas for what their imagined hotel would look like when they got out. Once they had accepted their new conditions, time went by remarkably quickly. I would go so far as to say that they look back on their confinement if not with affection, then with a certain amount of satisfaction at getting through the ordeal and emerging at the other end unbroken, even strengthened.

Then began the really hard work. With prison records, the usual lines of credit were off limits. But they had found a block of condemned buildings in the Cape, just perfect for a restoration project. Quite apart from fundraising problems, they faced a battle-royal in persuading the city authorities to lift the demolition order on the buildings, and in getting consent to restore them. Perhaps it came from some new found determination, some obstinate tenacity developed during the prison years, but these two finally won the day. Furthermore, little by little they raised the necessary money via friends and a growing band of other believers.

Now, years later, the results are impressive. It isn't called the Rose Bed Inn for nothing. Not only is it a mighty comfortable hostelry, but what were wastelands at the rear of the buildings have been transformed into a tasteful oasis of ponds, flowers, and greenery. There is the one main building, plus two others on this once-condemned block. One is converted into guest apartments, and the other leased out to local residents. The trials of the past are over. Today, Eldon and James have amassed combined assets thought to be worth around $5 million.

I DO NOT WANT to leave the Cape. It is an attractive, friendly, inspiring place: big enough to lose yourself in, yet small enough to feel a part of. I have met people during my brief stay, some not mentioned here, whose company I would very much want to enjoy again. I'm not done with this place yet. Coming from a curmudgeonly cynic like me, that is saying a lot.

From that point of view, Mark Twain was right. Cape Girardeau is the 'Athens of the Mississippi'. It doubtless has its problems, but it also has more than its share of class, grace, and good taste.

Fourteen

MISTER 'SIPPI'

SOME 40 MILES SOUTH of the Cape lies the town of East
Prairie. On the Missouri side of the river it is the nearest place to
a completely isolated dot on the map called Dorena, from where
a small ferry shuttles back and forth to the port of Hickman,
Kentucky, with not a bridge for 60 miles in either direction.
Forever on the hunt for a story, my picky little brain has become
intrigued by the life and times of the ferryboat pilot who works
this remote corner of the Mississippi; a man whose daily life is
defined by, and confined to, numerous trips each day between
one riverbank and the other.

I pedal along the flat, quiet streets of this somewhat strange
Missouri town. It seems tight and inward looking. Then I realise
that East Prairie is several miles west of the river, an inland
ranching community without that 24-hour connection to the
Mississippi, and which very possibly has some long term
residents who have never even laid eyes on it. People who live
by the river really *are* different. In some way, it appears to

influence their lives in the same way that the sea does to those who've been brought up with the tang of salt air. A fishing village will have a wholly different collective attitude to that, say, of a country town. Expanses of water seem to make a difference to a way of thinking and a way of life.

Which is not to say that East Prairie is without its quirks. My lodgings for the night tells me so. The Bell's Grade Inn is odd indeed. At street level it is an antique store, with zero to tell you it is an hotel. No name, no reception area and no receptionist. Someone has to come by and hand me a key. Up a flight of stairs, I find on one side a private restaurant and ballroom for hire, both of which are closed. On the other side of the corridor are five or six bedrooms. Mine offers the poor and dingy view of a towering brick wall right outside.

Sylvie Barker, a woman of late middle age, is the nearest thing East Prairie has to a PR representative. She comes by in the early evening to take me to dinner along with her husband Sam, a big, jovial rancher. We go to a simple family café where small children squawk, squeal, and wriggle while the grandparents tuck in.

Sam at least is a river man, in so much as he occasionally trails his open skiff down to the water to go duck hunting. He's got a story for me about that, but it will have to wait because just then we are joined by friends of theirs, a local family. The husband and father of three tells me that for one day each year, he too becomes a cyclist.

John Gruber is in his 40s, the owner of a farm machinery dealership. Every summer, he says, East Prairie hosts a 130 mile bike race, which he always swears that he's never going to enter again but always does. I respect him for that. During my coast-to-coast ride across the USA, one particular leg was a 118 mile haul across the empty Arizona desert, with only the one diner/truck stop in between. It had been tough going, a one-off distance that had to be completed on the same day, and which I've no desire to repeat, let alone race.

Sylvie has arranged for me to meet up with the ferryboat

pilot tomorrow afternoon. She will take me there herself she says, because Dorena and its ferry landing are a good 12 miles away. A little later I dawdle back to my strange hotel with its equally strange atmosphere. Along the corridor, doors creak open and bang shut. There is something almost sinister about the footsteps passing my own doorway. I find this place really quite creepy.

The feeling doesn't go away. Sunday morning dawns and the town is silent. The occasional car drives along overcast streets which are seemingly devoid of human life. A lone dog stops to scratch itself, then hurries on its way. I eventually find an open gas station where I buy a large cup of takeaway coffee. It may just be my imagination, but there seems to be a sombre mood hovering over East Prairie, as if it's a town of guilt and dark secrets which only the tight lipped, tightly-knit townsfolk know of.

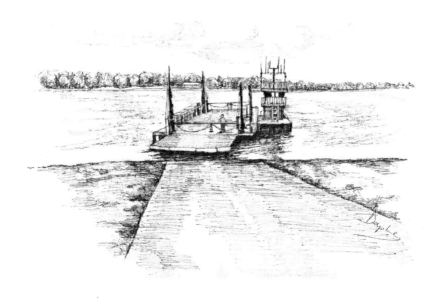

The car ferry that runs between Dorena, Missouri, and Hickman, Kentucky. There is no bridge for 60 miles in either direction.

147

Sylvie shows up early afternoon and we drive through the rural flatlands to the tiny settlement of Dorena, then on down to the ferry landing. It is merely a ramp in the middle of nowhere. There is a post with an electronic push-button bell that notifies the ferryman you are waiting. Finally we spot him coming round a bend in the river, a towboat-like vessel with a flat-bottomed barge tied alongside. It draws up to the landing and a woman swings open the barge gate once the steel platform protruding from the bow has met the concrete ramp with a resounding clang. A stream of vehicles disembark. There are just three takers on this side of the water. Sylvie leaves her car where it is and we walk aboard.

CAPTAIN STEVE STANIONIS is a stoutly built man, early 50s, balding but with a bushy beard, and quite a CV to his name. We are high up in his pilot house, an all mod-cons domain of marine electronics and an unusual steering system. Instead of a helm, Steve guides his boat by flicking at a thick pair of switches, something that I find disorientating to watch when my own natural way to go about this is with a wheel. He concurs, admitting to 'one or two' errors and near-misses when he first took over the boat.

We spend much of the afternoon criss-crossing the Mississippi, ten minutes downriver to Hickman, 15 minutes back upriver to Dorena. Before taking over this ferry service, Steve had variously been in the Coast Guard, running search & rescue boats; captain of a cruise boat in San Francisco Bay; skipper of a number of offshore oil support vessels in the Gulf of Mexico; captain of a gambling boat, and wackiest of all, a year spent as a lighthouse keeper in remotest Alaska.

"That must have been a lonely time" I suggest.

"Yeah, it was 100 miles west of the nearest town, so not too many people to talk to. But every couple of weeks I'd get a delivery of mail, movies, food, and five crates of beer. In some ways, it was real good to be away from all the hassles of the world. Just to be on your own, nobody riding your ass."

I well know what he means. Some years ago I spent a month alone on an uninhabited Caribbean island and came to understand how liberating it is to be without any human company. It's like having your own little kingdom with your own set of rules.

So what brought Steve Stanionis to this point in his life, I ask.

"Well, I was the master of a casino boat down in Carruthersville. By law, those boats have to have a qualified captain aboard, even though the only decision he's ever likely to make will be to do with the boat itself, and nothing to do with the river. Like making sure it'll get through its next Coast Guard inspection. I grew tired of never going anyplace. Then one day I was reading that magazine (he points to a copy of *Waterways Journal Weekly* lying on a tabletop) and noticed an advertisement by the Missouri Port Authority for someone to operate this ferry. I saw it as a chance to work for myself at last. So here I am."

The way it works, he says, is that the ferry is jointly owned by Mississippi County and the Missouri Port Authority. Steve operates it on their behalf though not as an employee. Instead, he is on a cut of the takings. He does alright too. Even in this quiet spot, he shifts an average of 16,000 vehicles a year, plus 30,000 passengers.

"Cruising backwards and forwards to the same two points all day is better than going nowhere at all. Matter of fact, it can be a lot of fun." He is grinning slyly. "Have you ever heard of river-dating?"

I haven't.

"See, there are people who live say, on the Kentucky side. They are almost sure to be married and living in some small town like Hickman where everyone knows what they're up to. So if they want to strike up an on-the-side sexual liaison with someone, then that someone will live across the river - because never do the two sides meet. It's like they are not just different counties and different states, but different *countries*. The chances of being caught out by the wife - or husband, because both sexes are at it - are therefore much reduced.

"Well anyhow, let me tell you that I know a river-dater when I spot one. They've got a pattern. Then the day will come when they stop using my ferry, and you know that one of two things has happened. Either he or she has been dumped by the other, or the spouse has begun to ask too many awkward questions. Either way, they've been smart enough not to actually get caught outright; smart enough to leave a decent margin for doubt by playing away on the *other* side of Old Man River.

"I always have a chuckle when I see a river-dater drive aboard. He or she will get out their cars and walk the line of vehicles, pretending to stretch their legs. They are in fact checking that they're not being tailed. They all wear that same expression on their faces: a look of relief, tinged with hints of both guilt and smugness."

There seems much to keep Steve entertained in the cross-river ferry business. "Being a captain allows me to marry people in mid-river. I've done that countless times because it helps keep my wallet warm. But the couples have to go with the flow, and not mind that my other passengers are watching on. I normally perform wedding ceremonies when going upriver. It gives me five minutes longer than the other way. And the same goes for burials, though I've yet to slide a corpse overboard. But I've scattered the ashes many a time."

Steve has carried some amusing live cargo across his patch of water. "Mules, covered wagons, and buggies are not as uncommon as they sound in these parts; neither are the small time crooks and fugitives fleeing the county line in a hurry. I even had a guy riding a horse all the way to Alabama where he was going to visit a sick uncle."

I flick through the magazine, noting the assorted ads from towboat companies. I need to make contact with one of them if I'm to experience the trade for myself, so I jot down a couple of numbers. Steve says that he thought of towboating himself, but he didn't like the idea of the one-month-on, one-month-off rota system. "Four weeks is a long time to go without a drink" he says with a wry smile. "and another four weeks is too long to be ashore with nothing to do *but* drink."

He's got a point there: what *do* you do with the drunken sailor?

We drive back to East Prairie where Sylvie's husband waits to relate his very own Mississippi tale. But first we call in at the Grace Inn, a small motel and the only other hostelry in town. Over such a long career in journalism and travelling, I've slept in some very strange places indeed, which include the tarmac of an outdoor car park, and on a stack of hay bales, so by comparison the Bell Grade Inn is luxury indeed. But Sylvie has picked up on my small disquiet about the place and will not let it go.

"Small town politics, my dear. I booked you in there not because the owner needs the business - he's a multi millionaire anyway. It was so he can say that the BBC has been to stay, which is a big thing around here. Also ... I was told you wanted to experience anything that's out of the norm. " I get that familiar sideways glance and raised eyebrow.

Touche. Sylvie has done her job quite brilliantly, given the tightness of this little town. And now she's doing it again in the company of a big, tough looking chap called Gary Hancock. He is tall, broad, dark haired, plenty of muscle, no bullshit, and as forthright as a stevedore in a vile mood.

"You wanna stay here buddy, then stay here" he says, reaching for a room key. "No charge. I only charge people who I don't like the look of."

I can't believe I'm hearing this. But about 30 seconds later in walks a swarthy looking man in jeans and a leather jacket. He's a trucker and has broken down; needs a room for the night because it is Sunday, and he can't get the vital spare part until tomorrow.

Gary looks him over. Finally he says, "I can put you up on the garage floor. You'll be sharing a mattress with the dog, okay?"

The trucker, not one to give ground easily, stares back at him. "You're fooling with me, right?"

"Nope"

"I'll sleep in my cab."

"Park it right outside. That'll be $30 for the night."

"Hey, screw you!"

Gary suddenly bursts into roaring laughter. So do I. Sylvie follows. Then even the truck driver manages a chuckle. Gary hands him a key and a sign-in card. "I like a little sport, feller. That's all."

So it would appear. Gary Hancock, the former sheriff of East Prairie, now hotelier and town prankster tells me that last week a young businesswoman stayed over for a few nights. When it came to checking out, Gary sprung one on her. The brief exchange went something like this:

'Before you go, you might want to see some security footage.'

'How do you mean?' she asked, surprised.

'We've got security cameras in every room. There is film of you naked in the shower, and using the toilet. You can either buy it for $50, or I'll sell it on to one of the East Prairie perverts.'

'What!' she screamed, outraged.

'Just kidding, lady.'

"She didn't appreciate the joke" he says with a beaming grin. "When she left moments later, the tyres squealed."

The trucker is doubled-up in laughter.

THESE DAYS, SAM BARKER calls the Mississippi the 'Mister 'Sippi' and "when you hear my story, you'll understand why." It goes back to one sunny Saturday morning in the winter of 1989 when he and six friends went duck hunting on the river; three in Sam's boat, four in a second boat. As they set out from Dorena on placid waters, there was nothing to suggest that the day would end in high drama.

"It was sunny, but cold" Sam recounts as we sit in an East Prairie diner. "All the trees were bare, but the water seldom ices over this far south. And the ducks were plentiful, so it looked like we were going to have ourselves a real good day. But the river can be very deceitful, believe that. Conditions can change without warning.

"It was early afternoon as I recall. Very suddenly the sun disappeared and storm clouds blew in from God knows where. It went from light to pretty damn dark in a snap of the fingers. The wind whipped up the water and in no time at all, the river had become an angry sea. Duck boats have flat bottoms and a very low freeboard; they're not made for choppy waters, and we knew we had to get back - and fast.

"So we're just half a mile from Dorena, and the next thing I see is a big sharp wave attack the other boat just ahead of us, the one with four guys in it. It lifted it onto its side and then overturned it completely. Fortunately, the water killed the outboard dead, or else there'd have been a propeller slicing the air, just to add to matters. All four guys were now flailing around in icy water, fully clothed. They had lifejackets on, thank God, but we were still that half mile from shore.

"Well by now, my own boat was starting to fill up with water, the rough stuff coming at us from every which-way. I probably had two or three inches of clear freeboard before I really started to ship water, so the dilemma was this: I couldn't chance going any faster because that would have guaranteed a catastrophe; but I couldn't afford to hang around either - because the men in the river were not going to last long in those temperatures. So I put my two companions ashore, then straightaway came back for the others, two at a time maximum."

Sam pauses for a moment, grimly reliving events inside his head. "I got back out there and decided the first two guys had to be the ones most in need. Well hell, they were *all* in need, but the two I picked up were already close to passing out and drowning. I do not know how I managed to haul them aboard amid all that heaving water - some special reserve of strength, which I guess just comes out at a time like that - and shouted to the other two that I'd be back as fast as I could. To tell you the truth, I thought they might well die in the meantime, it was so damn cold.

"Anyhow, I lurched the boat back to shore where my two buddies could look after them. I told them to strip these guys naked inside the cab of the truck, and to get the heater going full blast. Then I went back for the others, and somehow repeated the exercise. It was as black as night out there. One of them passed out on the boat, the other was rattling and shivering like a human vibrator, wanting to say something but unable to get the words out. I've never seen such a look of shock on anyone. He was way into another world, and it wasn't someplace you'd be wanting to visit neither."

He pauses again, a thin smile crossing his face. "I suppose in all this, there was a certain amount of dark humour. Once all four of them were squeezed inside the truck's cab and it was clear they were going to survive, we three in the other boat had a small laugh at their expense. Like can you imagine it? Four straight, married, middle aged rednecks, all of them stark naked, huddling together over the cab's heater, each blaming the other for what had just happened. It would make a damn funny movie sequence, right? In reality though, it had been no joke. No joke at all."

Once again he pauses, and the smile widens further. "Three of them four guys had never been to church in their lives. The next morning, Sunday, all three were there in the pews."

Sam says that they still attend to this day, but that two of them refuse ever to venture on the river again. As for the other two, it took three years for them to even look at the Mississippi again, let alone board a boat. "After that experience, they now refer to it as the 'Mister 'Sippi'. And so do I."

Fifteen

KING BISCUIT TIME

THE RAIN BUCKETS DOWN on East Prairie, bouncing high off the motel forecourt before settling into deep puddles on every square metre of uneven ground. Cars drive by with their headlights on and wipers going at full speed. The sky is dark, with no sign of a let-up anytime soon. It has long gone dawn, but it might as well be nightfall. I am not leaving in this.

There are some places in which you can start to believe that you'll never get out of. When I was a teenage youth, I went out to Australia for a couple of years to jackaroo on a cattle station in New South Wales. Following that, I went north to Queensland to work on the prawn trawlers, and for eight dangerous months I found myself trapped in the remote and claustrophobic fishing port of Tin Can Bay. For a while, I thought I was never going to get out of there. In 2003, while riding my bike from north to south down through Australia, I went back to that little port - and the same thing happened there that is happening now. Forever down came the rain, the fallout from an offshore cyclone, and I thought, 'My God, I'm never going to get out of this place; coming back here was a mistake'.

East Prairie has that same tight feel about it, as if it dictates events whether you like it or not. For one thing, I've got another puncture in the rear tyre (how that happened, I know not, since I haven't ridden the bike since Saturday). And for another, the map has me running out of road on my way to Carruthersville, some 50 miles south. All possible routes seem to join up to Interstate 55 on which I am not allowed. On top of this, the rain; the relentless, teeming rain.

As I'm fixing the puncture inside my room, Sylvie Barker comes by with the news that she and Sam are going to Blytheville, Arkansas this afternoon. Carruthersville is on the way, and in this weather would a lift be of any help? Apparently it is forecast to stay this way at least until tomorrow evening.

I have no hesitation in accepting. I shall get out of East Prairie today after all. Two nights in this town is really enough.

Later in the day while speeding down the Interstate, I am once again reminded of my own distaste for the four-wheel culture. But it is not the poor old car that I've got a beef with. It is the way we humans revere them and abuse them at the same time. Even with the rain pouring and the wipers slapping, the Interstate traffic dices impatiently and perilously between busy lanes; trucks chuck out their ceaseless, blinding spray; horns are slamming; a cop car shoots by, its siren blaring and red light flashing. Four wheels I can occasionally do with - particularly today. But the culture that goes with them, I can most certainly do without.

It is coming down even heavier as they drop me at a riverside hotel opposite the Casino Aztar, presumably the same gambling boat that Steve Staniosis had once been master of. Sam makes an extraordinary and most generous parting gesture before we go our separate ways. He fishes out a $20 bill from his wallet and presses it into my hand. "I've got this feeling you're gonna get lucky tonight" he says. "Here's a little something to help the process along."

Well, that's my evening taken care of. Thank you, Sam.

Carruthersville is my final stopover in Missouri, about 15 miles north of the Arkansas border. In this weather, it is not a place I'm going to explore on my bike, though from what I've seen of it through today's bleakness, it appears to have a significant divide between the middle classes and tumbledown ghettos. The accent is now unmistakably Deep South, and there are undoubtedly many more blacks than whites living here.

Some time long after dark, I wander into the casino with the firm intent of spending Sam's $20 only. There are vastly more men than women playing the green-baize tables, and vice-versa playing the machines. The women are all middle aged to elderly and mostly unsmiling. The house must be doing well tonight. How much I'd like to alter that.

Sam was right. I am lucky tonight. After two hours of pressing buttons and watching the reels spin, I walk back to the hotel. Fortunately for me, the casino is $80 the poorer.

The sky is still grey and heavy next morning, but at least the rain has stopped. So I saddle up and pedal away along uninspiring streets with bumpy sidewalks. Today's route to the inland city of Blytheville means a couple of very quiet back roads before joining up with Highway 61 again, the Great River Road. Once I'm out of town, I reach the turn off for a road so minor, it has no numerical designation. After a few miles of riding through empty ranch land, I reach the junction to Highway 164. Before I can turn onto it, a backfiring rust bucket pulls up in front of me and a young black man steps out.

"Hey, I've got an invitation for you!" he exclaims, ambling towards me.

"What invitation? I've never seen you before in my life."

He thrusts a pamphlet my way. "It's an invitation from God" he answers, pointing a forefinger towards the sky. "From Him up there." He turns and walks back to the car, then disappears down the road in jerky wheezes and bangs.

I stare at the pamphlet entitled 'The Invitation'. *Come unto me, all ye that labour and are heavy laden, and I will give you rest*, it begins. But right now is not the time or place for me to be told that *'publicans and sinners might pretend to be content with the sensual and the earthly, but in their hearts are distrust and fear'*. I stuff it into a pannier bag, maybe - and only maybe - to glance at it at some other time.

At a place called Steele I turn onto the Great River Road, even though the Mississippi is a good eight miles to the east, across from which now lies the state of Tennessee. Just half an hour later I cross into Arkansas - the 'Natural State' they call it - and half an hour after that, into Blytheville itself. Between the border and the city, the ranch land of Missouri has given way to that telltale crop of the Deep South. The land is wall-to-wall cotton fields, about which so many blues songs have been written over the past couple of centuries: acre upon flat acre of brown stalks, atop of which lies an ocean of white fluff.

Seeking directions to the Hampton Inn, someone points me down through tree lined avenues and into a very pleasant park. On this (by now) bright, warm afternoon, I pass a black woman fishing by the side of a pond, casting her line with expert strokes. Some kids are playing with a Frisbee nearby, and an old man is asleep on a park bench. All seems very relaxed, until I reach the other end of the park and emerge onto a busy road lined with all the usual gas stations and fast food outlets. At this point, Blytheville, a city of 17,000, loses its character, becoming just another neon-lit nonentity, indistinguishable from anywhere else in built-up America.

JANA GREENBAUM describes herself as the 'calling card of Arkansas'. She is in her 40s, petite, with long, wavy locks of blonde hair, and has driven 185 miles from her office in the state capital of Little Rock just to say, 'Hi there, good to see you, welcome to the state of Arkansas'. She is, of course, the PR lady for the Arkansas Office of Tourism. So today, I am part of her workload.

Over dinner we discuss a few of her story ideas for my ride through Arkansas, but only one of them cuts it for me, and that won't be until I reach the little port of Helena in two or three days time. I tell her not to worry; I'll find the goods somehow, or more likely they'll find me. It just seems to happen that way.

Jana has gone by the time I get up next morning, but she's left a note at the front desk to say that we'll meet up again in Helena on Friday, and to keep the night clear because we're going to an official banquet of some sort. Well now, I don't know how I'm expected to turn out for an occasion like that, but what they're going to get is someone in loafers, corduroy jeans, and a crumpled shirt. I don't pack dinner jackets for sweaty bike rides.

It is an easy trip today, just 25 miles to a port called Osceola where I meet with the river once more. The day is breezeless, the land as flat as an omelette, and the traffic light along the Great River Road: one of those relaxed days when it is a pleasure to be doing what I'm doing.

Ten miles from town is the settlement of Luxora where I pull in at a small gas station for some fruit juice. It looks to be the town's only trading store, selling everything from booze and magazines to groceries, as if petrol is a mere sideline. A big black guy is filling up a flashy red-and-white 4x4 at a pump when I wander back outside. He is eyeing the *eZee Torq* with intense curiosity.

"Hey man, wozzat big silver thing doin' on your bike?"

He is referring to the battery. I give him a few details. He says, "Man, that is so cool. You wanna do a trade-in? Your bike for my Chevvy, plus the difference in cash?"

"I don't think so. Thanks anyway."

"No man, listen to me. Your bike plus $5,000. You can drive it away right now."

Is this chap serious? As if I'd be carrying $5,000 in cash. And his car has to be worth a good $15,000. The bike retails in the USA for one-tenth of that sum. Anyway, I politely decline the offer again and pedal away. I'm about a quarter-mile down the road when he passes me with a friendly toot-toot.

Shortly after, a police car belonging to the Arkansas State Troopers whooshes by. And shortly after that, I see them slap the cuffs on my friend at the side of the road. From what I can make out from the terse grunting language universally adopted by cops, the fellow had stolen the smart 4x4 in Blytheville, little knowing that it came equipped with a tracking device. Or if he had known, then he clearly figured that $5,000 and the possession of a getaway electric bike would be a better deal than the one he is facing now.

I carry on into Osceola, a really pleasant little place with low-rise buildings and leafy avenues leading down to the river. I ask someone directions to my designated motel for the night. He says to follow the main street right to the end, turn right onto Keiser Avenue and follow that road for about eight miles. The Best Western is way out there in the sticks, he says. Well if that's the case, I'll find somewhere to buy a bottle of wine for an evening in. I'm certainly not riding eight miles back into town again.

At the end of the main street is a bottle store. I park the bike against a tree and go inside - and am instantly transported back to the Sportsman's Grill in faraway Ferryville, Wisconsin. It is 3pm and the place is buzzing. Then someone shouts, "Hey, you must be Quentin!" He thrusts a big paw my way. "Beau Butler, Osceola Chamber of Commerce. Jana asked me to fix you up with a motel room. Have a drink."

I'm easily recognisable I suppose: tee-shirt, shorts, cycling gloves, white socks and trainers.

This place is supposed to be a liquor store and nothing else; an off-licence, USA style. But everyone is using the long counter as a bar. Even the guy behind it, a doppelganger for Richard Gere, is pouring himself shots from a scotch bottle. There are probably 15 men in here, and every one of them is at it.

Beau Butler is a short, dark haired individual in his late 30s. He introduces me to a few of the regulars, and to the Richard

Gere clone behind the counter. He is the owner, at once friendly and at once generous. I tell him that I've just slipped in for a bottle of wine. He responds to this piece of news by telling me to pick out two bottles; the second one, he says, is on the house because "you're gonna drink it in here with the rest of us."

Oh my, I'm back by the Mississippi again. Hallelujah brother.

But this is a take-it-very-easy time for me. Tonight is a broadcast night, so I soak up the ambience rather than the wine, still marvelling at the hospitality of all these people who live beside the big river. Even though drinking in here is technically illegal, that doesn't stop the town sheriff from calling in on a social visit. He says howdy to one and all, has a shot of something himself, then gets back in his police car.

The unconcerned owner watches him go. "You know, that sheriff was so loaded one afternoon, he smashed his car right into the wall outside." He shrugs and grins. "Osceola is that sort of place, buddy. A combination of frontier town, river port, and southern culture."

Eventually I take my leave from this amiable bunch and pedal for a good 30 minutes before meeting with the Best Western. I notice a couple of eating houses close by, so I shan't go hungry tonight. But before that, I'll do the broadcast. On such days I am never completely at ease until that is over with, freeing me up for another week on the road and whatever it holds in store.

Tonight I get to talk about J.C. Harris, the Cape Girardeau piano maestro. At this, the presenter actually bursts into a Jerry Lee Lewis number himself, a dedicated fan of the old rock 'n' roller. He suggests that I find some way of hooking J.C. up to the programme when he performs at his fundraiser this coming Friday night. That should give the lad a boost.

The next morning, a man called Eric Golde turns up at the motel. He's from the Chamber of Commerce and has instructions to bring me back into town, as if I'm wanted for interrogation. Soon I find myself inside a sort of boardroom for a meeting of some sort. People begin to drift in and take their places; some sit at the long, polished table, others in chairs lined up along the walls. I have not the slightest idea why I am here.

The meeting gets under way, its delegates responding to questions from the chairman. *What is the position with the German engineering company thinking of setting up a new factory in Osceola? Tourism and hotel occupancy: was it up or down this past summer? The state of the chamber's finances, please - how much has been spent on what since the last meeting?*

I've a 40 mile ride today on down to West Memphis. All this stuff is holding me up. When the meeting breaks up 45 minutes later, Eric drives me back to the motel at speed. I ask him just what was I doing in a meeting of that sort? "Thought you'd like to meet Osceola's top dogs; observe how we operate" he replies. I suppose that's an answer of sorts but I hope he doesn't expect me to make a radio piece from this pointless experience.

I pick up the Great River Road again, stopping briefly after 20 miles at somewhere called Frenchman's Bayou for a rapid snack. Five miles further on I reach a junction and swing left onto Highway 77 for the final 15 miles into West Memphis. Experience has taught me that getting in and out of somewhere as big as Memphis, just across the river, is just too much hassle for a cyclist, so I've opted for West Memphis instead on the Arkansas side of the river. Alas, I am not going to see much of this place, which is a lot bigger than it seems from the map. It is heading towards dusk by the time I find my way to the Ramada Inn, tucked away in the delightfully-scenic and concrete setting of an industrial zone; and tomorrow I shall be gone early, on a 60 mile zig-zagging route to the river port of Helena, where I know that at least one good story awaits.

It turns into a physically punishing day; west for a few miles to get out of the city, then southwest for 40 miles along Highway 79 where I battle with a crosswind, then southeast for another 15 miles on Highway 44 into Helena - a route that takes me through the greenery and the silence of the St Francis National Forest and for a while, alongside the Arkansas River snaking its way towards the Mississippi and spilling into it just north of Helena. At one point, the road runs out of tarmac, becoming not much more than a broad dirt track cutting through the forest. Through the trees, sunlight dances on the Arkansas River. On the other side, the shoreline is a dazzling white beach that could almost be a glossy advert for the Bahamas. There is nobody else around. All I can hear on this sunny late afternoon is a gentle lapping at water's edge and the shrill chirping of the birds.

I cruise into Helena at twilight and find my way to the Magnolia B&B, a converted southern mansion close to downtown. I walk the bike along the surrounding veranda that overlooks sloping gardens, and press the buzzer. There is a rattling of bolts and locks before a dark haired woman of about 45 opens the door. She stares at me nervously, as if I've come to case the place over, intent on burglary. Just her head is outside the door, the rest of her remains indoors. Her eyes dart this way and that. This lady seems to be the serious type; rather jumpy, and hauling a big bucketful of worry. For someone who makes her living through the arrival of strangers, I can't help but think that she may be in the wrong business. On the other hand, this is a small town in the Deep South where cyclists are doubtless viewed as madmen.

She reluctantly hands me a key to an upstairs room and warns me to keep the front door locked at all times, even when I'm only out on the veranda for a smoke. No offence, she says, but she's had the kind of life in which she has learned not to trust anyone, nobody at all. I don't know if it's just her, but there is a heavy atmosphere lingering inside this large old house.

Past nightfall, I wander down into town and amble slowly down Cherry Street, the main thoroughfare that runs parallel to the river and its high levee. There is hardly anyone around on this quiet Thursday evening, but I find a bar/restaurant at the very end of the street which is doing some reasonable trade. I sit myself down at the small bar, ordering a cheeseburger and a glass of wine.

The bartender asks, "Where you from, buddy - Australia?" It is amazing just how many Americans ask if I'm from a country that's about as far away from England as it is possible to get. It is almost a daily occurrence. When I crossed from coast-to-coast, an inbred woman from a small town in north Louisiana had suggested the same thing, and I decided to have a little fun with her. Try the other side of the world, I said, observing her pained expression as she struggled with the geography. To put her out of her misery, I gave her an obvious hint that surely even she must get. I told her that I came from the country that created the English language.

"Sweden?" she'd replied hopefully.

I said for her to try again, but this great riddle was clearly becoming too much. Finally I let on. "England; Great Britain; the United Kingdom."

Her eyes lit up like a pair of disco strobes. "I knowed it!" she'd exclaimed. "I just *knowed* you was one of them North Polers!"

I have a couple of wine refills, and think to call it a night. When I ask for the damage, the barman hands me a bill for $4.50, the cost of the cheeseburger. I point out that I've had three glasses of wine too. He comes back with the news that the drinks are on the house - in case I feel insulted by being thought of as an Aussie.

I don't, I answer, telling him that the two nations are really very alike, particularly in a shared sense of humour. But he won't accept payment for the wine, and I once again put this down as having something to do with Old Man River, which is rolling by just across the road.

'SUNSHINE' SONNY PAYNE is a deejay like no other. Not only is he 81 years old, he has also been spinning the blues every weekday over the past 55 years without missing a beat. His programme is called 'King Biscuit Time', the longest running blues show in the world - and probably the world's longest running radio show of any genre. It has been going solidly since 1941. The programme is syndicated throughout the USA - something made all the more impressive considering from where it originates every day: Radio KFFA 1360 consists of one desk and two microphones tucked away in the corner of a large showroom called the Delta Cultural Center in tiny downtown Helena.

The room is a shrine to blues and jazz. Its walls are adorned with photographs and posters of just about everyone you can think of connected to southern music, and who at one time or another has called in at Helena to be interviewed on the programme: Louis Armstrong, Muddy Waters, Sonny Terry, John Lee Hooker, Fats Domino, Howling Wolf, B.B. King are among a list too numerous to mention.

Considering his age, the portly Sonny Payne is a sprightly chap. He retains just a few locks of grey hair these days, but his mind is sharp and alert. I had thought that I was supposed to interview him, but Sonny's got a different take on that. He is going to interview me, live on today's programme. Before we go on air, I ask him about the legendary Louis Armstrong, a man whose trumpet playing and gravel voice still fascinate me.

"I knew him well in the early days" Sonny says, "but once he moved up north from New Orleans, I only rarely got to see him. He didn't like coming back down south, which was all to do with the racial problems of the time. I never understood all that stuff because music transcends the colour issue. I still don't; but at my age, neither do I care any more."

On the dot of 12.15 Sonny speaks to the Mississippi Delta region. It is King Biscuit Time - a name that came from the station's embryo days when a local grain-processing company called King Biscuit Flour sponsored the show in return for the live-playing musicians' endorsement of their product. The name has stuck for the past 61 years. Sonny Payne has been here from the very start, firstly as a sweeper of the studio floor, and since 1951 as the resident presenter.

Legendary blues deejay, 81 year old 'Sunshine' Sonny Payne.

He plays a couple of tracks and then announces that he's got an unusual guest in the studio today, a strange Englishman who is riding a bicycle along the length of the big river. There is a brief pause as he turns and stares at me. Then he asks, "Why are you doing this, boy? For the exercise?"

"Hell no, not just for that!"

"Then why? Why beat yourselves up like this?"

It is a good question, and oddly difficult to answer to an audience that almost certainly views the automobile as sacrosanct, and the cyclist as a weirdo. But I explain as best I can, justifying my actions via stories for the BBC, not many of which I'd come across if I was travelling by car. "Let's face it" I say to him, "I would not be on your show at all if that were the case. I'm only on it because I'm also on a bike; doing something different, in other words."

The answer seems to satisfy my host, though I doubt his regular listeners will feel the same. They must be wondering what I'm doing on their show. This isn't the blues. It isn't even the news. It must be the booze. 'Sunshine' Sonny Payne must be on the bottle again.

Sixteen

GHOST CLOCK

THE DELTA AWARDS is an annual bash to honour assorted tourism officials from 15 counties in southeast Arkansas. Tonight it is taking place in the inland city of Dumas, some 60 miles west of Helena. Jana Greenbaum picks me up from the Magnolia B&B and we head away at once for what she terms 'the banquet'. We may be lucky to make it. Jana is exhausted, driving erratically and continually yawning behind the wheel. She takes a number of wrong turns which has us driving along some flat rural backwaters, adding to the journey time. Jana has been on the road more or less non-stop since Blytheville, but is obliged to show her face in Dumas this evening. She would rather be back in Little Rock with her husband, whom she doesn't get to see much of in her capacity as the calling card of Arkansas.

The Dumas Community Center is throbbing. You wouldn't automatically think of southeast Arkansas as a tourist destination, but it evidently must be. One thing is for certain though: these people intend to enjoy themselves this evening. There is a free bar offering every drink you can imagine, and two bartenders who cannot keep up with the demand. Tables covered with spotless white cloths are laid in readiness for dinner, and I doubt that they'll stay this starch-white for much longer.

Jana introduces me to a number of people whose names I forget as soon as I'm told them. This is a flaw of mine; I've always got to ask twice. But there is one guy whose name does stay with me, because in him I think there may be a good story. I don't yet know what it is, but when you happen to be a county judge, you're going to have something to say. Now is not the time to quiz Mark McElroy, the judge of Desha County back there on the river. But we instantly get along, and he slips me his card and says to give him a call over the weekend; maybe pedal on down to Arkansas City and stay at his house. I think I might do that. The last county judge I interviewed (on the coast-to-coast ride) kept me in so many fantastic true tales that I stayed over in his domain of Paris, Texas, for five days.

The evening settles down into first of all a superb feast of walleye and catfish, all you can possibly eat; and then into a series of slightly tedious speeches as various award recipients express thanks to their teams of workers, as if they have just received Hollywood Oscars. It becomes a trifle wearying to have to join in the clapping on no less than 20 occasions for these provincial Arkansas bureaucrats. All of them are from state government sponsored tourist councils. All the same, as usual everyone is extremely friendly and welcoming, and I'm actually rather pleased to have been invited here.

Jana has arranged for someone to give me a lift back to Helena, as she is going home to Little Rock straight afterwards. I like Jana, and I genuinely worry about her driving another 85 miles tonight. But she is determined to wake up in her own bed tomorrow.

The next morning I rise early with the intention of leaving this rather heavy B&B. But over breakfast a couple of ironies float into the proceedings. The first comes from an Australian couple sitting with some Americans at a nearby table. The Americans, instead of asking if they are from Australia, think they are from England. For obvious reasons, I find this amusing. The second irony, both occurring within a minute of one another, comes from inside the adjoining kitchen. I tap at the door and ask if I might have another cup of coffee. My edgy landlady is in the company of a bearded man with smiling eyes, who is somewhere in his mid-40s. He points to the percolator and says, "You sure can, buddy. Help yourself."

I call this an irony because whoever he is, he's the absolute chalk to her cheese. The body language tells me they are more than friends, but there is something in his manner that says he is worth talking to at some length. I wish I could explain this, but I cannot. It is an instinct developed over many years in this dodgy trade called journalism. I also sense a certain tension in the kitchen. She keeps her back to me, busy at the stove and saying nothing, while he maintains a telling distance from her.

Outside, it is a lovely sunny morning. I take the coffee onto the veranda and bask in the warmth. Shortly the Australian couple emerge with their bags and we exchange pleasantries. They are as delighted to meet with a Brit as I am with them. Despite the blatant sporting rivalry, our two countries really do share the same way of thinking, which is something they've been starved of since setting out on a six-week driving tour of the Deep South. Over an hour later we are still sitting there, nattering about matters of mutual interest. Such luxurious idleness has already ripped a hole into my plans for the day.

When they eventually leave, out comes the bearded chap for a cigarette. His name is Robbie Whatling, a local 46 year old who is apparently in some trouble with Miss Jumpy. "I didn't get back 'till five in the morning" he grunts. "Is it just me, or is that women don't never seem to understand such things?"

"No, it's not only you because I've just doubled it" I reply, recalling the two ex-wives and others, shouting at me and stamping their feet in what are meant to be the quiet hours.

Worse still are the ones who observe the time of night by point-blank refusing to speak at all. Once more, an innocent night out in the company of good friends that gets burnt to ashes by implacable female rage. I find myself in tune with this guy. He is his own man.

It transpires that on Friday and Saturday nights he plays the drums for a band called 'Borderline'. Last night an old friend had been in the audience, someone who Robbie hadn't seen in a long while. When the music stopped, they had a drink or two together. The trouble now is, he says, that the lady friend thinks he's been chasing skirt, and she's in real bad mood with him.

"Well, you can talk to me instead" I say, which Robbie seems happy enough to do - and it only takes a few minutes for me to know that I've got a rock-solid story in this softly spoken man. He is, you see, the survivor of not one, but *ten* airplane crashes.

I must put this into context. I'm not talking of passenger jets, but of the nearest thing that civil aviation has to fighter planes, namely crop dusters. At the age of 14, Robbie's father, a local rancher, taught his son to fly these forbidding machines. He didn't have a license or any formal air-school training, but the old man put him to work spraying crops on his ranch anyway, and on other nearby properties. Crop dusting is an extremely dicey occupation, requiring the pilot to swoop down to just six or eight feet above the ground, then fly straight-and-level at 100mph along the entire length of the field while discharging fertilisers onto the crop. At the far end of the field, he will then haul the airplane high into the sky again at a very sharp angle of attack in order to avoid the trees, the telegraph wires, the rooftops, the high fences, and other obstacles which don't take kindly to aircraft bumping into them. Then it is back to the other end of the field to start the process all over again.

"Two of the crashes were my own fault" he admits with a grin. "I ran out of gas both times, ending up nose-down in the middle of the cotton; embarrassing, that."

Is that an understatement, or what? He is quietly dismissive of his other prangs. "Sometimes a field can be a real tight spot" he states, "particularly when the crop is a bit too close to the trees. Clipping the treetops or the telegraph wires is occasionally unavoidable, but the planes are built with that in mind - as a probability rather than a possibility. When they hit the ground, they're gonna get bent some, but they're unlikely to be a total write-off."

"And the pilot?"

"Oh, he's gonna know about it alright, and then some. I've had broken legs, a fractured back, a broken jaw, concussion, and a badly battered face. I've got scars everyplace. But smacking-up in a crop duster isn't usually fatal, although my own dad was killed in one. But after that tenth incident, when I tore a wing off on impact with the ground, I figured I just might be pushing my luck."

Robbie Whatling, the survivor of ten airplane crashes.

173

Another slight understatement. Robbie suggests that we take a drive out to Helena Airport where these days he has an aircraft engineering and refurbishing operation - and where a number of bent crop dusters await his attention. I eagerly agree. With the total exception of the airline business, I find all other forms of aviation absorbing.

Helena Airport is really just an untidy row of old offices and old hangars. Somewhere beyond the unkempt grass is the runway. It has the strange feeling of World War Two about it. There are no scheduled flights in or out of Helena, only crop dusters and private traffic. All the same, Robbie would appear to be a very busy man. Inside his hangar are three dusters that he has to put back into shape, and a gleaming red-and-gold Beech 18 - a sort of much smaller version of the timeless Dakota DC3.

"You should have seen the state of it when the owner brought it in" he says, chuckling. "Half of it was in a bucket, and the other half was held together with chewing gum and bootlaces. The guy told me that he won it in a poker game, but after taking one look at it he thought the other guy might have been the winner after all."

Well, at least he's a winner now. Robbie has put his twin-engine workhorse back into great shape and it is now ready for a new certificate of airworthiness. It does not surprise me that this affable, unassuming man is held in such high esteem by the region's flying fraternity, because he can also boast that he also has the contract to maintain Elvis Presley's two aircraft, which are on display at Gracelands up in Memphis.

He invites me to his band's gig on this Saturday night in some town 40 miles away. Tempted as I am, I know that it is not a good idea; not if I'm going to get back at five in the morning and face a full day's ride to boot. As it is, I've got to ask a sour Miss Jumpy if she minds me staying over for another night because it's too late to get moving today. But that's okay. Robbie has given me a great radio item, sweetened by a little bit of Elvis.

I DEPART HELENA EARLY. Robbie is sound asleep, but the landlady seems in more cheerful mood this morning. I guess her man must have come home on time last night. Or maybe she is simply pleased to see the back of me. We do not have a lot in common.

It is a long, weaving ride south to Desha County and Arkansas City; some 75 miles of zig-zagging along several minor back roads. This really is the southern sticks, the sort of backwoods that Hollywood makes sinister movies about, in which the bigoted county sheriff and the crooked mayor dominate the downtrodden. But the judge says that he'll meet me along the way sometime in the afternoon, otherwise there'll be no time to show me around before dark. Suits me.

I head west to Poplar Grove for ten miles, then south to somewhere called Watkins Corner, southwest to DeWitt, then due south towards the one-horse town of Gillet. The surrounds are flat and sparsely populated, cotton fields everywhere, very quiet and hardly any traffic. Today is Sunday. Everything is shut in these settlements, except for the churches. Officially, segregation no longer exists in Arkansas, but when it comes to church services, black and white appear to go their separate ways: they may talk to the same god, but they've a different way of saying howdy.

Just before Gillet, the judge pulls up on the other side of the road and I wheel over. "You've made good time" he says appreciatively. "You must have covered more than 40 miles, maybe even closer to 50." He shakes his head in wonder. "I couldn't ride half of that."

"Judge, it's like taking the dog for a walk" I boast, quickly papering-over that untruth by adding that I couldn't preside over a county like he does.

"It has its moments" he comes back, eyeing me with a grin. Mark McElroy is in his mid 50s, a tall, slim man with dark-to-greying hair and eyes which dance with a sense of humour. He has that same aura about him of Robbie Whatling, in so much as not much appears to bother either man; each day to be taken in its stride.

He wants to show me his workday domain in Arkansas City, a tiny place these days with a population of just over 500. It is a spread out sort of town where the county court takes up most of the centre, its glistening white paint near-blinding in the sunshine and against the contrast of the deep blue afternoon sky. At the top of this imposing building is a clock tower. "There's a story in that clock" Mark says, "I'll tell it to you later."

We go up a flight of stairs to his actual courtroom, a spacious chamber in which the judge's vast polished oak desk stands supreme, overlooking the witness box, the lawyers' desks, and the public seating at the rear. Sunlight streams in through large windows. On this quiet Sunday, the big empty room has a slight - but definite - ghostly quality, though I daresay on busy weekdays the assorted defendants might find it worrying for other reasons.

The judge suddenly emits a loud chuckle. "Now if you haven't already guessed it, I am a rather informal individual who tends to turn up to work wearing jeans and cowboy boots. I'm telling you this because just last week I presided over a case to do with a contested planning application. On the day, I arrived here at about eight o'clock to find three hotshot New York lawyers hanging around outside, waiting for the court to open. They'd flown down here in their client's private jet, some developer who wants to build a riverside leisure complex in the county. One of these lawyer guys thought I was the janitor or some hick-town lackey, and he beckoned me over with his finger.

"He said, 'What time does this fucking court open, mister?' Another hour, I told him. He started cursing and blaspheming, and asked how anyone could live in such a shit town as Arkansas City. I hung around for a few moments until he glared up at me and barked, 'Well go on, get back to whatever it is you do around here'. I remained polite, but refrained from telling him who I was. I figured to let him work that one out for himself once the hearing got started."

Mark's eyes are twinkling with delight at this recent memory. "When everyone was told to 'rise for the judge', I made a point of staring down at those three suits for several moments. One of them turned bright pink, another began spluttering out loud, and the third guy dropped his jaw so low you could hear it hit the floor. I sat myself down, yawned, and put my feet - cowboy boots and all - up on the desk."

"And?"

"And man, did they grovel. I made them eat shit all morning." Judge McElroy has an ear to ear grin now. "The planning application was turned down. Their client hasn't got a good track record and the majority of Desha County folks were against the idea anyway. But I didn't tell the suits that. I told them I was turning it down on the grounds that they had not presented their case well enough or clearly enough." He pauses for another moment of eye-twinkling. "That should be enough to get them fired."

He turns serious for a moment. "Tell me something. Do you feel anything odd about this courthouse?"

I ponder on this, not wishing to sound stupid. "It's maybe because the place is big and empty, but I do sense a small eeriness in the air."

He nods. "I'm glad you'd said that. Sometimes I work late into the night - and whenever I do, I always get to hear footsteps in the corridor outside my office; but there is never anyone there. The others who work in the building won't remain here after dark anymore. There has to be some kind of presence lurking within these walls because I've heard those damn footsteps too many times."

On this note, we go back outside, where the judge points to the clock tower. "It could have something to do with that clock up there; it is over 100 years old and must have the weirdest history of any timepiece in the land."

He relates a story dating back to 1903 when Arkansas City had been a thriving river port. One afternoon, a steamboat

177

called in to unload a number of passengers. One of them headed straight for a gambling saloon where, over the course of the afternoon and evening, he managed to lose his entire life savings. The man, by then as drunk as a spinning top in slowdown, went on a vengeful rampage by setting the saloon ablaze. The fire spread and at least half of this riverside city was scorched to the ground.

"Justice was swift back in those days" Mark goes on. "The guy was rounded on by a lynch mob and dragged towards the nearest tree. But just before they hanged him, the culprit called out, 'Damn this town, damn you all! I shall be back to haunt you. Keep looking at that clock up there and you'll all soon see that I mean it!'

"Well now, it seems to me that he did just that - and that he is still doing it today. You see, ever since that night, the clock has done as it damn well pleases. The hands will suddenly jump an hour back or three hours forward. On the dot of noon and midnight, it'll strike 13 times. Every now and then, it stops completely, then starts again all on its own. When I took over here, I figured that we had to do something about it; so the city had it shipped down to a leading horologist in Florida, paid him $10,000, and received his guarantee that he would fix the clock for once and for all.

"When the clock was returned, everything was fine - for a week. And then it started to do that shit all over again. The horologist came up here from Florida on no less than three occasions. He assured us that the clock was in first class working order; that he'd taken it apart and put it all back together again, and that there was nothing, not a damn thing, the matter with it. He stayed over for several days to make his point - and it kept perfect time for all the while he was here. But as soon as he left, well, the clock went berserk. After his last visit, he told us he could no longer honour the guarantee, because the only possible explanation was that there had to be something to the hanged man's curse."

The courthouse clock at Arkansas City.
It has to be the most spooky timepiece in the country.

This is an extraordinary tale, belonging entirely to the Mississippi River. Only here could you find the 13th hour. I look up again and notice the hands read one hour earlier than it actually is. What a great radio piece.

"Maybe the footsteps you hear are his?" I suggest.

"Yeah, could well be. Spooky, eh?"

"Just a little."

The judge then takes me over to a single-storey wooden building standing on a rough patch of open ground. He unlocks the door and we wander in to what is quite obviously a bar: except there are no bottles or glasses, only a long bar top and about 30 stools. "I had to close this place down" says Mark, staring into another sort of ghostliness, devoid of all life. "There were just too many fights and it got out of hand; like if you want to be sure of a brawl, then come on over to this place. When someone very nearly got killed, enough was enough."

He unlocks a side office, pointing to the volumes of ledgers lining the shelves. "These days we use the building for storage. The early history of Arkansas City is in those books" he says. "Take a look through, if you like."

They are large, heavy volumes, written in a handwriting that never made it into our modern times: long, immaculate stokes of the quill that could almost be calligraphy. They contain details of the steamboat movements, their captains and pilots, passenger lists, cargoes bought and cargoes sold. There are weather reports, flooding details, court hearings, births, deaths, and marriages; the journals are the city's official daily diaries from another era, and so richly evocative of the period.

It is dusk by the time we arrive at the judge's house, situated on an open prairie a few miles from town. Before going inside, he suggests we walk the 50 metres over to his garage for a pre-dinner cocktail. In any language, a garage would seem an odd place to go for a drink, but then this is no ordinary car shelter.

We British have cramped garden sheds, where the man of the house can occasionally retreat for a little peace. Not so this American. He has a garage that would house four cars quite easily, except that the only vehicle in here is a gleaming silver-black Harley Davidson motorbike. The rest of the place is Mark's playroom. In one corner is a neon-lit bar with five bar stools. Around the walls are assorted posters, electioneering stuff urging the citizens of Desha County to vote for Judge Mark McElroy. The place is a home-from-home, a bachelor pad brimming with collectors' items; a wagon wheel and rare farm implements, a dartboard, a wood burning heater, easy chairs, a jukebox and fruit machine, a small library of paperbacks, a radio and TV.

I feel like claiming squatter's rights. It would be worth emigrating to Arkansas to live inside this unexpected gem, which has its own shower and loo as well. For a married man however, it has a strange drawback. "I'd like to spend a lot more time in here than I do" Mark says, "but anything more than half an hour makes my wife a little bit paranoid. It's like she thinks I'm trying to avoid her, or maybe I'm on the cell phone to another woman. If I tell her I just need a bit of thinking space, she simply stares back at me, saying nothing - which is actually saying a whole lot, if you know what I mean."

His wife is a charming woman, to me at least. And so is his well mannered teenage daughter. The evening passes away in a most congenial atmosphere, right through into the yawning phase. In the morning, all three are gone by the time I get up; the parents to work, the daughter to school. They have left a note beside a percolator of hot coffee inviting me to stay another night. Alas, I cannot. But I am grateful for the offer, and humbled by their leaving a stranger alone in such an expensive, expansive home. Miss Jumpy, with all her demons, may not trust anyone who comes to stay; but the judge of Desha County, for all his ghosts, has no such qualms.

Seventeen

AN OASIS OF BOOKS

IF I AM TO GET ABOARD A TOWBOAT, then I'd better get my skates on, because this far south I'll be running out of river before too long. This thought occupies my mind today as I head along Highway 65 on the 40 mile ride to Lake Chicot State Park, my last stop in Arkansas before crossing the big river into the state of Mississippi.

It is another warm, sunny southern morning; another day when cycling is more a pleasure than a drudge. At somewhere called McMillan Corner I turn left along a very minor road, Route 144, pedalling through quiet countryside in which I meet not a single vehicle for several miles. It eventually brings me to a lakeside junction, where I wheel along silent shores. This is one quiet, peaceful area.

Lake Chicot is shaped like a giant letter 'C'. At one time it had been part of the river, but is now a mile or two from it, cut off by the eternal shifting of the Mississippi's make up. It does as it pleases, this flowing snake; not as man pleases. But I've no idea why Jana Greenbaum has booked me into here; the state park is eight miles north of the nearest town, Lake Village, and in the middle of nowhere. Still, I'm happy if she is.

I am offered a superb lakeside cabin by the park's receptionist. She is an Arkansas Park Ranger, the official body that runs the state park, and which means that a loaded handgun is part of her uniform. Only once before in my travels have I been checked into a hotel by someone openly wearing a gun, but then that was in the Dominican Republic during one of its many political upheavals.

The lake shimmers in the afternoon sun. Someone is out there on a boat casting his fishing line, but it is otherwise empty. When sundown arrives, it is just breathtaking; a glowing ball of fire sliding gently down towards the placid waters, creating a lake of glittering gold. Close to shore, contented cypress trees protrude from the shallows, their roots firmly ensconced in the lakebed. This glorious eyeful is one definition of splendour, as if this particular sunset contains some sort of universal wisdom; like God is having a word with you.

It is not quite so splendid in the morning, alas. Determined drizzle sweeps along a misty lakeshore, but that isn't going to deter a pair of ardent fishermen who occupy a nearby cabin from getting out there on the water. They and I are the sole guests in this remote setting of several hundred lakeside acres. They have come here to go fishing, and that's what they're going to do, no matter what the weather. I have come here to, um, well actually, I don't know. But I shall use today to try and arrange that towboat ride. If every cloud has a silver lining, then there are certainly enough to go around on this ultra grey morning.

And a silver lining is delivered. The Ingram Barge Company of Nashville, Tennessee, offers to put up with me for a day or so aboard one of its vessels which endlessly ply up and down the Mississippi. The problem lies in scheduling. All kinds of stuff can go awry on this river, says the Ingram PR man: engine trouble, crew problems, cargo problems, *crunch-crunch* going aground problems, and a whole host of unforeseen permutations. I tell the chap that I'll be heading for Greenville, Mississippi in the morning, then on down to Vicksburg.

"Yeah, let's try for Vicksburg" he asserts. "We should have a couple of boats going through there early next week. Gimme a call on Monday when I'll have a better idea of the timing."

Today is Thursday, October 26. I've been on the road now for seven weeks but am certainly in no hurry to have this adventure over with; no hurry at all. Towards the end of every long ride, I begin to feel a little uneasy, wanting to put off the inevitable: when the freedom of what I'm doing draws towards a close, only to be replaced by a plane ride back to England, and to all the unopened brown envelopes, bank statements, and dreary weather.

Following a trip like this, home is not necessarily so for quite a while afterwards. In fact home can be quite an alien place. By strange contrast, hotel and motel rooms are not in the least alien to me, and I know the same sentiment applies to others who spend a lot of time away. I recall listening to a radio programme about touring rock stars, one of whom became so disorientated whenever he got home to Los Angeles, that he had a special bedroom designed inside his own mansion that replicated the standard four walls of a Holiday Inn suite. For several days after each tour, it is the only room he can properly relax in - despite the fact that his wife, kids, and all the familiar comforts of home are all under the very same roof.

I pedal through the afternoon gloom for the eight miles south to Lake Village to pick up some supplies for the evening. Maybe it's just the heavy damp and the greyness, but this place seems to be bleak and disarranged, with messy trailer parks, abandoned cars, and potholed roads. I stuff my shopping into a pannier bag and hotfoot it back to the cosiness of my self-catering cabin. It has been a lazy day.

The sky is blue again when I ride away next morning, back through a Lake Village that really doesn't look much better in the sunlight. I follow the lower 'C' of the lake, where it becomes

Highway 82 and which reconnects with the river, then pedal across the long Mississippi Bridge which fortunately has adequate shoulder space, finally arriving into what they call the Magnolia State. Ten north-easterly miles later, I enter Greenville, a river city that has had many a sentimental song written about it. At first sight, I wonder why; it is just the usual strip of parking lots, shopping malls, gas stations, used car dealers, a few office blocks, and dozens of the obligatory fast food franchises. With the wind more or less behind me on the northeast ride from the bridge, I've made such good time that I'm tempted to give this place a miss by heading due south for a further 50 miles to a little place called Rolling Fork, itself just 50 miles from that all important stop of Vicksburg.

I decide to give it a try, turning onto Highway 61 again - and straight into an impossible headwind. This one is like a tug-of-war in reverse. Five miles later I give up, knowing that after another hour of this, I'll run out of battery power completely. So I head back to Greenville - and do not have to turn the pedals once. The wind-assist hitting my back is so strong, I sail there instead.

As it happens, the wind has done me a favour. Down by the river and away from the gaudy strip is the Greenville they wrote the songs about; a quietly rambling old town, a bit run down, where people amble lazily and dogs are asleep on the sidewalks. Originally, I had not intended to ride through Mississippi at all and thus have no contacts here. But that is easily rectified alongside this river where a helping hand is always assured. I stop and ask a man who is peering into a store window where I can find the local CVB. He gives me directions and says to ask for a guy called Bill Serrat. Here in the old Greenville, he adds, everyone knows everyone else.

Minutes later I am shaking the big welcoming hand of Bill Serrat. He's a tall, beefy individual, early 50s, with a warm, lived-in face. Bill is genuinely delighted that I've pounced on him like this, though not at all surprised. "Been expecting you" he says cheerfully, as if I'm part of his scheduled remit. "I knew you were in the area someplace; just didn't know where exactly."

I find this puzzling, since I've made no connection with the Mississippi tourist office. But somewhere along the line a whisper came Bill's way; as a moderately keen cyclist himself, he has apparently been following my weekly blog on the internet - and figured I'd come calling sooner or later.

He books me into a hotel across the street, then suggests an agenda for the afternoon; experience the delights of Greenville - a town, he says, that once buzzed with life, and which he is trying to have buzzing with tourist-life once more.

First stop is a small blues museum, which I'm sorry to say has nothing on the Delta Cultural Center back in Helena; but the next stop is unusual and quite amusing. Stuck away from it all in the watery Greenville 'suburb' of Deer Creek is a shrine to that idiotic and irrepressible muppet, Kermit the Frog. For here is where he was 'born'.

Greenville, Mississippi. Birthplace of Kermit the Frog.

Deer Creek was actually the home of Kermit's creator, the late Jim Henson and it clearly holds Kermit in some reverence. If the puppets of our own much-missed 'Spitting Image' TV series maimed our senior politicians with such damning effect, then the power of the puppet is obviously not to be underestimated. Even the harmless Kermit continues to draw in the tourists on a year round basis, I'm told. The shrine is basically one small room crammed with muppet memorabilia, in the middle of which is Kermit himself inside a big glass case, sitting on a log and finger-picking a banjo. But I guess the main attraction for tourists is a two-seater settee where a life size version of this demented frog will sit with you, his arm wrapped around your shoulders, while you pose for the camera.

The third port of call I would not have expected to find in a frontier port like Greenville. The McCormick Book Inn; not a hostelry of any sort, but a true oasis for book lovers, especially if they happen to be interested in any aspect of the American South: there are works on southern politics and politicians, on southern history and folklore, on southern travel, and numerous biographies of southern characters, be they famous or infamous; and there are volumes and volumes of southern fiction. There cannot possibly be another bookstore anywhere in the world so comprehensively devoted to the south, and nor a bookseller more thoroughly versed in it. Hugh McCormick, the tall, erudite, quietly spoken proprietor has the very considerable distinction of having read every single book up on his shelves, which amount to thousands.

The remarkable thing is that down here in the Delta (where according to Hugh, there are 'more writers than readers'), he appears to be doing a very brisk trade. The phone seems to ring ceaselessly, incoming emails ping out their electronic signals, and the flyscreened door to this out-of-the-way establishment situated in a leafy, non-commercial street opens and shuts with human traffic every other minute. He says that Delta people will think nothing of driving 100 miles and more to pick up a book they've got on order, and that the McCormick Book Inn has become a landmark for tourists. Hugh also claims that the store's worldwide mail order catalogue has never been in more demand than now.

This is no Waterstone's or W.H. Smith. This is what a bookstore should be. It is the sort of place you could stay all day, and indeed some browsers do just that. Amid all this Deep South knowledge, are rocking chairs for his customers where they can peruse in comfort for as long as they wish.

His father started the place 41 years ago, when Greenville might well have been a rather different place in terms of culture and beliefs; a time when the redneck way of life, personified by an extremely active Ku Klux Klan, was widespread and when the issue of segregation had not been resolved. My learned host says, yes, you're right - but wrong when it comes to Greenville itself.

"I don't know what it is about this town, but it's spawned so many writers, painters, and people of the arts, that it became a place of rebellion and debate during the Martin Luther King era. Sure, the place had its bigots and it still does; but almost uniquely in the south, it had more than its share of liberals and thinkers - people you wouldn't find in, say, Skinnertown, Alabama, or some other ignorant backwater."

Instantly the mysterious Mississippi comes to mind. "Do you think that could have anything to do with the river?" I ask, interested to hear his take on this.

"It's a possibility" he replies. "Just ask yourself why Greenville has had no fewer than 35 nationally-published authors, and the non-river towns in this area have none, with the exception of John Grisham ... who, by the way, calls in here from time to time ... but yes, it could well have something to do with that. You raise an interesting point."

Hugh goes to his desk and pulls out a pamphlet, reading it through before handing it to me. "Read a few of these quotes from Greenville writers. They may not answer your question, but you'll see that they didn't come from Skinnertown."

One passage in particular does actually answer the question in a roundabout way. It is by a Canadian born author called Bern Keating, who settled here after World War Two, and who died here just a couple of years ago. It reads:

'I am a writer and my entire factory is the size of a portable typewriter. I can live anywhere in the world that I wish. Nevertheless, I wouldn't live anywhere in the world but on this sun-blistered mud flat. Why? Well my neighbours are more often kind than cruel; they are never indifferent. Yes, they are feckless and improvident, but unrestrainedly generous. They hold an artist in a vague kind of respect. They never return anything they borrow, but on the other hand, they'll give you the shirt off their backs. I don't know why, but I love them.'

In my limited experience, Keating's honest appraisal of Greenville could be applied to most of the small towns here on the river. I think he's nailed it dead centre.

Before leaving, Hugh takes me out to the back garden to show off his 'bottle tree'. This is yet another oddity of the Lower Mississippi. It is something between a bush and a small tree, on which the many branches are pruned into short, thin projections - thin enough for each to accommodate the neck of a wine bottle. Every available branch and twig supports an empty bottle of all possible colours - clear glass, light and dark greens, light and dark blues, shades of reds and yellows. In the sunlight it looks like an exploding firework, a multi-coloured fountain spouting in all directions; it is a strange yet oddly pleasing creation. But what, I ask, is its purpose?

"Evil spirits" Hugh answers without a trace of irony. "Bottle trees are a real superstition around here. They're supposed to keep evil spirits at bay, in the same way that daylight keeps Dracula wrapped in the darkness of his coffin." He eyes me with a wry smile. "I grew up here, and I've lived with bottle trees all my life. They work for me, I'd say."

Fair enough. I mean, how many people wear crucifixes and lucky charms in the belief they will somehow steer them out of harm's way? And in this unlikely setting for what has become an *international* bookstore, Hugh's bottle tree would appear to be doing a pretty good job. I have thoroughly enjoyed the company of this thoughtful, well educated man, and I silently thank that wretched headwind for leading me towards a certain radio piece.

Bill Serrat thinks that Greenville has one more surprise for me today, but says it'll have to wait until this evening. He drops me off at the hotel where I wallow in the luxury of a hot bath and watch a bit of CNN, which is in hot political mood today as the mid-term elections grow ever nearer. It continually repeats an advert by a website called *Don't Vote.Com,* portraying a slimy congressman kissing babies, grinning from ear to ear as he pumps hands with the multitudes, and generously hosting a barbecue for adoring voters. The message is clear; the guy is untrustworthy; a liar and a crook. At the end of the ad, a voiceover says, 'Don't vote for this man or anyone else - until they have given satisfactory answers to all your questions'. Despite the European trend to think that American voters remain naïve about their politicians, *Don't Vote.Com* is a clear sign that political cynicism is at last warming up in this country.

Sometime after dark, Bill picks me up again and we take a drive into what is clearly the black part of town. "We're gonna have dinner here" he says, pulling up across the street from a tumbling old brick building with a worn, creaking sign that hangs from a post, and is swinging in the evening breeze. It reads, *Doe's Eat Place.*

"Yeah, I know the place is an eyesore from the outside" Bill grunts, "but wait 'till you taste their tamales." We cross the street and go inside, which instantly supplies surprise number one: we have entered via the kitchen, where the chef and another man are working up a sweat over the stoves. Someone else is busy scrubbing giants pans. There is a lot of clanging going on in here. Next, in walks a waitress, yelling out menu orders. She says hello to Bill and beckons for us to follow her. Further inside is the dining area, two cosy bistro-style rooms with tables covered by red-check cloths. The place is alive and humming - with a wholly white clientele.

Bill's wearing his ever-present grin. "Bet that's the first time you've entered an eating house through the goddam kitchen, eh?"

He's right; doesn't Doe's Eat House have a separate entrance?

"It's a tradition" he replies, "dating back to 1941 and the days of true segregation in the south. It's actually quite a good story, which is why I brought you here."

He insists that I try a tamale as a starter, to be followed, he claims, by the biggest, thickest steak I've ever seen. Once we order, he sets about giving me the lowdown on this evidently thriving establishment set in a scruffy, unlit part of town. He is right again; it turns into a compelling story so completely in keeping with the eccentric ways of all these small Mississippi ports.

Back in 1903, a man known as Big Doe Sigma moved his family to Greenville and took over this building. Even back then it was a black neighbourhood, to which Big Doe catered by turning the place into a grocery store. He did reasonably well until the devastating flood of 1927, the worst flood of all; the one that wiped out so many up and down the river. He then went into bootlegging for a few years, producing moonshine from a still that could produce up to 40 barrels of firewater a day. This underground activity nevertheless got the family back on its feet, affording it enough money to put the badly damaged building back into habitable form, and to re-open the grocery business. But as we've already seen elsewhere in this narrative, floods have a habit of driving people from an area, many of whom are never to return. The store struggled to survive.

Many years later in 1941, somebody gave Big Doe's wife a partial recipe for these too-spicy-for-me tamales - a food not tasted before north of the Mexican border. The locals took to them big time, and even though they were sold as takeaways, that was the start of Doe's Eat Place - possibly the most unpretentious name for a restaurant that I've ever heard.

By that time, the front part of the store had evolved into a honkytonk, strictly for blacks. White people wanting a tamale entered through the back door, a sort of apartheid in reverse. One day a doctor was invited to stay for lunch, usually a tamale and a steak. Soon the doctor brought other white professionals along with him to sample Big Doe's grub. Over time, the family went from being grocers to bootleggers to highly popular restaurateurs - and not simply because of the food.

As 'Sunshine' Sonny Payne had said to me in his Helena studio when talking of Louis Armstrong, 'music transcends the colour issue'. It surely does, because the whites who entered Doe's Eat Place through the back door were, ironically, as much there to listen to the black musicians - whose twangings and wailings were clearly audible from the screened-off honkytonk - as they were for the menu.

Talking of the menu, the tamales and steaks arrive at our table. I gingerly have a go at the former, but cannot get through two mouthfuls. As for the latter, there can be no other steakhouse like this one. Not one, but two huge, sizzling steaks the size of ping pong bats are on our plates, each of them a good two inches thick, and accompanied by half a dozen giant prawns. Inside this oddball bistro built of flood-battered bricks and set in a dark, uncelebrated part of town, the packed house of well-to-do whites is tucking into its fare as if it were Marco Pierre White out there in the kitchen. Whoever is doing the cooking is an unknown hero of the celebrity chef culture.

Yes, it is another odd story, made odder still by the subsequent decision to close the honkytonk and turn it into the present-day kitchen, through which all customers are obliged to enter and depart. But then again, what else should I expect in these parts, where being out of the norm *is* the norm? Along this river, to be normal in the conventional sense would have the local quacks and shrinks booking you into a psychiatric ward and signing you off as a certifiable case.

Eighteen

PREACHER MAN

*T*HE WIND HAS DONE ME a major favour today by swinging
180 degrees from yesterday's direction. It is blowing just as
hard, but is now at my back and I'm wondering if I can make
the full 100 miles to Vicksburg on this warm and sunny
Saturday. Bill Serrat makes the decision a little easier by offering
to take me and the bike a few miles out of town, and well onto
Highway 61. I'm going to give it a crack.

Bill and I get along really well, to the point where he starts
telling me some personal stuff. By the time he's through talking
about a particularly difficult aspect of his life, the miles have
whizzed by. So he makes life easier still by saying that he'll
drop me off at Rolling Fork, leaving just 50 miles to pedal. With
this following wind, I should get to that famous civil war city
long before nightfall.

Rolling Fork is the birthplace and former hometown of that
blues giant, Muddy Waters, which is about as much as I can say
about this town of 2,000 people, situated ten miles east of the

river. Aside from the 'main street' (basically Highway 61 with just a few buildings spaced well apart from each other), the rest of Rolling Fork seems to be hidden among the trees.

Bill, bless him, has already made contact with his Vicksburg counterpart, ensuring that my run of good luck along the Mississippi continues over the weekend. And it begins with the wind, which is being so uncharacteristically helpful that I find myself singing out loud while I pedal. After just three leisurely hours of cycling along a completely level highway, a road sign informs me that Vicksburg is only five miles distant.

But wait … what is this coming up on my right? Am I hallucinating or what? Firstly, there is this multi-coloured bus parked off-road. Next to it is the weirdest structure I have ever seen, like a berserk, 20-foot tall obelisk, sharp angles and corners protruding from everywhere. It too is multi-coloured; white, pink, yellow, and red. And next to that, in the same blinding colours, is a one-storey building where a tall, ageing black man is holding court out on the porch, surrounded by eight or ten white people. Somewhere amid all this, a sign written in an appalling scrawl announces this to be a house of worship for Gentiles and Jews.

There has to be a story here, and I resolve to come back tomorrow to have a chat with the old man. From what I can see and hear from the roadside, he isn't short of words. They are tumbling from his mouth like a verbal waterfall, and his 'congregation' seems agape with awe.

I carry on into Vicksburg, where the hills begin. It is a lovely old town standing high on a bluff that overlooks the Mississippi. I can feel the history, the American Civil War, the last-ditch stand taken by the confederates in which Vicksburg was the very last Mississippi port to fall to General Grant's union army. This feeling of history comes easily this afternoon, as I stop and listen to a brass band playing in the gardens of some magnificent old building, and witness a gathering of people dressed out in the garb of the mid 19th Century; the men are in long jackets and top hats; the women wear bonnets and puffy ankle-length dresses Some of them are dancing on the grass, a twirl of bygone days.

A lady with the name of Colleen Stafford May is waiting for me at the CVB in the city's sloping main street, a bubbly woman in her mid-50s and to whom I warm easily. This may have something to do with the fact that, apart from my two sisters, she is the only person I have ever met in my entire life with the same middle-name as myself, Stafford. Colleen gives me directions to my lodgings and we arrange to meet there this evening. I freewheel back down the slope, then turn up another hilly street leading away from the river. At the top is the house I'm looking for - not really a B&B, but a mini-mansion whose wealthy socialite owner utilises it for the sole purpose of accommodating visiting friends and dignitaries. She is waiting for me out on the porch.

Betty Bullard is a youthful 72 year old, immaculately dressed, and strikingly refined in that Southern Belle manner. She takes me on a tour of the mansion, known as George Washington Ball House, who was a descendent of George Washington and one time owner of this splendid residence. Betty says to make myself at home, pick a bedroom as there are several to choose from, and to stay as long as I want, no charge. There doesn't appear to be anybody else around, and she confirms that I have her spare mansion entirely to myself. The ceilings are high, the bedrooms huge, and the walls are adorned with paintings and sketches of Vicksburg history. The civil war is coming at me from all directions. Ensconced in a ground floor bedroom, I am soon alone with the past.

Mark Twain's description of the city's stand during the civil war concerns a six week blitz on the place by Yankee forces, from May 18 to July 4, 1863. In his book, *Life on the Mississippi*, and in the parlance of his time, he wrote the following passage:

'Signs and scars still remain, as reminders of Vicksburg's tremendous war experiences; earthwork, trees crippled by cannonballs, cave-refuges in the clay precipices, etc. The caves did good service during the six week bombardment of the city.

They were used by non-combatants - mainly the women and children; not to live in constantly, but to fly to for safety on occasion. They were mere holes, tunnels, driven into the perpendicular clay bank, then branched Y-shape within the hill.

Population, 27,000 confederate soldiers and 3,000 non-combatants; the city utterly cut off from the world - walled solidly in, the frontage by gunboats, the rear by soldiers and batteries; hence no buying or selling with the outside; no passing to and fro; no God-speed to a passing guest; no welcoming a coming one; no printed acres of worldwide news to be read at breakfast - a tedious, dull absence of such matter instead; hence, also, no running to see the steamboats smoking into view in the distance, and ploughing towards the town - for none came, the river lay vacant and undisturbed; no rush and turmoil around the railroad station, no struggling over bewildered swarms of passengers by noisy mobs of hackmen - all quiet there; flour, $200 a barrel, sugar $30, corn, $10 a bushel, bacon, $5 a pound, rum, $100 a gallon; other things in proportion: consequently, no roar and racket of drays and carriages tearing along the streets; nothing for them to do among that handful of non-combatants of exhausted means; at three o'clock in the morning, silence; a silence so dead that the measured tramp of a sentinel can be heard at seemingly impossible distance; out of hearing of this lonely sound, perhaps the stillness is absolute; and all in a moment comes ground shaking thunder-clashes of artillery; the sky is cobwebbed with the red lined criss-crossing streaming from soaring bombshells and a rain of iron fragments descends upon the city; and along empty streets which are not empty a moment later, but mottled with dim figures of frantic women and children scurrying from home and bed toward the cave dungeons - and encouraged by the humorous-grim soldiery who shout, "Rats, to your holes!" and laugh.

The cannon-thunder rages, shells scream and crash overhead, the iron rain pours down, one hour, two hours, three, possibly six, then stops; silence follows, but the streets are still empty; the silence continues; by and by, a head projects from a cave, here, there, and yonder, and reconnoitres cautiously; the silence still continuing, bodies follow heads, and jaded, half-smothered creatures group themselves about, stretch their cramped limbs, draw in deep draughts of the grateful fresh air, gossip with the neighbours from the next cave; maybe straggle off presently, or take a lounge through the town if the stillness continues; and will scurry to the holes again, by and by, when the war tempest breaks forth once more'.

Six weeks of that must have been hell - the 27,000 confederate troops as much there to ensure that the townsfolk didn't capitulate, as they were for the fighting of a detested Yankee foe - a feeling still held by many southerners today. The residents of Vicksburg refused to observe July 4, Independence Day, for 81 years after its eventual fall.

*F*OR A CITY OF 26,000, Vicksburg has surprisingly few restaurants, although it isn't short of floating casinos, four in all. Colleen picks the only place in town where we can relax with an after-dinner cigarette, which is precisely what everyone else in here is doing too. Hooray for the diehards.

Later, we go down to the river and onto a gambling boat. The casino is jam packed with punters. This industry has become the lifeblood of the state of Mississippi, once classified as the fourth-poorest in the entire union. Gambling has turned all that on its head. But there is no profit to be made from me tonight. I am pleased to say that I walk away from the slots $130 better off.

In the morning, Colleen picks me up again and we drive up to a viewing area on top of the bluff overlooking a big bend in the river - a spectacle that may not seem too exciting, but which is nonetheless a real treat for the eyes. The whitewashed city shines down on today's blue, blue water, and the water shimmers back at it, as if inviting the population down for a swim. This is the Mississippi with the big friendly smile on its face; not a hint anywhere of the plans for its next victim.

199

The Preacher's strange obelisk.

After a spot of lunch somewhere, we drive back out to that strange house of worship. She warns me that the Reverend Dennis has got this reputation for talking a blue streak, and that it's nearly impossible to get away from him once he gets into the rhetoric. We pull up outside the house, where the old man is once again sitting on the porch, preaching to a young white couple. He looks up and eagerly beckons us over, the more the better. The couple seem relieved to see us, like it's now someone else's turn for a good ear bashing.

"Welcome, welcome, welcome" he says, offering a bony hand. "I am the Reverend Dennis, and this house of God is my home, shared by my good wife inside who is the same age as me, 92. Praise the lord and hallelujah."

The Reverend Dennis is in remarkable physical condition for a man of his years. He is a tall, slim individual with short white hair. He wears a white shirt, grey tie, and a pair of grey trousers held up by braces. His shoes are polished to a gleam.

At the first opportunity, I ask him to explain that structure over there, the erratic tower-like obelisk. He stares at his bizarre creation, then goes into a long diatribe about good and evil, most of which I cannot understand because his words flow so rapidly that they punch, jump, and bump into one another like 20 sparring boxers all in the same ring. His arms wave and flail like twanging rubber bands, and his eyes roll into some kind of fiery trance. I can pick out a few references to God and Satan, some hallelujahs delivered in lieu of punctuation, and something to do with St. Peter; but other than this his explanation leaves me even more baffled than I was before.

But he's got real spirit, this vociferous man of the cloth. Whatever it is that he's saying, he clearly believes it. Shortly he invites us inside to meet his wife, Margaret, and what a lovely old lady she is; calm, unruffled, 100% all there in the head, and very long suffering. She tells us that this front room used to be her own grocery store, and there still seems to be evidence of that: shelves stacked with jars of this and that, an early cash till, large container tins from another era, and what must be the

201

earliest of bacon slicers, maybe even the actual prototype. She closed the store down 20 years ago, figuring it was time to put her feet up and settle into a life of ease. But ever since, she says, more people have turned up to hear the preacher spout off than ever came into her store.

I ask her about the unfathomable obelisk outside, that deranged totem pole. She tells me to ask the preacher about that.

"Margaret, I tried. I couldn't make out a word he said."

"Well, I guess he's explained it to me once or twice, or maybe 100 times, I wouldn't know. When you live with the Reverend Dennis, you learn to switch off; just to nod your head at appropriate moments. It becomes automatic, elsewise I'd have gone crazy years ago. Every night, or just as soon as you good people have gone, he starts preachin' on me 'cause he just cain't shut it up. So I just say to him, 'Give it a rest, preacher. I cain't hardly hear the news'. That stops him - for about 30 seconds." She smiles up at me, this wonderful woman. "You know how much them 30 seconds mean to me? They be like glorious sunshine after a bad storm."

Margaret gets my sympathy and my vote. I then ask her about the hand-painted bus next to the mysterious obelisk. "The preacher got it from a school when it got too old for them to keep it on the road. The bus is his church, and worth lookin' at. Mind, he sees *anywhere* as his church: the porch, the roadside, on top o' that hill across the road, inside the bus, street corners in Vicksburg - except he don't drive to town no more, too old. Wherever he can get himself someone to preach at, he'll be there. Don't a night go by without him preachin' in his sleep even."

The Reverend isn't listening to any of this. His lips move continuously, audible at intervals, and miming his thoughts at other moments. It's like he's engaged in a quiet spiritual chant, or silently preaching to an audience that only he can see. I feel for his wife. Someone who preaches non-stop from sunrise to bedtime and then carries it on into his sleep, would be a serious test for anyone. Yet he is immensely likeable, and well meaning beyond a doubt.

Such a person living in such bizarrely colourful surrounds cannot fail to become a local attraction. By now, another visitor has joined our foursome, a professional photographer from St Louis who snaps away furiously at his new subject. The Reverend, used to all this, appears not to notice. Instead, it seems to inspire him into a blasting tirade against sex and alcohol, two of America's most popular indulgences. He is still going on about this as he leads us to his bus, one of those old bangers from the 1950s.

At the far end he has installed a figure of Jesus Christ, and a kneeling cushion upon which to pray, one person at a time. At the near end, just behind the driving seat, he has established a pulpit that is draped with multi-coloured cloth, beads, and tassels. Between are the 50 year old passenger seats, some with the springs poking through, which serve as the pews. The five of us sit down while the Reverend moves to his pulpit.

It is impossible to get the gist of this random sermon. One moment he thunders on about the satanic forces amid us, and the next, with a stern finger wagging in the air, he shouts something about Icarus, the winged messenger of Greek mythology. It is hot in here, the sun beating through the bus windows while the Reverend belts out whatever it is that's going through his mind. I can feel a headache on its way.

After another few minutes of this, I realise that the only way we are going to get away from these rantings is by walking out, something I am loath to do. I wanted the story, and this is the price for it. Instead, I opt to test an exercise in human nature by pulling out a $10 bill and stuffing it into the donation box next to the pulpit. This has immediate impact. The others instantly follow suit, and the preacher is assuredly not going to do anything to prevent these proceedings. His voice fades into humble mutters of thanks as the coffers swell. We quickly descend from the bus and into the fresh air of mercy.

The Reverend Dennis has a parting shot in store as Colleen

and I scramble for her car. With his hand tapping on my shoulder, and with surprising clarity, he says to me, "Now hear this, boy. Get fornication outta your mind; and you stay well clear o' them gambling boats. That's an order from the Lord; hallelujah."

THE INGRAM BARGE COMPANY has a towboat passing through Vicksburg at around midnight. It won't be stopping, but Ergon Marine, the company's agent here in town, is willing to take me out to it on a service boat. I'll climb aboard as it moves along, and don't be late because the boat won't wait. So says the Ingram PR man over the phone from Nashville on this sunny Monday morning. He gives me Ergon's address and suggests I nip down there to firm things up. I'll do that, I tell him. I'll do that right away.

I pedal to the southern outskirts of town, then down a steep incline into a combined parking lot for a floating casino and the riverside offices of Ergon Marine, where I've got two office buildings to choose from. Neither has any sign of what is what and who is who. I pick the one on my right, but before I can reach the door an urgent voice barks at me from outside the other building.

"Hey! Come over here, mister! Right now!"

I walk the bike over, coming face to face with a serious looking man in his early 50s. He's got cropped hair and a pockmarked face. He wears a grey suit and I notice the ominous bulge of the shoulder holster under his left armpit. He flashes some sort of official ID card at me, but allows me no time to inspect it. "I'm from Homeland Security" he growls, "and I wanna know who you are, and what is your business here."

"I'm looking for Ergon Marine" I answer. He is eyeing me with suspicion, possibly because I've arrived on a bike and am attired in tee-shirt and shorts. On a weekday morning, people do not normally visit a commercial premises looking as I do. I explain my mission, but he seems unwilling to take it in. He glares at the bike, demanding to know what is inside my pannier bags - which is precisely zero. All my belongings are back at the mansion. Nevertheless, he insists on a search of both me and the bags.

"I dunno" he mutters, clearly disappointed that I'm clean. "We're on all kinds of alert at present, and you don't look nor sound right to me."

I have been a traveller long enough to read the signs. This bloke is just itching to snap the cuffs on; to cut a proverbial notch on his barely-covered gun; to justify his position in the quiet city of Vicksburg. Under the orders of George W. Bush, the homeland security people have been given immense powers following the 9/11 attacks, and as far as this agent is concerned, I represent an unusually tempting opportunity to display his authority around here.

"Show me some ID" he snaps. I've none on me, and his eyes narrow further. "I dunno" he says again, "I'm gonna have to check you out, buddy. You're not playing the part right." This idiot belongs in a far right-wing Chuck Norris movie.

"Why don't you simply ask the boss of Ergon?" I suggest.

He doesn't have to. Right then the door behind him swings open and out strides a rotund, red faced man with an unlit cigarette twiddling between his fingers. It does not remain unlit for long. But before lighter meets tobacco, the man spots my bike and says, "You gotta be the guy boarding the Ingram towboat tonight, yeah?"

"That's me, boss."

The homeland security agent expels a disappointed sigh - then contritely says, "I've been probing him, Dan. I think he's probably kosher."

Daniel L. Koestler is vice-president of Ergon Marine, and once he's had his smoke he invites me into his office for a coffee. "Don't pay no mind to that zealot out there. He likes to think that he's a secret service agent or something. Truth is, we don't have too many terrorists in Vicksburg, so there's nothing like a new face to get him up and jumping."

Dan is keenly interested in a foreigner's thoughts on the Iraq war, and once we get on to that topic, I can't stop him spluttering his endless rage at American involvement in a lost cause. Even this far south, deep into what is supposed to be redneck territory, I've still to meet *anyone* along the river who supports it. Eventually we get on to the purpose of my visit. Dan hands me his business card and tells me to be here by 11pm at the latest. "I won't be around at that time, but I'll pass the word for the night staff to expect you. If anyone gives you hassle, tell them to call my cell phone. The number's on the card."

He says that the boat, the *Dennis C. Bottorff*, will carry me south for 24 hours to its next scheduled stop at Baton Rouge, the state capital of Louisiana. After that, it's a two day ride to New Orleans, which will leave just one more day of pedalling - to the very end of the Mississippi River. The 18 feet wide, four-inch deep pond back at Lake Itasca - the very beginning of the Mississippi - suddenly seems like a dim memory from another time.

Nineteen

TOWBOAT

*A*T HALF PAST MIDNIGHT the *Dennis C. Bottorff* comes steaming round a river bend, pushing 24 cargo-laden barges. The boat is lit up like a fairground and its powerful searchlight is trained on the arches of the Mississippi Bridge. Me and the bike are aboard a small service boat, which after a brief chase out in mid-river, catches up with the towboat where two crewmen secure fore and aft lines, thus towing the little vessel along while I transfer bags, bike, and body onto this big 170-foot tug.

The mate welcomes me aboard and says we've got a little paperwork to get through before anything else. We sit inside the warmth of the crew's mess room, and he passes me an indemnity form to sign, releasing the owners from any liability should I meet my maker while aboard their vessel. He then runs through some written safety instructions and gets me to sign those off as well. By the time we're through with this, the lights of Vicksburg have faded from view.

He takes me on a short tour of the boat, which begins with the galley. If I get hungry during the night, take what I want from here, he says, opening the door to a giant fridge that is crammed with pre-cooked food. Then we climb a companionway up one deck, where I dump my bags in the small but comfortable guest cabin. Next, we climb further still, past the captain's cabin and on up into the darkened pilot house where the chap at the helm is lost in concentration. This is not the time to start quizzing him, but at least I know my way around the boat already.

We go back down to the mess room and drink coffee - the one absolute law on these boats is that alcohol is a big time no-no, a definite firing offence, and illegal under Coast Guard rules. After a while, I think to call it a night. I have got all day tomorrow, and most of the night as well to glean whatever stories I can from the ten-strong crew.

AT SOME TIME DURING THE NIGHT the boat passes the city of Natchez, another high-bluff town on the east bank of the river. During my coast-to-coast ride in 1999, this is where I crossed the Mississippi from Louisiana on a chilly January evening. I mention this because it was in Natchez that I had a strange experience that I still think of occasionally and one that I think is worthy of mention here, since it is a Mississippi story. I'll follow that with a short tale from this peculiar city with a truly bloody and violent past. Both the following stories are derived from my notebooks of that ride.

'I follow the signs to downtown Natchez, searching for the King's Tavern at 619 Jefferson Street. Gliding along these streets of proud old southern mansions and rolling lawns, I neither see nor feel any reminders that this city of 20,000 had once been officially designated as America's most violent town. I only sense that tonight is going to be the weirdest night of all in my TransAmerican odyssey. For the tavern has the reputation of being the most haunted house in the state of Mississippi, where previous guests stayed long enough to check in, though not long enough to check out. They were gone in a hurry and they're not coming back again.

I park the bike outside the tavern and enter into the warmth where a log fire is blazing, casting shadows along a low-beamed ceiling. Dining tables are spread about, softly lit by flickering candles. In one corner is a small bar. A few diners are talking quietly in an ambience of gentle informality. Down here at ground level, it is not unlike a traditional pub in the English shires.

The tavern has just the one guest room. A waitress directs me up a narrow flight of creaking wooden stairs, and then up a second flight to the very top of the building. My quarters consist of an old bathroom, and a bedroom designed to give the visitor an instant chill of the spine - and that's not simply because it is pretty damn cold up here anyway. The floorboards are bare; a forlorn four-poster bed is up against a wall, its posters imbalanced at a ten-degree angle; there is an antiquarian writing desk with an inkwell, and a large antiquarian book lies open on a wrought-iron lectern next to an empty fireplace. I can either sit on an uncomfortable, dusty chez-longue or creak to and fro in a spindly rocking chair. At the foot of the four-poster is an antique traveller's chest. An imitation oil lamp next to the bed casts its light through the silence. This spooky room belongs to a long-gone era. Judging by the dust, nobody has been up here for weeks. The bed is unmade, as if its last occupants had fled in the middle of the night - which they quite possibly did - and the maid is clearly of no mind to come up here and straighten things out. A silent presence seems to exist within these walls. I cannot see it, but I *can* feel it. Let's call it an acute metaphysical awareness, which follows me into the bathroom and which might as well turn on the old brass taps for me, so that steaming bathwater can flow into the ancient tub - one of those tubs that stands on four iron legs. It is eerie up here.

The King's Tavern is the city's oldest building, first

appearing in the public records as a drinking house in 1789, and owned by a man named Richard King. This three-storey structure of cypress wood and brick has been through a number of incarnations since that faraway year, and is now operating as a pub/restaurant once more under the stewardship of a relatively new owner. She is Yvonne Scott, a tall middle-aged woman with wavy blonde hair and a slightly nervous disposition. She tells me that she always carries a loaded .22 calibre pistol in her purse.

"Well, that's not going to bump off a ghost, is it?" I suggest.

"No, it won't. But there can be bad karma out on the streets as well as inside here. A few years ago my husband was gunned down in a Natchez bar following an argument. He had a reputation for a mean temper, and the culprit walked free from the court after a plea of self-defence. I've carried the pistol ever since. It makes me feel better." She pauses for a few moments. "Sometimes I dream about my husband, and he is always pushing me to exact revenge." Ghosts, old and recent, would appear to surround Yvonne's life.

The ghosts of the King's Tavern have, she says, been around almost as long as the place itself - though it wasn't until 1930 that a possible explanation of who they are came to light. Yvonne points to the glowing fireplace. "It was during some renovation work that a female skeleton was discovered at the back of the fireplace. She had been stabbed to death and bricked up, along with a 200 year old knife. Researchers later discovered her to be the lover of Richard King, and the assumption was that King's wife had her killed in a fit of jealousy. She is our most apparent ghost. The last sighting of Madeline - that's our name for her - was only two days ago."

In apparition mode Madeline appears as a distressed young woman, roaming the tavern at random and occasionally swiping at glasses from trays and tables, smashing them to fragments. Her favourite place is the ladies loo, where female diners have been known to shriek and freeze in horror as she presents herself to them while their knickers are down.

"Plenty of women have come screaming out of the can, tripping over their own underwear" Yvonne says, enjoying a rare smile. "One of them publicly fainted in that embarrassing state."

She goes on to tell me about a second ghoul who wanders the tavern. "Now he is real *creepy*" Yvonne says with a genuine shudder, "a stern, old fashioned guy in a chinchilla coat who sways a kind of power over you, if you can understand that. He often appears over there (she points towards the bar), and he just glowers at me, nasty-like, and with a look of total disapproval. He is *mean*."

So where had this gentleman come from, I wonder aloud. "After finding Madeline, the renovators unearthed two more skeletons from the basement floor, both male. They had been murdered, and I guess he must be one of them. After the continuing appearance of this guy, I withdrew the tavern as a place for overnight guests." She eyes me uncertainly. "Except, that is, for the occasional journalist like you or researchers of the paranormal." Ominously she adds, "Don't be surprised if things happen up in your room tonight. I haven't had the tavern very long - but long enough to know what goes on here. And it does go on, my friend." There is no doubting Yvonne's sincerity. This is no publicity stunt; she means what she says. Worse still for me, I can feel that she is right. But then I volunteered for this, all in the name of a brief radio story.

Yvonne lives over the bridge in Vidalia, Louisiana. She has twice stayed over after a late night, but not any more. "No way" she says emphatically, "I've had too many experiences already, even in broad daylight." She relates a recent story about the man in the chinchilla coat. It happened during the afternoon while preparing tables for the evening's trade. Yvonne was in the kitchen, which you get to via a swing door next to the bar.

"I had a tray in my hands, loaded with cutlery and stuff. Normally I just bump the door with my shoulder and pass through. But something stopped me. I froze right by the door, suddenly knowing that he was on the other side, waiting. For a few minutes the kitchen turned as cold as ice, honest. He's like that, this man with the coat. He likes to mess with my head."

She presumably slept up in my room on her two stopovers. "Yeah, and thank God I was knee-walking drunk on both occasions. Frankly, that room gives me the shivers."

The waitress, a young lady with the name of Lashay, clears the plates from our table. She has worked at the tavern for a year and seen plenty of smashed glass. "It's like one moment I'm trotting along with a tray of wine glasses, and the next thing is that three or four of them are flying across the room. It's happened several times."

At 11pm, the place closes up for the night. Yvonne hands me a front door key and bids me goodnight. Shortly I am alone with just the dying embers of the fire for company. When I can avoid it no longer, I switch out the lights and climb the creaking stairs.

The bedroom is enshrouded in pin-dropping silence. Outside, the elegant streets of Natchez are deserted. Each step I take on the bare floorboards sounds like a deep, ghoulish groan. I am conscious of my own breathing. After a while I climb into the unmade bed and switch off the imitation oil lamp.

I let my eyes adjust to the dark, then drift into an uneasy sleep for a few hours. At around 3.30am I suddenly awake, my imagination flying like one of Lashay's wine glasses. Assorted creaks and knocks are audible from below, as if a scuttling pack of rats is gnawing at the woodwork. I am expecting an apparition to appear at the foot of my bed at any moment. It is not the thought of a ghost that bothers me, so much as the sudden shock of one appearing from nowhere. Not very good for the heart, that.

I do not see it - but I do suddenly feel it. I'm lying on my back when an unseen pressure pushes my right arm firmly down onto the mattress. I am unable to move it for several moments, and when I finally do, it is like lifting weights. This is not imagined. I am very much awake and alert now. A moment later, the pressure transfers to my left ribcage. Something is

212

trying to push me out of bed. After a while it eases and stops. Whoever or whatever is the cause of this is certainly making a point: that it is the boss of the house, and I'm not to forget it. In the end I lapse into an exhausted sleep, waking again at dawn feeling jaded and a little irritable.

Daylight should bring some relief to supernatural activity, but the King's Tavern seems to keep its restless spooks locked in a tight compound. Even with the early sunlight streaming through the downstairs windows, the presence remains. It isn't menacing, but it is pronounced. Inside these walls, I have as much expectation of meeting with a ghost at midday, as I do at midnight.

From ghosts I'll now switch to blood and gore. Earlier I mentioned that Natchez was once considered the country's most violent and dangerous city, which might seem a bit odd since at the time it was also the nation's wealthiest city per-capita because of cotton. But between the years of 1776 to the outbreak of the civil war in 1861, the city was split into Natchez-over-the-Hill and Natchez-under-the-Hill. The former was the strict preserve of the cotton barons and rich socialites, a city of splendid avenues and big mansions. The latter was the precise opposite; a swarming commercial waterfront at the bottom of the bluff that attracted some of the worst rogues in the land: wanted murderers, escaped convicts, swindlers and cardsharps, professional beggars and pickpockets, bare-knuckle prize fighters, guns-for-hire, river pirates, whores, drunks, snake oil salesmen, charlatans and religious phoneys. They headed for Natchez-under-the-Hill like gold rush prospectors - and were followed into town by a good many enterprising morticians and undertakers who sensed sombre fortune. It was like a Klondike for the criminal classes, only twice as rough.

Among this motley bunch were Davy Crockett and Jim Bowie, two big-name frontiersmen, each famous for different reasons and who were both to later lose their lives at the Alamo. Street fighting, any sort of fighting, was in their blood and it is therefore no particular surprise that both men turned up in

Natchez-under-the-Hill.

Davy Crockett came here from Tennessee with one aim in mind: to become the 'Cock of the Walk', a title then held by another brawling roughneck called Mike Fink. It was a revered, no-holds-barred fighting title, enabling the champion to strut around town with a big red feather in his hatband. The feather told everyone that he was the meanest guy in town and never to be messed with. Whoever wanted to take the title from him, had to fight him for it; hard, dirty stuff, with killing permitted.

I can imagine the scene: a waterfront setting of loud bars and busy brothels; sidewalks littered with hustlers intent on ripping off the steamboat passengers and drunken crew members. If a body lay in the street, it was either drunk, dying, or dead. On this particular waterfront, a corpse was just another corpse; a visible item of Natchez-under-the-Hill's dirty underwear.

Crockett challenged Mike Fink for the title. It was to be a street contest that would draw the crowds, and where serious bets were taken. According to Don Estes, a renowned local historian, "Those two assholes fought all day - and I mean *all day*. They beat the shit out of one another in a way that few other men could have survived. Neither would entertain the thought of losing or quitting - yet neither could overcome the other. By nightfall they had to call it a draw, which meant that Mike Fink got to keep his coveted feather."

Jim Bowie on the other hand, was a man who didn't go looking for trouble; trouble came looking for him. When he arrived in Natchez from Louisiana, he witnessed such violence in the under-the-hill part of town, that he devised the legendary Bowie knife as an item of self-defence. It had three features which differed from other knives of the day; an effective handle guard; the curve of its long, broad blade; and a lethally-honed edge that ran one-third of the way up the blunt side.

"Bowie did not design it to cut twine" says Don Estes. "He designed it to kill people. If you got into a knife fight in this town, it was to the death. If a lawman came by, he'd either put money on the outcome, or shrug and leave them to it. Life was cheap back then. Murders were an hourly occurrence. Sometimes the dead got buried; other times they were simply tossed into the Mississippi."

Bowie, he says, had a strong sense of fair play even in a place like this. Estes relates an incident that took place outside a barber's shop in Natchez-over-the-Hill. The shop was owned by a free slave called William Johnson who witnessed the event and recorded it in a diary later found stuffed up a chimney. "It was kept up that chimney because blacks were not supposed to read or write in those days. It could have lost Johnson his freedom. Back then, white people thought that a little education made them dangerous."

Johnson recorded that two men waiting to have a shave and haircut got into an argument while Jim Bowie was in the barber's chair. The dispute spilled out onto the street, and Bowie stood up to watch the proceedings. One man was clearly getting the better of the other, resulting in the loser pulling out a small pistol from his pocket and shooting his opponent point-blank dead. In Bowie's eyes, this was a dirty tactic requiring suitable redress; an eye for an eye.

He marched out onto the street, challenging the gunman. Bowie and his knife attacked with lightning speed, taking two bullets in the process. It was a disembowelled gunman that fell to the ground. He had been gutted with just three swipes from Bowie's blade. When word of this incident spread, the Bowie knife was officially adopted by the U.S. Army.

As for Jim Bowie himself, he moved on to Texas and fought at the Alamo. His own demise was no less violent than his own life. New research reveals that he was captured by the Mexican Army, severely tortured for several days, and was then buried alive.

Today, Natchez-under-the-Hill is little more than a waterfront strip of concrete, a convenient berthing place for a floating casino, and for the many replica steamboats which call in on the town during the tourist season. All the whorehouses, saloons, and steam packet offices have been demolished.

I AWAKE TO THE THROB OF TWIN DIESELS, totalling 7,200 horsepower. It is October 31, but down at this latitude it is sunny and warm outside. The water is a muddy brown around the boat, yet a startling blue 50 metres either side of it. We are obviously in shallow water, with the propellers and the boat's wake stirring up the riverbed. It must take some nerve to pilot one of these machines.

I go down to the galley for a light breakfast. On this boat, the crew works two six-hour shifts a day, and the men on the early-hours watch are already tucked up in their bunks. The only other person at the table is Mark Battise, the chief engineer who hails from that hurricane-bashed coastal city of Biloxi, Mississippi, a place bowed and humbled after Katrina tore it apart. The outside world automatically thinks of New Orleans whenever Katrina is mentioned, but Mark insists that it was his own hometown that took the real brunt. He was there at the time, and he's got over 100 images of this disaster stored on his laptop computer which he offers to show me when he gets off his watch.

Assorted crew member come in and out, snatching a piece of toast or cups of coffee. They are all instantly friendly, offering this 24-hour visitor a welcome that you could only find on, and alongside, the Mississippi. There is no resentment at my presence; just an immediate acceptance, and a willingness to help in any way at all. It is an odd mix of give and take. The mate on this watch is deeply interested in my bike, which is relaxing in the mess room. Mark Battise is curious about the BBC, to which he frequently listens on the internet; a deckhand asks me about England, the country that his grandparents came from, and which he is determined to visit someday. And the cook, a reading obsessive who is fascinated by Mark Twain and his river, is eager for a few of my own tales on the journey so far.

I should not be - but am - mildly surprised to find a female cook aboard a boat like this, which I had previously imagined would be a floating bastion for the hard-swearing, the misfits, and the damned. In fact, it is very civilised within the confines of these 170 feet by 50 feet, where unexpectedly high IQ's exist among the crew, and where Kay, the plump, cheery, middle-aged cook is entirely at home.

"Books are my main love" she chimes. "I get plenty of free time to read on a towboat. I've got my own cabin and bathroom, and all the privacy I could want. Cooking is my talent, so I'm in the right job; and rivers really do interest me. They always have. With one month on, and one month off, I don't think I could ask for a better deal."

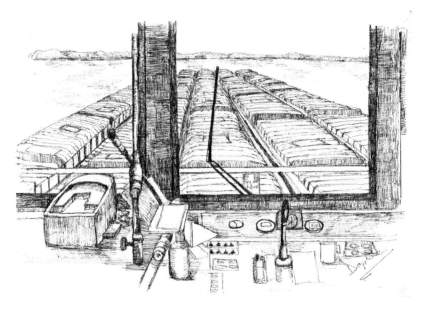

The towboat Dennis C. Bothorff pushing 24 laden barges.
View from the pilot house.

A little later in the morning I climb up to the pilot house to introduce myself to the captain, a short, curly haired, bearded man in his mid-50s. He is wearing a blue denim jacket, matching blue jeans, and a pair of moccasins on otherwise bare feet. A pair of small, rimless glasses is perched on the end of his

217

nose, giving him the slight look of a dishevelled academic. His handshake is firm and his demeanour warm. He and I are going to get along.

Up here in the pilot house, the high domain of the boat in all senses, you get an immediate picture of the enormous responsibility that Capt. Dwight Shinley bears. He has not just got a few million dollars worth of boat to command, but many more million dollars worth of cargo in those 24 barges directly ahead of us. Underneath the boat, he has only two or three feet of spare depth before crunching aground. "Damn river is abnormally shallow this year, but we'll be okay" he says with his boyish grin. "Been in a lot worse spots than this and I figure on a few more before we get down to Baton Rouge tonight."

The steering is an hydraulic tiller system, a thin metal lever in comfortable reach of the pilot's swivel chair. Every conceivable electronic navigational gadget surrounds him, including a colour sat-nav flow of the river, which moves along with every metre we travel. The pilot knows every last detail of the immediate situation: wind direction and wind speed; the weather up ahead; our pinpoint location; our precise ground speed and precise depth; the exact mileage to the next significant port or point; and he knows the names and call signs of every towboat ahead of him, behind him, and heading towards him, and how far each one is away. Whatever would Christopher Columbus have made of all this electronic assistance, I wonder.

"Yeah, this stuff helps, that's for sure. But the thing about the Mississippi is that it shifts and changes all the time, making some of the software obsolete. Trust me, this river will deceive the very best of advanced electronics - and then straightaway it'll deceive them again. It is one sneaky son of a bitch, and anyone who takes it for granted is a goddam idiot - and I speak from over 30 years of towboating up and down, when half these new gadgets didn't exist."

Dwight's comments are well supported by Mark Twain, who wrote the following in his Mississippi narrative:

'One cannot easily realise what a tremendous thing it is to know every trivial detail of 1,200 miles of river (between St Louis and New Orleans), and to know it with absolute exactness. If you take the longest street in New York, and travel up and down it, connecting its features patiently until you know every house and window and door and lamp-post and big and little sign by heart, and know them so accurately that you can instantly name the one you are abreast of when you are set down at random in that street in the middle of an inky-black night, you will then have a tolerable notion of the amount and exactness of a pilot's knowledge, who carries the Mississippi in his head. And then if you will go on until you know every street crossing, the size, character, and position of the crossing stones, and the varying depths of mud in each of these numberless places, you will then get some idea of what the pilot must know in order to keep a Mississippi steamer out of trouble. Next, if you will take half the signs in that long street, and *change their places once a month*, and still manage to know their new positions accurately on dark nights, and keep up with their repeated changes without making any mistakes, you will understand what is required of a pilot's peerless memory by the fickle Mississippi'.

THE MATE AND DECKHANDS are roaming along the 1,000 feet of barges, checking that the connecting systems which keep the 24 barges together are holding fast. "Do you know that this load we're pushing is stopping not far short of 1,000 trucks - or 940 to be exact - from clogging the roads?" Dwight Shinley asserts. "Each time I get to thinking that I'm not living a worthwhile life, I remember those numbers and hope that I'm doing some good after all."

Not living a worthwhile life? Keeping nearly 1,000 of those treacherous 18-wheelers off the road makes him a big-time hero in my eyes, a saint even. This thought leads me to prod him on his actual status on the Mississippi. Since the demise of the steamboat pilot, surely the towboat captain is the new hero of the river?

"I wouldn't use the term 'hero'" he answers, "and neither would the environmentalists who think of us as polluters, not saviours. I guess when you add up all the towboats on all the Midwest rivers - not only this one, but the Missouri, the Ohio, the Tennessee, the White River, and the Intracoastal running west into Texas - it becomes not a case of who is the hero, but who is the least-worst offender. See, there has to be at least 1,200 boats working these waterways, so we're obviously doing some environmental damage. On the other hand, without all these towboats there would be well over a million more trucks out there in the highways. I honestly don't know if we're the heroes, the villains - or if it is just that the world is fast on its way to hell anyhow."

"The world itself, Mother Earth, is in fine shape" I reply, since he's on to a subject close to my heart. "It is the human race that's in dire need of repair."

Dwight nods. "You know, one of the attractions of my job is that it takes me away from all the shit going on ashore: the politicians, the corporations, the cheating and scheming and money-madness. When I'm up here alone on watch, then for six hours it's just me and the river, and I love that."

He is an interesting man, this calm and thoughtful towboat captain. I ask what he would do in lieu of this particular job if the occasion were to arise. He thinks for a few moments and says, "Carpentry. Not construction-site stuff, but handmade furniture or maybe traditional wooden boats. I like working with my hands, and I love wood as a material." As a surprising afterthought, he adds, "And perhaps a bit of blacksmith work as well."

Now there's a forgotten art if ever there was. He would, in other words, go back to the traditions of craftsmanship which came from a gentler and more caring age, which has me liking and respecting him all the more. By and by I take my leave, but Dwight says for me to be sure to join him again on the night watch, and chat some more.

The boat is steaming along at a ground speed of 10mph and following the river's endless curves and bends which take us not only south, but east, west, north, and northwest in order to head south again. I sit out on a small afterdeck next to my cabin and bask lazily in the sunshine, my thoughts drifting here and there, the way they do if I stare at rippling water for any length of time. Sometimes I think of home, though not often: other times of the two ex-wives, old girlfriends, my scattered family. And of the people I've met more recently along this mystical river. Would I, should I, change anything about the way I live? No, I don't think so. My intention is to grow old really quite disgracefully.

After lunch, Mark Battise shows me his pictures of a blown-apart Biloxi. The trees are down, roofs are down, entire buildings are down, everything is down in crumbled heaps strewn across the acres of devastation. Biloxi had been a stopover on my coast-to-coast ride, but I barely recognise it from these images. "I dunno why the media goes on about New Orleans" he grumbles. "Apart from the Lower 9th Ward and some flooding along Canal Street, you wouldn't really know that Katrina had hit the place at all." I daresay this is a minor understatement, but judging from his photographs, I'm inclined to agree that Biloxi should have got better coverage than it did.

He takes me on a tour of his spotless engine room, which requires the wearing of ear mufflers. Two enormous white diesels of 3,600 horsepower each are growling thunder and slurping the fuel at the rate of several gallons per mile. The second engineer is now on watch, but Mark automatically checks that all is as it should be before retiring to his cabin for a nap.

I do the same, but am awoken by a rap on the door. There is a phone call for me up in the pilot house. I dash up there, where Dwight's second-in-command - otherwise known as the pilot - passes me the handset, the wiring of which somehow entangles with the tiller during the transfer, causing a brief tug-of-war.

"Hey!" he shouts angrily, "Will you let me steer the goddam boat!"

I apologise instantly for this boo-boo on my part. The pilot, a tall and slim man of early middle age nods solemnly, on the verge of a silent seethe. But he gets his composure back, then suddenly grins and salutes, military style. The incident is already forgotten.

"What was all that about?" asks the female voice at the other end. Her name is Sophia Dettmer, a programme planner at the BBC in London, and she wants to know what I've got for her on tomorrow night's slot. I always ensure she has a contact number for me on the day prior to broadcasting, which today happens to be the number of a working towboat. I give her a rundown of the week's likely stories, of which this vessel is certainly going to be one of them.

Once I'm off the phone, the pilot holds out his hand. "David Reeves" he says, "from Ash Tree, Arkansas. As you see, I'm the pilot."

Now here is an odd fact. In the steamboat days, there was also a captain and a pilot aboard every ship. But the captain was only the captain of the actual ship itself and of its passengers. He had no authority over the pilot whatsoever, except to tell him which ports of call to make for. If he thought the pilot was heading for some mid-river disaster or was about to go aground, he simply had to button his lip and let it happen - even though in rank he was above the pilot. So in effect, steamboats had two captains: one who steered the ship, and the other who tended to mundane managerial details.

"It's not quite like that nowadays" David says, "although there are parallels. When Dwight is off watch for six hours, then for that time I am effectively the captain of the ship - so you could say there are two captains aboard, just like there are two engineers, and two mates. But Dwight has the last word on everything - not that it ever comes down to that. Everyone on board, from the cook to the captain, knows what they have to do and when to do it; so we all just get on with the job. I'd say that this boat pretty much runs itself."

On that note I slip back to my cabin for a little shut-eye. If the boat is going to offload me in the middle of the night, then I'll be using the wee hours to seek out some accommodation in Baton Rouge, of which I have none at the moment. I drift in and out of sleep, coming awake whenever the engines change their pitch, or when the boat comes to a complete stop. I know by now that the pilot will be navigating a tricky passage and manoeuvring his barges through a deceitful stretch of water. I don't show my face again until the evening meal, served from six to seven o'clock, when dusk turns quickly to darkness, and the night enshrouds the vessel.

A while later I go back up to the unlit pilot house where Dwight Shinley is back at the controls. He seems pleased for my company and I feel honoured. We chat about all kinds of stuff. I learn that he avoided marriage until his mid-40s, and that the one-month-on, one-month-off can be tough on such unions. "Absence makes the heart grow fonder, sure. But that's only when you're away! Once back at home, cracks can appear in the relationship and a little friction creeps in. In my case, it comes to a head if I have more than a couple of drinks in the evening. My wife doesn't like that one bit; but I say to her, 'Look, I've been gone four weeks without a drop; so give me a break, lady.'"

I ask what his most memorable experience is in 30 years of plying the river. He chews this one over for several long moments. "They all kind of run together over the years. Yeah, plenty of things have happened - but I suppose the one time that stands above all the rest was 9/11. I was asleep at the time. When I awoke, I switched on the television in my cabin - and came out of bed with a jump. I couldn't believe what I was seeing, those pictures of the Twin Towers and all. I know that it's all part of history now, but at the time it was beyond shocking; beyond an outrage even; it was beyond belief. The whole crew was in a mighty subdued state for the rest of the trip, trying to come to terms with this atrocity, and I knew that things would never be the same in this country ever again."

At least he's had no major mishaps in a 30 year career and more. "Just one or two incidents - like back in 1983 when I clipped a bridge on the Tennessee River during high winds. That was bad judgment on my part. I should have stopped the boat. And I've bumped the riverbed a few times, but who the hell hasn't?"

It seems that we're in some peril of doing that right now. Dwight brings the boat to a standstill and trains the searchlight onto the starboard bank. Ahead is a 90-degree left turn, and there are three sandbars that the captain knows of between here and there. "I'm looking for which way the water is gonna swing the barges" he explains calmly. "It'll tell me where I've got depth and where I haven't. We call this exercise 'flanking'.

Do they. I shut my trap and allow him to concentrate, but I'm as absorbed as he is in all this. Even though I have very many sea hours under my belt, I cannot pretend to follow Dwight's thinking. All I know is that we remain stationary for a good 20 minutes, with the searchlight constantly switching focus from shore to river bend; then ever-so-slowly we get moving again, cautiously inching our way to, and around, the bend. The captain has successfully nudged his 1,000 feet of barges and 170 feet of towboat between two nasty sandbars with just one foot of water between barge and riverbed. Then the water gets deeper and he picks up speed once more. The navigational software has been of no use at all. Getting us through that particular tight spot was all down to the knowledge and instincts that people like Dwight Shinley, David Reeves, and all the other pilots along this river have developed over time. Classic, brilliant stuff, and they go up several notches in my esteem.

Such esteem equally applies to the crew members. Deep sea trawling is generally regarded as the world's most dangerous occupation, but these river men face similar dangers. High up on a bluff, overlooking the river at sunset from the safety of land, the sight of a towboat pushing its load along can be an almost romantic spectacle. But it is a different perspective for the men out on deck; hands and fingers frequently get crunched between barges; arms and legs get broken, and on occasion a deckhand will be crushed to death; in wet, slippery weather, others have simply vanished overboard, and probably sucked under by the sheer industrial power of a towboat's prop wash.

The 'flanking' exercise has delayed us a little and it isn't until nearly one o'clock in the morning that the lights of Baton Rouge come blazing over the port bow. Dwight pulls his load over to the opposite bank, alongside some idle barges. "We're gonna drop four barges right here, and then pick up another ten" he says. "So this is where we say so long, and it's been good to have you aboard. A service boat is coming out for you."

The past 24 hours have been an eye-opening experience for me, and I'm boyishly thrilled to have done this thing in the company of such fine people - men who in my opinion, possess more top notch celebrity status than movie stars ever will. God knows what America would do without them. They are its unsung heroes.

Twenty

To the City of my Dreams

*I*T CAN BE A FUNNY OLD LIFE. One moment I am comfortably ensconced on a towboat, the next I'm standing on bumpy gravel in the pitch dark, attempting to load up a bike that is intent on toppling over on this uneven ground. After much cursing, I eventually get it all together and then stumble up a steep dirt track, cross some railroad tracks, and wheel into the downtown silence of a post-midnight Baton Rouge.

I have been here a couple of times in the past and failed to find inspiration of any sort in a city of grey government buildings and dull government employees. I guess this is an embedded aspect of the city that even the Mississippi cannot add colour to, preferring to give Baton Rouge a resigned shrug as it gathers pace towards the relative dazzle of New Orleans.

Everything is as I remember; two principal streets running parallel with the river and a number of crossing side streets. At a set of red lights I ask a cab driver for directions to any motel or inexpensive hotel. He throws his head back in mock laughter.

"Buddy, there are just two downtown hotels these days, and both are going to hurt your wallet. You're looking at $200 a night, minimum." He gives me directions to the Sheraton anyway, and I slowly pedal towards it, devising a cunning little plan as I ride.

It is not the actual $200 that's the problem; it is the *principle* of paying such a sum merely for a few hours sleep. Overpriced hotels are a real bugbear of mine, one of the great corporate confidence tricks of our age, and I refuse to play their game. Instead, I'll play a little game of my own.

In my bag I have some previous email correspondence from Jeff Richards, the PR for Louisiana's tourism industry and a Baton Rouge resident - and he's someone the senior Sheraton staff must know well. I walk the bike into the plush, empty lobby, causing the clerk to view me with some worry. I explain who I am, the BBC and all that, then ask the clerk if there is a reservation for me placed by Jeff Richards - knowing full well that there won't be because we haven't been in touch of late.

The man is confused, not quite knowing what to do: in the light of the Jeff Richards connection he is clearly unwilling to shoo me away; but neither does this go-by-the-book corporate employee have the power to authorise a complimentary room - and there is nobody for him to turn to at this hour of the night. My plan is purring along perfectly and I've already decided what to do with the remaining hours of darkness. I tell him that I'll sort things out in the morning; meantime, would the Sheraton be good enough to store my bags?

His relief is palpable: of course, it'll be a pleasure sir. I unload them from the bike and ride away towards the 24-hour casino down on the river. I lock the bike to a railing, then wander inside to chance my arm on the machines once more. Inside these gambling boats, time does not exist. There is no day and no night; there is only the moment. By now I've got less than five hours before the city opens for business, and I'm hoping they will be hours well spent - literally. Well, whatever happens within this time warp, at least I've got warmth and a roof over my head for the rest of the night. Resolving not to lose more than $100, that will still put me $100 ahead of the price that the Sheraton would like to relieve me of. Like that first puncture back up in Minnesota, I am simply following the line of least resistance in the circumstances in which I find myself.

What I do find surprising in these wee hours of a Wednesday morning is the volume of people gambling their way through the night. Baton Rouge is not a tourist city, yet the boat is more than one-third full of punters, and they are mostly people of working age. What it says about this government metropolis, I don't know. Is it a regional statistic of loneliness, poor marriages, and divorce? Or of a local addiction to gambling and the resulting financial desperation? Or is there an abnormal amount of bored salesmen passing through? Or are they all disconsolate government employees trying to find a different meaning to life? The only thing that I am sure of is that nobody is in here for the same reason as me.

Time flies by. I win a pile, then manage to lose it. But at 7.30am, when I wearily stagger out of here, I've retained exactly the same amount as when I entered. It has been a hard tussle with the machines through the dark wee hours. I feel a bit like Mike Fink and Davy Crockett after their own ferocious day-long battle in the streets of Natchez. But in one sense, I've at least come out as something of a winner.

Later in the morning I meet up with Jeff Richards, a slim, fast-talking, dark haired man in his early 40s. We hit it off right away, he being an ex-journalist who "grew a little weary of chasing cops cars to the scene of the crime, usually homicide." The switch into public relations allows him more time at home, but he remains a journalist from head to toe, and a bit of a hustler to boot. His delivery of words is short and sharp, and his crisp sentences echo those of the hardboiled pulp-fiction writers. His fingers snap as he talks. This is a man who is far more at home in the company of cynical cops and overworked morticians, than in the world of suave PR practitioners. He is the right man in the wrong job. Jeff's phone call to the Sheraton is brief, to the point, and effective. With a snappy grin, he tells me that my room awaits.

For obvious reasons, I sleep much of the day away. In the evening, and following my BBC slot, I roam the empty streets of this hushed city in search of somewhere to eat. In a tucked away corner of a tucked away square, I find a place called *The Cathouse*, so named I gather because it had once been a notorious brothel. Latin American music is coming from within, filling the night air. If it was once a house of ill-repute, then it has most certainly changed its ways. Inside, tables have been pushed aside and a smartly dressed clientele is dancing around the floor in exaggerated movements. They are all doing the tango with a little help from some South American musicians booming out from a CD player.

"It's a once-a-week thing" explains the chap next to me at the bar. "Romantic, eh?"

"If you say so" I answer, unconvinced.

"Yeah, I know what you mean. But there's not much nightlife in Baton Rouge; not for us middle-aged people anyhow."

"What do you do? For a living, I mean."

He sighs. "I work for the government of Louisiana, what else? I'm at the Department of Transport." The man is fairly typical of his city: friendly enough, but a tad tedious. If I ever came to live by this wonderful river, it would not be in Baton Rouge. I wolf down my cheeseburger and bid this harmless fellow goodnight.

I ride off next morning along a minor road called Route 30. For a while it runs along the river, and I pedal along the top of the levee which is actually paved, though only for a few miles. When it becomes grass and gravel I move back down to the road where traffic is light on this sunny morning. I realise after a while that I've made life difficult for myself today. I should have gone straight onto Highway 61 as I'd been advised, instead of this twisting rural route.

About 15 miles down the road I encounter an unusual sight. Slowly moving my way is a gang of men in orange jumpsuits.

They are picking up litter and debris from the road. A pick-up truck idles along behind them. The men nod at me as I pass. Inside the pick-up is a chap in uniform, accompanied by a guard dog and a pump-action shotgun. The man's elbow pokes out of the rolled-down window.

"Prisoners?" I ask him.

"That's it, buddy; low-risk cons."

I pass the settlement of St Gabriel, then turn east onto Route 74 towards a place called Gonzales, which will put me back onto Highway 61. The headwinds are blowing my way again. By mid-afternoon I'm heading due south, intending to stop over at somewhere with the strange name of Grammercy Lutcher. But today has turned into one of those days when each mile seems more like two. And that guy from the Louisiana Department of Transport has some answering to do. The shoulder of this major highway is an insult to tyres, wheels, and man, with a surface you would only expect to find on Planet Mars. The November sun is sliding fast by the time I reach this settlement of little more than a few houses, a gas station, and a bar. The map says it to be much bigger than it is, and I'm much annoyed to learn that there is zero overnight accommodation here.

I sit in the small café inside the gas station, pondering this latest dilemma. Nightfall is fast approaching and the next town along is a further 15 miles. But one thing I'm absolutely *not* going to do is to ride along this appalling shoulder in the dark. So I either have to hang around here all night or try to get a 15 mile lift on to LaPlace from one of the gas station's customers. Alas, the downside to being no more than 50 miles from the big city of New Orleans has set in. Suspicion of strangers is obvious, and the friendliness has become superficial. Nobody is interested in helping out. Finally, a female employee at the station rings her husband who, because she has told him to, reluctantly comes to my aid and takes me on to LaPlace, a garishly-lit town with the usual neon strips of burger joints and used car lots.

I find a reasonably priced motel, grab a takeaway, and retreat from the world. Tomorrow it will be the Big Easy, the Crescent City, or as one country & western singer calls it in a lyric about the city's annual Mardi Gras festival, *'The City of my Dreams'*. I lived and worked there for almost a year between the latter part of 1999 through to the late summer of 2000. I shall be intrigued to see how it has changed, if at all.

NATURALLY, IT HAD BEEN BECAUSE OF A WOMAN. New Orleans had been on my coast-to-coast route, where I spent a few days out of the saddle, utterly enchanted by this most European of U.S. cities. I stayed in a small, intimate hotel in the Lower Garden District about a mile from downtown. I not only fell in love with the place, I also fell in love with Denise. She was a professional artist living in Gulf Shores, Alabama, and like me, was in the Big Easy for a few nights. It was one of those male-female encounters that the brakes could not possibly hold. It had been sheer magnetism, accompanied by sparking, crackling electricity.

Back in England, I could not get this woman with the flowing auburn hair out of my mind, and it reached the point where I had to make a decision: to go or to stay. I went without regret; not then and not now. At the time, the idea was that I would live in New Orleans, and Denise would make the 120 mile drive from Gulf Shores on weekends. So I went to live in that same small hotel where the owner gave me a free room in return for helping with the guests on a rota basis. A popular weekly newspaper called *The Gambit* hired me as a freelance writer. It covered politics, the arts, entertainment, along with the offbeat and the bizarre - all of which were in great supply in the New Orleans of the day. For several months the Big Easy had indeed become the city of my dreams. But by and by the affair began to wane. By the time it was no longer, I moved back to England.

I relate this piece of personal history because I have not yet got New Orleans 100% out of my system, and I'm hoping this coming weekend will do just that. But first I have to get there, and I've this dire feeling that it is going to be one almighty ordeal: not simply due to the road surface, but because of the traffic-clogged urban sprawl of Kenner and Metarie, two of the city's outlying areas which I know to be extremely hostile to cyclists.

It is yet another warm, sunny November morning as I set off from LaPlace along Highway 61, a road that here is simply known as 'Airline' because it passes the city's Louis Armstrong Airport. Apart from the road condition, all goes smoothly enough until I pass the airport at Kenner. The shoulder comes to an end and the nightmare begins.

There are no sidewalks to ride on, only occasional patches of roadside grass. It is Friday afternoon and the traffic is thick, thick, thick, and about as erratic as a fox running loose in a chicken yard. Horns slam, and not always at me. Vehicles speed by within inches of each other and within inches of myself. This is at least as bad as those hours spent trying to get into the St Louis conurbation. At one point I have no choice but to ride on the wrong side of the road down through an underpass, wheeling precariously along a raised stretch of concrete just two feet wide and with a three foot drop. Cars and trucks growl by, head-on. If I fall, then I'm done for, no question of it. Harrowing moments like these truly concentrate the mind. This is enough to get New Orleans out of my system for good and always.

It goes on like this for another few miles; sometimes I run a very risky gauntlet indeed, other times I walk the bike along rough verges. But at least the signs to downtown are becoming prevalent, and I finally enter an area where the sidewalks begin - albeit, sidewalks as jagged and uneven as mountain peaks. Gradually the city starts to smarten up: shabby, unpainted clapboard houses make way for tidier homes of brick; garbage-strewn wasteland become gardens, some with sprinklers on the go; barred-up stores become going concerns. A big green sign directs me to Loyola Avenue, and suddenly I am amid the downtown towers of New Orleans.

I check in at a Holiday Inn named the Downtown Superdome. It is adjacent to the home of the New Orleans Saints, the city's NFL team, and which became a temporary shelter for the wretched multitudes forced to flee their homes when Katrina struck. From my 11th storey room, this part of the city seems entirely unaffected by the storm; the office blocks and skyscrapers glint in the late afternoon sun; on the street below traffic hums and flows; every couple of minutes comes the blast of a police or ambulance siren, their wails ricocheting off the tall buildings of this concrete canyon. It's all very familiar.

All the same, it does feel a little strange being back in a place that holds so many personal memories. I spend the evening walking through the past, firstly down to the Chart Room, a French Quarter bar on Chartres Street. My old friend Rusty the bartender has gone, he's left town the unsmiling barmaid says. And no, she's never heard of Victor Klein, an outrageous self-ordained archbishop with whom I spent many happy hours in here - in both senses of the term - laughing wildly at his stories and eccentric ways. I'll meet up once more with this unmatchable character a little later on.

What has changed is the atmosphere. The Quarter, as it's known locally, is fully intact and as attractive as ever, with its fine old French and Spanish colonial architecture. But something is missing, as if the spark has gone from it. Next, I cross the city's main thoroughfare of Canal Street and amble slowly towards the Robert E. Lee Circle, a large roundabout with an imposing statue of the great southern confederate General, and carry on up St. Charles Avenue towards the Lower Garden District. All the restaurants and cafes and bars are still in business, as indeed is my little hotel just a parallel block away on Prytannia Street. In a structural and physical sense there is no difference from the New Orleans I once knew, to the New Orleans that I'm in tonight. And yet there *is* a difference. It seems that the great storm - of which around me, there is no evidence whatsoever - has left the city psychologically battered and scarred; and these scars somehow hang in the air like unseen rain clouds.

I carry on past my old hotel, with all its many memories, and wander on down to Magazine Street, an arts & crafts district of bric-a-brac stalls, galleries, antique stores, and cafes. But to venture a block or two further south would be asking for trouble. This is where the 'projects' begin - a low rent, high-crime area for black families. At around midnight the shooting will start as the drug gangs continue their endless turf wars. I recall the nightly cracks of gunfire, audible from my room in the little hotel only a few blocks away: just as I recall the obituaries in the New Orleans daily paper, the *Times Picayune*; two pages each day, mainly concerning young black men under the age of 30. Without exception, they died from heroin overdoses, gunshot wounds, or cirrhosis of the liver. Chronic alcoholism is another issue down in the projects.

I amble back to St Charles Avenue and call in at a café/bar that I occasionally used back then. Nothing has changed in here either, except for the atmosphere; it is neither bad nor sad, just ... different. I order a big bowl of gumbo, a delicious Cajun dish of meat, seafood, and vegetables, and then walk back downtown to my hotel which sports an enormous lit-up mural of a jazz clarinet running from top to bottom of the tall building.

There is another odd sight, however. The hotel's parking lot is packed with military jeep-style vehicles, and I soon learn that this hotel also serves as the city's base for the National Guard which has all but taken over from the NOPD. Following Katrina, police manpower fell dramatically as disillusioned cops turned in their badges in droves, searching for a better way of life than controlling the chaotic aftermath of the storm.

My plan is to ride the final miles on Monday. That will take me across the Mississippi Bridge and down along Route 23, deep into Cajun country, much of which has been obliterated by Katrina. Jeff Richards will drive down from Baton Rouge and pick me up at the port of Venice where the river registers Mile

Zero, and where its rolling waters vanish into the salty expanse of the Gulf of Mexico. Following that, I'll remain in New Orleans until the next, and last, broadcast of the ride this coming Wednesday evening.

WARRANT OFFICER ROBIN WILLIAMS is 44 and hails from Oxford. He has lived in Louisiana for the past 14 years, but other than for an occasional twang he's not lost his English accent. Even the twangs disappear when he gets into conversation with me, a fellow Brit. We are in the hotel's ground floor command centre of the National Guard, which is hidden well away from the guests. Surrounding the banks of computers are numerous charts and street maps pinned to the walls. Myself excluded, everyone in here is attired in camouflaged jungle fatigues, the standard uniform of the NG.

Robin Williams and his sidekick Sergeant Major Kevin Allen are getting ready to take me on a tour of the outer city, where the storm did most of the damage: that is to say, on the shores of Lake Ponchartrain some way north of downtown, and the Lower 9th Ward, to the east of the city. Canal Street will take us all the way up to the lake, where the business district soon switches to modest residential areas. At one point we come across some obvious NG activity seeming to concern an entire block. The guys pull over to check it out.

"There's been an armed break-in" says a guardsman holding a walkie-talkie. "A black guy with a gun broke into that house over there. We happened to be patrolling nearby. The owner managed to slip outside and flag us down. We think the suspect is still somewhere on the block, lying low. A couple of sniffer dogs are on their way." We get out of the car and observe the search for the armed culprit. Soon the dogs arrive, their tails wagging like supercharged pendulums. The leashed dogs get down to it at once, eager to be of assistance. If anything can flush this chap out from his hole, it'll be them. Anyone attempting a burglary in the broad daylight of ten o'clock in the morning must either be utterly desperate or really know what he's doing, fearless of capture or retribution. After half an hour of this, it very much looks like the latter. The guards can't find him and neither can the dogs. He has stealthily and cunningly outwitted them.

We carry on through the northern suburbs until reaching the lake, where the evidence of Katrina's wrath hits me between the eyes: abandoned buildings; crumbled jetties; wrecked boats; and jagged piles of concrete and rubble everywhere. We cruise along Lakeshore Drive where an entire row of once-plush lakeview apartments is ripped to pieces, looking like a shrine to some insane sculptor who works with broken concrete and twisted metal. But at least one person views his wrecked property with a resigned sense of humour. *'For Sale'* reads a sign painted in rough scrawl across a semi-collapsed wall of an apartment that is now just bare ruins. *'Some Work Needed. Slight Water Damage!'*

Katrina damage, New Orleans. At least someone has a sense of humour about it.

237

"The storm dumped so much rain that the lake overflowed into the streets and rolled all the way downtown where the levees had broken anyway" Robin mutters. "I've not seen anything quite like it, ever. It was ten times worse than the usual downpours we get in New Orleans." Now that is saying something. I know from experience that when the rain comes down in this city, it comes with such voluminous ferocity that a wall of water can rise to your front door in no time.

Funnily enough, there is a cloudburst right now. Kevin, who is driving, switches the wipers on to rapid motion, but they cannot cope. This is simply too dangerous to drive in so we sit inside the stationary 4x4 and wait for it to abate, the windows steaming up fast and the vehicle completely enclosed in teeming, bucketing rainwater.

The short but fierce downpour doesn't exactly help with the dire vista that is the Lower 9th Ward. This is the section of the city that got obliterated, and it remains a tumbledown morass of deserted, shattered houses with corrugated roofing flung far and wide along uneven muddy lanes and overgrown weeds. Here and there are signs of repair, but the truth is that most of its former residents will not be coming back.

There is deep concern that this also may apply to tourists, without whom New Orleans is just another provincial city in a country with an over-supply of such places. It is a particular headache for poor old Jeff Richards, who had complained to me that he still gets worried phone calls asking if the flooding is still around, and if the streets are safe from looters and rioters. "It's a whole effing year on" he'd explained with such suave panache, "but the media insists on describing the city as battered, fallen apart, finished, like it is some goddam ghost town. The world out there doesn't seem to realise that New Orleans is back, and open for business because the press is only interested in calamity and disaster." He does have a point. The only things awry with the city today are those psychological scars and its wounded pride.

I HAVE NOT SO FAR CONTACTED anyone from the past, waiting instead for 24 hours to pass while immersing myself in my own thoughts and memories of New Orleans. But it is now Saturday night and I think that the company of the Reverend Victor Klein would be most apt. As you'll soon see, he is a true son of the Mississippi River; unique, bizarre, outspoken, outrageous, and occasionally quite dangerous.

I leave a message on the answer phone of *Ordo Templi Veritatas*, the fringe religion that Victor runs from a spare room at his home in the Garden District. You can never get this chap to answer the phone directly. Within moments he calls back. "Where have you been all this time?" he growls in his trademark gravel voice. "We've got some drinking to catch up on, asshole. I'll meet you in Lucky's at seven."

Lucky's is a bar on St Charles Avenue that I frequented back then, and where I made a lot of pals. However, I always made a point of keeping this place a secret from Victor until my final days in the city. This particular reverend and self-ordained archbishop can lose you friends in a flash.

Victor Klein is a stout 55 year old with dark wavy hair and built of rock-like muscle. He is a learned academic, a theologian, a confirmed bachelor, and a womaniser like no other I know. He is highly opinionated, and the gruffest of laughs always accompany his wild and wonderful sense of humour. Victor is also the author of seven books; three are about the reputed ghosts of New Orleans, of which there is an infinite supply; another three deal with the occult, to which he is no stranger; and the seventh is called *My Motto*, a demonic collection of 666 self-devised adages and maxims. To get an insight into this controversial man of the cloth, here are a few random, thought-provoking samples.

- We are all whores. Success lies in becoming the pimp.
- If Christ died for our sins, who died for Satan's?
- Stop Original Sin. Get an abortion.

- We are all on Death Row; time, place, and method of execution to be determined.
- If you believe in traditional religion, then practice human sacrifice.
- Rain never falls harder, nor colder, than when it falls on me.
- A man who does not eat pussy, has no soul.
- Judge a civilisation by its prisons.
- Suicide isn't the answer to all your problems. However, it is a great way to start.
- Government isn't even a clever hoax.

Victor believes strongly in life after death, but refuses to allow his thoughts on the matter to be restricted by organised religion. His transient, spasmodic 'congregation' tends to be a ragtag following of confused agnostics and disillusioned Catholics, mainly women - and Victor has no qualms about seducing every last one of them.

He is nursing a bourbon and coke when I enter Lucky's for the first time in six years. The place hasn't changed at all: a long bar to the left, a large pool table in the centre, a few booths and tables to the right. And neither has the Reverend. He is exactly the same as I remember him; tough, fit, and unlined. It's as if his high intake of bourbon and non-filter Camel cigarettes provide him with a magic formula for eternal youth. We take up exactly where we left off, quickly catching up with the years. There are a couple of other guys in the place, and an attractive brunette on her first night in the job of tending bar and whom my friend has clearly got designs on. She is perusing copies of his *New Orleans Ghosts* trilogy, and is impressed because she wants to become a writer herself. Victor, I recall, always keeps a few copies to hand in case of such an encounter. It is an opening ritual of his well-practised seduction prowess.

Let me put the man into perspective. His home-grown religion, the Order of the Temple of Truth, is officially acknowledged by the state of Louisiana, as is his reverend and archbishop status. He can legally marry couples and he can bury the dead, both of which are bread and butter activities for him. He is not some fanatical TV evangelist - although he would make a cracking television host, engaging and enraging his audience at the same time. Quite simply, Victor Klein is a one-off, and as unique as it is possible to be. To illustrate that assertion, during the course of the evening he relates this fairly sinister story, something that occurred since we last met.

"If you want to go to church on Sunday and be a good boy, then that's fine because I don't care. But if you want to really *understand* why you're in church in the first place, then you have to explore the other side of the wall. There is no point in praying to God without having some idea of what God's perceived opponent is really like. Who is to say that you might not find Satan a more attractive proposition? How could you know that unless you hear the guy out? It's like saying you'll only vote for an asshole like George W. Bush because you're a dedicated right winger and you cannot stand the Democrats. But unless you listen to what the Democrats are saying, how can you judge who has the better ideas? It's the same with God and Satan - so, my good friend, I decided to have a parley with the so-called bad guy: to let Satan have his say."

"You arranged an encounter with the Devil?" I ask. Little could surprise me about the Reverend Klein.

"Bet your ass I did. I even went to the expense of hiring an old plantation house for a whole weekend, Friday night to Sunday night. Including me, we had a party of 13 devotees of *Ordo Templi Veritatis*. I guess that 666 would have been a better figure, but I haven't got that many donation-paying followers. So 13 people of both sexes seemed an appropriate number under the circumstances."

And what circumstances they were: a dozen naked people sitting in a circle around an equally naked archbishop chanting a code from the occult that only he knew. On the second night in a remote three-storey plantation house many miles from the city, things began to happen. They used up less than an hour in calling up the perceived Devil, getting warmer by the minute as a response started to emerge.

"It was a hot, sweaty night" Victor says. "But then a sudden cold came over the room, like you'd walked out from the heat and straight into a giant freezer. Everyone began to shiver, looking jumpily at each other, suddenly nervous. But I carried on with the spell because that is what I went there to do; to try and find the truth between this God and Devil stuff. I was as cold as a pack of frozen beans myself. It was obvious that something was about to take place."

He is looking at me seriously. Victor is not lying; I know when he does that. This is a memory he is re-living. "Gradually a smell - slight at first - overcame the room to the degree that we could barely inhale. It turned into a dreadful, awesome, indescribably sickening stench." He pauses for a puff on his cigarette. "What followed made it worse. Amid the stench, a dark green cloud began floating over the room. I can tell you that *something* was forming in there, getting ready to present itself."

I am now spellbound myself, because I am one of the few people who gets this man. In a day-to-day sense, Victor Klein is fearless. He will take on any bar room brawler, and I've seen him do so even while wearing his dog-collar. His rival did not rise from the floor for ten minutes, during which time the Reverend calmly downed two more bourbons and then helped the battered man to his feet. But this event at the plantation house ... well, that was another matter entirely and of which he had suddenly lost control. In a moment of earthly wisdom, he scrambled into his clothes and joined the fleeing group. They got out of there 24 hours ahead of the rental expiry date.

"What I saw for myself during that incident was that outside forces exist, although I knew that anyhow. Yet did I call up the Devil himself? You see, I do not believe all that is in the Bible. It was re-written by the monks in the 6th Century and from that time on its teachings have been controlled by kings, queens, church leaders and politicians in their attempts to scare and suppress the masses, which they are still trying to do today. So I asked myself this question: what if the foul stench and the green mist had just been a bunch of fraudsters and murderers who've passed into the next world but who can't let go of their earthly side? You know, people like Richard Nixon, Pablo Escobar, and that serial killer guy, Ted Bundy. It's a theory that's got merit, because those people must occupy the dark side of the afterlife, and would have had no problem picking up on my code-chanting."

Even with the distance of an ocean between us, Victor and I will always be buddies. He has ideas and thoughts which appeal to that offbeat side of me.

We eat, and the night wears on. Nobody I knew from the past enters or leaves. It is a new bunch these days, although Victor recognises one or two of them and says howdy. They give him a brief smile and several metres of space. He is that kind of a guy, utterly incomprehensible to the mainstream. In here tonight is a mainstream from elsewhere; hucksters and transients trying their luck in a city where there is nothing to lose and possibly all to gain: commercial mercenaries hoping to cash in on the bad times and present them as money-making opportunities. Hard female predators with cast-iron mouths outnumber the men. The Satan-seeking Victor is interested in banging the lot of them, although tonight he only has eyes for the bargirl, who tells him she'll get off her shift soon, and not to fall asleep at the bar. I leave him to it, with the promise of another session together before I depart the city.

Twenty One

THE LAST BOAT ON THE RIVER

THE NATIONAL GUARD SAYS there is none too much left between New Orleans and the port of Venice. They tell me to expect no gas stations or other services along the highway because Katrina closed them down. The guardsmen add that many of the people remaining along that empty stretch of road are living in emergency trailer parks, and that the region is now even more of a wilderness than it was before.

The exact distance to Venice is 77 miles in a south-southeast direction. If I'm to face more headwinds, I can't see the bike making it on a single battery charge. It is a problem that I ask the NG to help me with: would someone take me across the bridge and for a few miles further until city's edge? This would serve two purposes. Firstly it will save the battery about 15 miles; and it will also spare me a repeat of that murderous hassle I had on Friday afternoon. If I'm to expire along the Mississippi, then at least let me make it to the end of the line.

They are a good bunch, these fatigues-clad people, and far

more popular with the locals than the police have ever been. They willingly agree to the request. We'll leave the hotel at six o'clock tomorrow morning, Monday. I reckon to complete the remaining miles in about four hours. I call Jeff Richards at home, who says he'll aim to be in Venice by one o'clock, and if he doesn't pass me on the way, then to wait for him at the only gas station-cum-general store in town.

I spend much of this Sunday pedalling aimlessly along quiet streets, and find myself riding towards a club called *Tipitina's* down on Tchoupitoulas Street next to the river. I don't know if they still hold the regular Sunday afternoon *fais-do-do*, but I used to go to it often. It is a Cajun term for a dance party, when the accordions and violins get everyone in the mood for a form of Cajun footwork and body reeling which I have never been able to master, and where the family atmosphere is always happy and innocent: mothers dance with young sons, fathers with their daughters, old men of 80 with young teenage girls. It was a most agreeable way to pass a Sunday. Alas, it is closed.

I carry on through the warm sunshine. On the river a small cargo ship with Liberian registration is steaming towards the port area. The Mississippi is 700 metres wide at downtown New Orleans and some 30 metres deep, capable of taking much larger ships than this one. The port, a little quieter now than it once was, nevertheless still handles around $8 billion worth of cargo annually. Across the water is the residential area of Algiers. One of the really magical sights along this river is night-time New Orleans as seen from Algiers. The rolling water glistens in the reflection of bright downtown lights, and the city alluringly beckons you over.

On the way back to the hotel I pass a group of cops inspecting an overturned car. Now this is strange; no other car was involved and Baronne Street is as flat as a sheet of paper. How would it be possible to overturn a vehicle in the middle of a road as even as this one?

"That's what we'd like to know" grunts a cop. "They've taken the driver to hospital, so we'll have to wait for the answer.

It beats me, I'll tell you that."

Well, I suppose this *is* New Orleans with the magic Mississippi cutting through it. And if that isn't explanation enough, then surely anything can happen in a city where 15% of the population still practice voodoo. I stay on Baronne, passing the office that had once been occupied by a well known human rights lawyer by the name of Clive Stafford-Smith. I knew him well when he was an ardent campaigner against the death penalty and once accompanied him onto Florida's Death Row to interview a client who for the past 14 years had been waiting his turn for that state's vile electric chair. Clive is also a Brit, and he too has since departed New Orleans in favour of home shores, from where he is now striving to free British-born internees from that monumental cock-up called Guantanamo Bay.

I feel my system at last beginning to free itself from the clutches of this fine city. I do not belong here like I once did. Victor Klein apart, there appears to be nobody here who I know any more. The city belongs to others now, somehow a different breed of resident; to pretend otherwise would be foolish. And that is all well by me. I am glad to have seen the place again - and I shall be just as happy to leave.

EVEN AT SIX O'CLOCK IN THE MORNING the roads hum with commuter traffic. The National Guard vehicle crosses the bridge into Gretna, part of southside New Orleans and a totally different place from across the river; a concrete landscape splattered with suburban shopping malls and numerous untidy industrial estates. We get onto the Belle Chasse Highway, also known as Highway 23, the road that will take me all the way down to Venice. The driver drops me off a couple of miles into open country, and thus commences the ultimate leg of this long journey that began near the Canadian border.

It is breezeless at this time of day and I make steady progress along the flat, empty road where houses are scant. The other spasmodic road users must wonder where the hell I am going on a bicycle. I won't call it Desolation Row; but I will call it remote multiplied by two. It is quite unlike anywhere else encountered along the way; a road that seems to whisper that I've overstepped the boundary and placed myself on a long trek to some lost world. All I can hear is the sound of two tyres whirring along rough concrete.

As the morning warms up and the miles go on, signs of Katrina become evident. Aside from roofless houses and collapsed farm buildings, there is a striking amount of forlorn trees stripped of their bark. At one stage, the entirety of a small forest is in this rather lamentable state, as if it had been the object of an unfriendly nuclear experiment. Small settlements, really small, come and go without much sign of life. If they once had stores and gas stations, they don't now. I seem to be passing through a time warp that is stubbornly inhabited by hardened recluses and forgotten people. I wave whenever I spot someone, but rarely do they wave back - something that is wholly inconsistent with the citizens of this amazing river - and I can only put this down to the probability of a residual bitterness that continues to linger long after the storm had shattered and blown their lives to pieces. I do not know; it's only a guess. But if Washington ignored the people of New Orleans for as long as it did in the Katrina aftermath, it wouldn't have given these remote communities south of the city a single thought.

I continue on through a sub-tropical wilderness; what little headwind there is gives me no special trouble, requiring just a few light jolts of electric-assist every so often. Nowhere does the scenery alter; at three feet above sea level, it is flat, scrubby, and vacant. There are no roadside billboards. If someone is offering a service of some kind, it is advertised on scrawled cardboard and staked into the ground by the entrance to their properties.

Towards Venice, makeshift trailer parks come into view; small compounds of mobile homes known by the acronym FEMA, meaning Federal Emergency Accommodation. They are principally for the workers of Venice, the first port along the river for visiting ships. Even the government could not ignore Venice. It is where the pilots board each incoming vessel to guide them up to New Orleans and Baton Rouge, which is as far north as ocean-going ships will travel up the Mississippi.

The river is about one mile to my right, but nowhere along the way is it visible, and there do not appear to be any tracks leading towards it. This disappoints me. I would like to watch it flow downstream for one last time; snatch a few minutes and sit on its bank: maybe puff a cigarette, and think back on the past weeks; to reflect on their magic moments and on their darkest horrors, both of which are as integral to a journey like this one as they are to Victor Klein's more ambitious quest for God and Satan. But memories are for the future. All I must do now is complete the job by reaching the end of this mystical body of water, and witness it disappear into a timeless sea.

With just five or six miles to go a 4x4 toots from behind, passes, and pulls up ahead. Jeff Richards springs out. I reach him and we shake hands. "You know" he says with a slight sigh, "when you first contacted me from England, I thought to myself, 'who is this guy? Is anyone mad enough to ride a bicycle from one end of the Mississippi to the other?' Frankly, I reckoned your plans would die of malnutrition - and that even if you went ahead with them, you'd quit somewhere along the way. But you didn't - and here you are."

"Almost" I remind him. "Anything could happen in the last few miles."

"How about a ride?"

"Thanks, but no. I'll catch up with you in about 20 minutes."

"You've got it, buddy. Well done. You've earned my honest admiration."

Coming from a sharpshooter like him, this is high praise indeed. Jeff is not the type to acknowledge personal achievement with anything more than a short prehistoric grunt. He speeds off and I remount. A short while later, broken, dilapidated houses and more FEMA trailer parks come into sight and Highway 23 transforms into a disarranged street of battered buildings, a few parked cars, and the gas station and general store where Jeff's vehicle stands on the forecourt. I don't think they'll be twinning this place with that other watery city of Venice. I wheel into the gas station, where Jeff is inside knocking back a beer.

"Hey, champ" he grins, "have a beer or two to celebrate." In a few minutes, I tell him. First I have to pedal to where I'll run out of road; to the very end of the line. Jeff says to carry on for no more than 500 metres. After that, he says, I'll be going nowhere but backwards.

He is right. The road becomes a gravel lane, with water on both sides and ahead. To my left is an oily looking marina. To my right is the Mississippi River, now looking more like a confusing expanse of lake than a rolling waterway. Ahead of me is a road sign. It very simply reads: DEAD END. If the source of the river back up in Minnesota is a tourist attraction, then the tail end of it is the precise opposite.

I park the bike against the sign and walk as far as it is possible to walk, about 25 metres, until the lane comes to an end at a cluster of thick mangroves by the water. Steaming into the marina is a blue workboat of some kind; a service vessel for the oil and gas rigs out there in the gulf. Five minutes later it comes steaming out again, and seems to be in one hell of a hurry, as if urgently going in search of a drowning man.

It is, quite literally, the last boat on the river.

So this is it. I want to linger awhile in this place they've dubbed 'the end of the world', but the mosquitoes will not permit me that small courtesy. They are out and biting, swarming around my bare arms and legs. I take one last look at the Mississippi as it turns into saltwater, then flee the scene.

Out of curiosity, I ride over to the marina, an untidy basin of idle shrimp boats - the ones that survived Katrina. Others, not so lucky, are lying abandoned on their sides as a reminder of the storm - as if the settlement of Venice needs such a thing. I turn around and wheel away, heading for that celebratory beer with Jeff. My Mississippi marathon is over.

Clean out of road. Journey's end, Venice, Louisiana.

MY HAIR, OR WHAT REMAINS OF IT, NEEDS CUTTING.
Not far from the hotel is a small one-man barber shop on Union
Street. I lock the bike to a lamp post by the barber's glass door,
where I can keep an eye on it. Sitting in the chair with an itchy
bib around my neck, the barber begins asking questions while
he snips. By the time he's through with me, three more chaps
are waiting for the scissors. This does not deter him from
making them wait another five minutes. He is intensely curious
about the concept of an electric bike and is eager to check it out
for himself.

When the impatient next-in-line shouts at him to get back
inside and "cut my goddam locks, man", the barber scribbles
down the address of a nearby bar on the back of his business
card. "If you can" he says pleadingly, "meet me in there at five.
I wanna talk a deal with you."

Patrick Ricks, hairdresser to neither the rich or famous, is sitting at the bar when I roll up, and he is beaming with pleasure that I've kept the appointment inside this small, dark saloon - a place that would also appear to discourage celebrity clients. Patrick is a tubby individual of around 45, a bachelor whose recent circumstances forced him to go back and live with his widowed mother. He is, it appears, just another of Katrina's fallen, spewed out with the rest of them into the ceaseless torrent of disaster stories.

Before the storm - possibly the world's most publicised natural disaster along with the tsunami - Patrick had his own downtown office-supplies business. It may not have thrived, but it did well enough to bankroll a couple of employees and pay the rent. Until, that is, the day that the water level rose to the point where it washed his business away. In common with everyone else in the city, he only had hurricane insurance - but no flood cover. He is, to say the least, pretty damn sore about the refusal of insurance companies to fork out, since it was the hurricane that caused the flooding.

"No pun meant, but those slippery bastards killed me dead in the water" he spits out. "The business drowned, and I drowned with it. For months afterwards I walked around in a daze, a stupor, and I'm only finding my way out from it around now."

Patrick is not seeking sympathy or spinning me a line. I know how to spot the genuine from the bogus. He is merely telling me of his personal Katrina disaster, and for reasons I'll come to shortly, I am finding this mild mannered person quite intriguing. Earlier in life he had qualified as a barber, but after too many years of standing up all day and working for others, he quit to buy up his office-supply company. Patrick's tale is an everyday story of an everyday man, who wants not much more than to be his own boss and pay his own way in life. Working on the principle that people need to have their hair cut more than they need paper clips, he returned to the barber trade as a way to make ends meet. By this time he was on his uppers.

He moved back in with his mother to save on rent, and managed to borrow just enough from friends and others to set up shop on Union Street, which has now been in business for six months. But during the storm he also lost his car, and now gets to and from work via a tedious bus journey. "The thing is this, man. I've been thinking all afternoon, and if you're willing I'd like to buy your bike - but I can't hardly pay nothing because I'm paying off all my debts every week. But I really *want* that machine. I've never seen an electric bike before. It's a great notion, and it would free me up from the goddam bus."

I can tell by the pleading look on his face that this amiable chap is verging on the desperate. I have been up and down financially too, but as it happens I'm in no special need right now. What I *am* in need of takes a brief explanation. The *eZee Torq* has been with me all the way along the river. By now I know its every twitch, its every idiosyncrasy, its every stubborn mood, and its every act of kindness. The fears I had at the start of the ride that it might turn into my direst enemy proved unfounded. It has been a true and reliable friend. We have been in this thing together from start to end, to the extent that a bond has developed between man and machine. I have feelings for it.

I have a choice. I can either lug the bike back to England, or I can find a home - a good home - for it here. The former option is not especially practical for a number of reasons, but it is what I was resigned to doing - until I went for a haircut. Patrick is a caring individual, a victim of events outside his control, cash-strapped and struggling, yet open and honest. I cannot think of a more deserving person to take over the bike's welfare. And besides, in my innermost-self, I think that this particular machine *belongs* by the Mississippi River. If machines have souls - as many prominent engineers believe, oddly enough - then towboat pilots aside, this two-wheeled electric soul knows this river as well, and probably better, than anything and anyone else.

"So" he asks edgily, "if you're willing to sell, how much do you want?"

The *eZee Torq* retails for $1,500 in the USA. I tease him for a while, making him aware of this troublesome fact. His face falls into a deep hangdog and disappointment sets in. He fiddles with his glass on the bar top, staring at it miserably. Another dream hits the rocks.

"I'll sell it to you for ... "

The tiniest flicker of hope jumps from his eyes.

"... for a bottle of Cutty Sark."

"What!"

"You heard."

Patrick is spluttering and stuttering. He thinks I'm messing with his head. This is America where the dollar reigns supreme and debt collectors live in style. Nobody ever *gives* anything away, unless it is absolutely worthless. He is actually eyeing me now with a sudden and deep suspicion.

"Your bike for a *bottle of scotch*?"

"That's what I said."

"Nah, can't be true. You're playing games, man."

I shrug. "Take it or leave it."

It slowly dawns on him that I mean what I say. "I'll take it!" Patrick gasps, pumping my hand and showering me with thanks. I quietly explain to him why I'm doing this, and he solemnly swears to look after it well; to treat it as he'd treat a wife, if he had the fortune to have one. Now I'm no saint, but I believe that buried somewhere inside the human spirit, mine included, is the need to do a little good for others - and just to witness his glow of sheer delight at this unexpected slice of luck is reward enough for me. That the bike is going to a Katrina victim and will stay by the big river, makes it all the more worthwhile.

Today is Tuesday. I broadcast tomorrow and will leave here on Thursday. I tell Patrick to have that bottle ready first thing on Thursday morning, when we'll make the exchange. "Good buddy" he says, slapping a grateful hand on my shoulder, "I'm gonna make it *two* bottles."

See what I mean about the human soul wanting to do good

for others?

Other than meeting up with Victor once more, I've not much left to do in New Orleans. I spend much of Wednesday mooching around the French Quarter for no other reason than passing time, and where I pop into a café/bar for a light lunch. There is just one other customer inside, a middle-aged female tourist from Cincinnati. I know this small detail because she is swapping banter with the barman from the farthest table in the place, and volunteering her life story at the top of her voice. She then gets onto the never-ending topic of Katrina and asks the barman what it had been like.

"I rode it out in here" he calls back, "along with the owner." He points to a large photo up on the wall behind him. "That's her; name of Alison, one L." From where I sit Alison, one L, looks an unpleasant, ageing termagant. She has a tight jaw, thin mouth, and mean eyes. I do not much like the look of her.

"You rode it out in here?" the tourist from Cincinnati asks incredulously, as if that commanded double-time plus danger money.

"Yeah, in here. And lady, I went through hell."

"I'll bet. I'll bet you did!"

"Yeah, it was hell" he says again. "I had to spend a whole 24-hours boxed in with that bitch." I suppose that is all New Orleans can do with Katrina now - poke a little fun at it. I laugh, because it probably was hell, and the barman's delivery is good. The tourist lets rip with a throaty cackle that echoes off the walls. This guy has made her day.

I stroll down to the river for one last look. It sparkles in the sunshine on its ceaseless flow towards the gulf. My own worldly needs are simple; really just the bare essentials and an occasional dose of magic. The Mississippi has given me that. But in a couple of weeks it will look different. The cold will arrive - it can get very chilly here, though never icy - but the shivering will only last for six weeks. The spring comes fast to New Orleans; then it will slowly build into the stifling heat and humidity of a long, sweaty summer, to be replaced once more by the comfortable autumnal warmth that I'm basking in now. Then will come those six weeks of chill again.

And, like the river running through it, so it goes on.

Epilogue

HEADING NORTH

'Good Morning America, how are you?
Don't you know that I'm your favourite son
I'm the train they call the City of New Orleans
And I'll be gone 500 miles when the day is done.'

SO GOES THE CHORUS to the Arlo Guthrie country song romanticising the train that I'm now aboard; the big, shiny diesel that runs daily between New Orleans and Chicago, a 19 hour journey. I am on my way north to a wintry Minneapolis via a long weekend back up in Cape Girardeau, one of my favourite places along the river. I could have flown, but aside from the carbon footprint issue, I've plenty of time and prefer the train anyway.

There is a lady in Cape Girardeau by the name of Connie. She is a presenter at Kape Radio 1550 and who interviewed me on my way through. We ended up having dinner together and have remained in touch since. I'll be staying at her house over the weekend, which might feel a little strange after God knows how many nights spent in B&Bs, hotels and motels.

The *City of New Orleans* rolls on through the flatlands of Louisiana and Mississippi. When darkness falls, I make my way to the dining car for a bite. It is white cloth napkins and silver service, even if the food does come straight out of a microwave. The prices reflect the silver service; the food reflects a microwave overdue for a service. Rita, my waitress is a black woman in her 40s and turns out to be yet another Katrina statistic. Her story is a tough one.

"We was livin' in the Upper 9th Ward and saw that storm a'comin'. Knowed it was gonna be a real bad one, so me, my husband, and the kids, we grabbed a few clothes and some useful items and piled into our tired old car. We took off for Texas, a place called Kerry, near Houston, where we knowed a cousin or two would gives us shelter.

"Trouble is" she goes on, "we're still there. Tried to get back to N'awlins but by then the rents had doubled, and we cain't afford 'em no more. So if you wanna know how that is for me, hear this. My routine is seven hours on a Greyhound bus from Houston to N'awlins. Then I join the train and work for 19 hours until we make Chicago. I get a little sleep durin' the day, but when the train starts rollin' for N'awlins again, that's another 19 hours on my feet. Once there, I head for the bus station and sleep the seven hours back to Houston. And man, I got me less than 48 hours before the same thing starts all over again. And that don't mean I'll be seein' my husband neither. He's out on the oil rigs, workin' the shifts." She shakes her head at this continuing run of poor luck, and I feel for her. "All I wanna be is a normal housewife, but we cain't afford for me to stay at home. The cousins gotta take care of the kids when I'm away. It ain't a good time for us right now." This is a *Desperate Housewives* tale in reverse, and another sorry example of how Katrina wrecked so many lives.

It is way into the night when we roll into Memphis, a merciful 20 minute stop where all us politically-incorrect inhalers can go outside for a puff. For the duration of the stop I pace to and fro along the platform, keeping warm against a chill

The Last Boat on the River

that has yet to hit New Orleans. The train pulls out again on the dot of schedule, passing a vast lit-up pasta restaurant with the name of *Spaghetti Warehouse*. It looks more inviting than the dining car.

It chugs on through the dark, clearing Tennessee and Kentucky. At three o'clock in the morning the train comes to a halt at Carbondale, Illinois; my stop. Connie, bless her, is there to greet me. This is the nearest stop to Cape Girardeau, 60 miles southwest of here. It is a misty drive through the heart of the deer hunting season. Connie has to swerve and brake whenever a deer leaps out onto the road.

We enjoy a most pleasant, relaxing weekend here in the Athens of the Mississippi. I meet her three sisters, one of whom has only just hit her 40s and has been married a staggering six times. "On the day she announced her fifth divorce" says a chuckling Connie, "she'd had *four more* proposals of marriage by lunchtime of the same morning." I can only put this bizarre statistic down to the river once more; a river that is still a dazzling blue despite the fallen leaves and bare branches. Winter is setting in; warm clothing is now required.

On Saturday night we get talking to a middle aged couple who end up inviting us over for dinner for the following Sunday evening. Nelson Sparks and his lady friend live in a large old house that, as property developers, they have renovated into a mini-mansion. It is in a part of town where the black and white neighbourhoods meet. There is no point in turning a blind eye to this: segregation, apartheid, call it what you like, exists around here as a natural state of affairs. On the opposite side of the street by a lamp post lies a scrappy pile of unwanted household items outside a run-down house; an old fridge, torn cardboard boxes stuffed with old clothing and dirty blankets, and a number of other discarded items. "That's what is left of an eviction that took place this morning" Nelson says with distaste. "A bunch of crack addicts lived there, but they didn't pay the goddam rent, low as it is. The law officers who threw them out also chucked their belongings onto the street.

259

Word got around fast. By nine o'clock, it was one big free-for-all among the Cape's looting classes."

Just then, a young man wearing a hooded coat wanders to the same street lamp and lingers underneath its dim orange glow. "Drug dealer" Nelson grunts. "He'll do five or six deals before moving on. Shit, man; I'm trying to clean the area up - and I'm reaching the point where I'm prepared to wave my gun in their faces."

Paradise, I know from experience, always has its dark side. But he's a determined individual, this big man with a proud and bushy moustache, and I daresay that he will eventually manage to shoo, rather than shoot, these people away. Over dinner I suggest that he nips over the bridge into Illinois and then on down to Cairo sometime. If ever an opportunity exists for developers, it has to be in that barred-up city. Nelson is intrigued by this thought. Someone like him has got to give that wasted place a shot.

Early on Monday, too early for my liking, I'm back at Carbondale railroad station to carry on up to Chicago, where I'll switch trains for a further nine hours on to Minneapolis. This first train, alas, is not the *City of New Orleans*, but a stop-start chugger that, among others, is carrying a large group of prisoners towards some jail or other. They are all young black men, wearing the same hooded cream-coloured tops, and under a police guard. They are openly derisive of whites, making a good number of loud derogatory remarks, and not caring who hears. The police remain expressionless, immune from it all. Is there really *anywhere* that is truly integrated? I do not believe there is, and I'm not convinced that there ever will be.

At Chicago, I board the *Empire Builder*, a train that runs between Chicago and the far west city of Seattle, and am pleasantly surprised by the amount of people willing to go the full distance by rail rather than take a plane. A couple of hours from Minneapolis I go down to the buffet car for a sandwich and one of those tiny bottles of white wine which contain two glasses at most, and which budget airlines and train companies are so fond of selling you at three times the normal price. The chap behind the counter, a no-nonsense type who knows how to deal with troublesome customers, gives me a cool glare when I quip about the wine being on special offer at a thrice-the-price sale. He spreads his hands on the counter and says, "Oh, I've got me a live one here; tough guy, huh?"

I respond instantly by jabbing my finger at him. "Sure I'm tough. I've been known to tear apart a bread roll with my *bare hands.*"

The riposte has him rollicking with laughter. He pulls out another little wine bottle. "This one is on the house, buddy. I gotta remember that line. It's ace." I very quickly zip my lips from admitting that I've plagiarised the quote from a Raymond Chandler novel: one that just happened to spring to mind at exactly the right moment. With my free bottle, now would not be the time to tell him that.

*T*HE TWIN CITIES SIT UNDER HEAVY SKIES, accompanied by an icy wind down on the ground. The big river has turned cold and bleak, yet it still has one more surprise in wait. In America, anything can happen. Beside the Mississippi, it most probably *will* happen.

I am due to fly home this evening, Tuesday, 14 November. The ever-helpful tourism executives for Minneapolis/St Paul suggest a decent lunch somewhere to send me on my way. They say to meet them at a restaurant called the *Bubba Gump Shrimp Company* situated on the third level of the Mall of America.

The mall is in the Bloomington district of Minneapolis, and for a first-time visitor like me it is a jaw dropping, gasp-inducing experience: an indoor city within a city, the like of which I've never seen before and will probably never see again. Not being of materialistic mind, modern shopping malls normally make by blood freeze, and thank you, but I'll take the long way around to avoid such bastions of consumerism. Yet the moment I step inside the Mall of America, I know that I'm in for something special. It is a gigantic, futuristic complex that oozes innovation and good taste, and I am very quickly swallowed up in an atmosphere that is somehow other-worldly. The Twin Cities and the poor weather outside become irrelevant and forgotten. If ever the day comes when humankind makes its exodus to faraway planets, then those pre-planned galactic cities up there will surely be modelled on this astonishing place with a controlled year-round temperature of 70 degrees Fahrenheit.

In addition to its 520 stores, 30 fast food outlets, and 20 restaurants, what other shopping mall in the world contains the following? Not one, but *two* universities; a million gallon walk-through aquarium; a vast indoor amusement park complete with roller coaster and ferris wheel; a four-storey Lego showcase; a 14-screen movie theatre; a performing arts centre attracting some big-name acts; a computerised NASCAR motor racing track; four flight-deck simulators; its own church and its own police department; and a wedding centre called the Chapel of Love where to date over 4,500 couples have tied the knot.

I hope eventually to stumble upon the Bubba Gump Shrimp Company. I am up on Level Three, so let's see now ... ah yes; the address is 396 South Avenue.

And this is *indoors*?

A while ago I would have shaken my head and said, 'Only in America', but the past weeks have narrowed the focus somewhat. Now I say 'Only by the Mississippi': only by that eccentric, enigmatic, deceitful, moody, ever-rolling stretch of watery mysticism that possesses a sleight of hand all of its own making, and which in some way exerts its own very special influence over those who inhabit its 2,552 miles of twisting shores.

There is no other river in the world like the Mister 'Sippi. It is the boss.